CW00663995

VOICES ON THE PATH
A HISTORY OF WALKING IN WALES

to Woody

with best wishes,

Andrew.

Voices on the Path

A History of Walking in Wales

Andrew Green

First published in 2024
© Andrew Green

All rights reserved. No part of this publication
may be reproduced, stored in a retrieval system,
or transmitted in any form or by any means, electronic,
electrostatic, magnetic tape, mechanical, photocopying,
recording, or otherwise, without prior permission
of the authors of the works herein.

Andrew Green asserts his moral right under the Copyright, Designs and
Patents Act 1988 to be identified as the author of this work.

ISBN: 978-1-84527-952-3

Published with the financial support of the Books Council of Wales

Cover design: Eleri Owen
Cover image: from Hugh E. Page, *Rambles and walking tours
around the Cambrian Coast*, London: Great Western Railway, 1936

Published by Gwasg Carreg Gwalch,
12 Iard yr Orsaf, Llanrwst, Wales LL26 0EH
tel: 01492 642031
email: books@carreg-gwalch.cymru
website: www.carreg-gwalch.cymru

Printed and published in Wales

My feet is my only carriage
And so I've got to push on through

Bob Marley and The Wailers, 'No woman no cry'

As I walk, solitary, unattended,
Around me I hear that eclat of the world

Walt Whitman, 'As I walk these broad, majestic days'

The river is gentle in the soft evening,
And all the steps of my life have brought me home

Ruth Bidgood, 'Roads'

I Carys, Catrin ac Elin

Contents

Foreword

Since I was around one year old I've been a biped. It's always been an advantage, in my experience, to have two legs and two feet. More than that, using them has been a source of great pleasure, a pleasure that's increased with age. About ten years ago I started to walk the 870 miles of the Wales Coast Path. Since completing the Path, it's become a habit, even an obsession, to cover long distances on foot. For the first time I began to think seriously about the act of walking. That isn't something most people do, any more than they think about their heartbeat or breathing. But, as Rebecca Solnit says in her book *Wanderlust*, there's nothing simple or straightforward about walking. It's an activity loaded with all kinds of social, cultural and economic associations.

Walking has a history, too. Over the centuries people have walked for many reasons, and they've held very different views about walking. Different kinds of walking have come and gone. Wales, thanks to its varied landforms and distinctive history, has a rich tradition of foot travel. It's especially rich in certain types of walking, like pilgrimage, droving, mountain walking and social protest. This book aims to capture some of that variety, and in doing so to shed a new, and perhaps unfamiliar, light on the history of Wales.

I tell the story of walking in Wales in broad chronological order, starting with footprints left in intertidal mud in the Mesolithic period and finishing with the urban stroller of the present day. For almost all of this time, because walking was an everyday, unobserved activity, the historical record of it is sparse and intermittent. But from the eighteenth century, as carriages, trains and then cars arrived to supplant moving feet, walking came to be noticed and sometimes valued as an activity in itself. Sources become more frequent, and it's possible to hear the voices of many people who've walked and thought about walking.

In following the long path of my story, I pause from time to time along the way to spend time with some of the most interesting of them: Samuel Taylor Coleridge, Catherine Hutton, Iolo Morganwg,

Anne Lister, George Borrow, Francis Kilvert, Gerard Manley Hopkins, Ursula Martin and others. My definition of 'walking' is a broad one, though I've excluded running and paid only glancing attention to 'vertical walking', mountaineering and rock climbing.

This isn't an impartial book. I've a preference for walking. In the later chapters preference stiffens into partisanship, as walking becomes marginalised by the car and motor traffic inflicts more and more damage on the earth's climate and natural environment. A resurgence in walking and other low-impact forms of transport, it seems to me, is essential for the sake of the futures of our children and grandchildren. It's time we all got back on our feet.

Many people have had a hand in making this book. The following were generous with information, guidance and encouragement: Jess Allen, Diane Bailey, Chris Baker, Julie Bromilow-Nicklen, Alun Burge, Mary-Ann Constantine, Jim Cowie, Jane Davidson, Andrew Davies, Stevie Davies, Richard Daugherty, Hugh Dunthorne, Elizabeth Edwards, Mari Evans, Michael Freeman, Gerald Gabb, David Greenslade, Quentin Grimley, Aled Hughes, Iwan ap Dafydd, Delyth Jenkins, Dafydd Johnston, Gareth Jones, Mark Lewis, Angela Maddock, Maredudd ap Huw, Theresa Nolan, Dave McGlade, Gareth Pierce, David Pope, Andrew Prescott, Gareth Richards, Sioned-Mair Richards, Shan Robinson, Richard Scriven, Elen Simpson, Helen Tatchell, Karmen Thomas, Dafydd Trystan, Iain Tweedale, Peter Wakelin, Alexander Wade, Chris West and Simon Whitehead. I'm grateful to the staff of libraries and archives in Wales, especially in the National Library of Wales, Bangor University Archives and Special Collections, Swansea University Library, Swansea Public Library and the Richard Burton Archives, Swansea University.

Every effort has been made to trace copyright holders for permission to reproduce quotations from written works. Thanks are due to the following for giving permission and disclaimers: Jess Allen ('All in a day's walk' website), Martin Bidgood (Ruth Bidgood, 'Roads'), Carcanet Press (Robert Graves), Stephen Davies (B.L. Coombes, *These poor hands*), Hannah Engelkamp (*Seaside donkey*), Felix de Wolfe Ltd (Gwyn Thomas, *A Welsh eye*), Peter Finch (*Edging the city*), Jon Gower ('The land they shall lose', in *I know another way*, ed. Jon Gower), HarperCollins UK Publishers Ltd (Walter Wilkinson, *Puppets in Wales*), Emily Hinshelwood (*On becoming a fish*), Honno Ltd (Ursula Martin, *One woman walks Wales*), Delyth Jenkins and Y Lolfa (*That would be telyn*), Y Lolfa ('Llwybr y glannau' by Dic Jones, in *Yr un hwyl a'r un wylo*), Harriet Monkhouse (Patrick Monkhouse, *On foot in north Wales*), Robert Newell ('Robert Newell artist' website), Open Government Licence (John H. Barrett, *The Pembrokeshire Coast Path*), Hilary Osmond (Osi Rhys Osmond, 'Coracles and cromlechs', in *I know another way*, ed. Jon Gower), Ann Pettitt (*Walking to Greenham*), Plaid Cymru (Kate Roberts, *Traed mewn cyffion*), Dewi Prysor (*100 Cymru: y mynyddoedd a fi*), Iain Sinclair (*Black apples of Gower*; *Lights out for the territory*), Rhys Trimble (*Swansea automatic*).

Thanks are also due to all those who provided illustrations: they're acknowledged in the captions.

Myrddin ap Dafydd, Dwynwen Williams and Eleri Owen at Gwasg Carreg Gwalch supported me throughout the making of the book. Diolch o galon am eich cymorth ac amynedd.

Introduction

On 23 March 2020, as cases of Covid infections multiplied, the British government ordered everyone in the country, with some exceptions, to stay at home. Only essential shopping was allowed. We could take only one daily form of outdoor exercise. Most businesses and other venues were told to close, and gatherings outside the household couldn't exceed two people.

This 'lockdown', intended to slow the headlong spread of the disease and backed by the most draconian legislation since the Second World War, had an immediate effect. Almost everyone obeyed the rules, with the exception of some of those who had set them. Silence descended on cities, towns and countryside alike. Vehicles stood idle on roadsides and in drives, and beach car parks were locked off. Shops remained shut, or open to just a few nervous customers. Families huddled indoors, waiting for more news and instructions.

But outside the weather was freakishly warm and sunny. Many people were eager, even desperate, to take advantage of their single outdoor exercise a day. The streets around our house were emptied of their usual cars, and you could walk down the centre of any road in safety. Birdsong became louder and more intense. The skies were free of the vapour trails of aeroplanes. I thought I knew all the public rights of way within an hour's walk of our home, but in those strange days I discovered many more paths, often obscure and underused. I saw more fellow-walkers than normal. Many of them, I supposed, ordinarily used their cars for even short trips, but they were now exploring their surroundings, for the first time, on unaccustomed feet. A new neighbourliness began to grow, even in the absence of physical closeness. People came out of their houses at set times to stand on the street and clap health services staff and other 'key workers'.

It didn't last. The strictest of the regulations were soon relaxed, and a more normal pattern of life began to resume. But for that brief period a whole way of life had changed. Of all the changes, the most striking were the near complete absence of cars, vans and lorries, and the revival of human means of getting about, mainly walking but also running and cycling. We're normally unaware of how tyrannical the rule of motor vehicles is in our outdoor lives, and how completely the practice of walking has become subservient and peripheral. But in those magical, silent days it was possible to imagine how things were before the internal combustion engine, that stubbornly persistent technology – a time when most people walked to work or school, and walked much longer distances that we do today.

Many people look puzzled when you suggest that walking might have a history. Walking seems such an elementary activity, moving the body forward by putting one foot in front of the other and repeating the action. Few people give it much thought, especially if it hardly features in their everyday lives, as is now common. But walking does have a long history. Few books have been written about the historical and cultural significance of the breathing of the lungs and the beating of the heart, or any other unwilled bodily movements. But walking isn't unwilled, and it's always carried a wide array of meanings and associations, some of which have changed through time. Rebecca Solnit, one of the pioneers of walking history, wrote:

> The most obvious and the most obscure thing in the world, this walking that wanders so readily into religion, philosophy, landscape, urban policy, anatomy, allegory, and heartbreak. The history of walking is an unwritten, secret history, whose fragments can be found in a thousand unemphatic passages in books, as well as in songs, streets, and almost everyone's adventures.[1]

Many animals walk, but only humans and their immediate ancestors are regular bipeds (we began our career on two feet around 3.5m years ago). Human feet, each of which contains twenty-six bones, thirty-three joints and more than a hundred muscles, tendons and ligaments, have evolved as exquisite walking machines. With two feet we can balance ourselves and hold our bodies upright. Walking upright, we're able to scan our surroundings, use our arms and hands freely, and let our minds move in a hundred directions. When we humans left our original home, Africa, around 100,000 years ago, it was on foot that we explored other continents. Walking, you could argue, is the only truly human means of locomotion. All others, even that most perfect of inventions, the bicycle, rely on some kind of external contrivance. They also create an artificial divorce between travellers and the world they travel through. Walking, by contrast, sets up a healthy balance between the outer and the inner person, and between the person and the world:

> Walking, ideally, is a state in which the mind, the body, and the world are aligned, as though they were three characters finally in conversation together, three notes suddenly making a chord. Walking allows us to be in our bodies and in the world without being made busy by them. It leaves us free to think without being wholly lost in our thoughts.[2]

An action that is at once simple, adaptable and fluid, walking opens doors to different worlds. Think about the dozens of words in English used as varieties of the verb 'to walk'. Some of them – amble, stroll, wander, saunter, perambulate – convey a lack of pace or firm direction. Others convey the opposite: stride, pace, drive. Others again suggest the effort and fatigue of excessive walking: plod, trog, tread, tramp. Hike, trek and ramble imply walking as a countryside recreation, while march and yomp suggest the progress of infantry soldiers. Modes of walking are legion. Walking to work and to school, walking for health and healing, walking to escape, walking solo and in groups, marching to war, or in solidarity to campaign and protest, droving animals, scaling hills and mountains, pacing to map the land, walking to examine or connect with the natural world, walking for money, walking as art or performance, promenading, walking to worship or on pilgrimage, walking to think or create, ambling along as an outcast or vagrant, tramping urban streets – throughout history the pedestrian has played all these roles, and many more.

The reason why walking has a history is because many of the uses and modes of walking have changed substantially over time, as a result of social, economic and especially technological change in its context. Some walking types, like pilgrimage, were common for centuries, fell out of use, and have now returned in a different form. Others are more recent in their origin. Marching as protest and demonstration became common as coherent social movements grew in the nineteenth century. Walking as an art form has developed only since the Second World War.

Wales is a fertile setting to explore walking through the ages. Its landforms – mountains and hills, moors and fells, wide and narrow valleys, and long, indented coastline, with only occasional plains and levels – are ideal country for the walker. Walking remained dominant long after horse-drawn carriages arrived, thanks to the inferior state of the roads. Wales was a poor country by comparison with its larger neighbour, and many people simply couldn't afford the cost of newer forms of transport, whether carriage, train or car.

There were certain modes of walking that Wales became known for. One of them was pilgrimage, since Wales had a large number of pilgrim destinations in the late Middle Ages. Later, another form of walking, cattle droving, emerged from the dependent patterns of agricultural trade that developed between Wales and England. In the nineteenth century, a tradition of solidarity and protest grew up among the new working classes employed in the iron and later coal industries. Their protests often took the form of mass marching to demonstrate their solidarity and strength.

Although almost all walking down the ages has been mundane, anonymous and unremembered, it's possible to trace in Wales many changes in how people have walked. Some of the clearest and most vivid traces are also the earliest. Usually, a walker leaves the lightest of traces behind, but there are human footprints that have survived, exceptionally, for millennia.

Another sign of walking is the path. New paths can be laid, but many paths we use today are clearly of old, or even ancient, origin, even if their history remains obscure. In Wales they often pick out an obvious route along a ridge or a hillside. Such paths have been trodden by countless feet over decades or centuries, and resemble palimpsests, manuscripts that have been rubbed out and rewritten countless times.

Paths are generally pacific. To conduct a war, you need a road. When the Romans arrived with their legions in Wales in 48 CE, roads were a crucial element in the conquest of new territory and the repression of its inhabitants. Military marching called for more road building during a later invasion, when Edward I launched his war of conquest and occupation in north Wales.

Walking for a living was the rule for individuals as well as groups of workers. Until quite recently, all kinds of people, from poets and ministers of religion to tramps and eccentrics, shared the roads and tracks of Wales.

Wales was among the first industrial nations. By 1851 there were already more workers employed in industries than in agriculture. If you worked in an ironworks, a mill or a coal mine you'd be likely to be fixed to a single location, but that didn't mean that you'd ceased to walk a long distance to get to and from your workplace.

For centuries Wales has attracted visitors, and many of them have been walkers. Before the eighteenth century they were relatively few in number. They tended to come for a specific reason, usually connected with emerging traditions of curiosity, antiquarianism and early scientific enquiry.

In the second half of the eighteenth century a critical 'turn' took place in the history of walking, in Wales as in much of Europe, that made a lasting difference to the way people travelled on foot. It was connected with the foregrounding of landscape as a motive for travel. Visitors chose to walk for new reasons: to place themselves in close connection with the natural world, to share a sense of the 'sublime' or the 'picturesque', to experience the pleasure of gentle ambling and strolling amid the conversation of genial companions, or to look inward to the self, to find or heal themselves.

The second major 'turn' in the story of walking in Wales happened in the second half of the nineteenth century, with the development of heavy industry and the spread of railways and motor vehicles. Gradually, over the following century, the new forms of transport came to change utterly the course of human walking. Their speed and convenience proved irresistible to people who could afford them, relegating walking to an inferior status, the resort of the poor and the desperate, or to the category of a separate, specialist activity labelled 'recreation'. An inherently egalitarian, social form of transport, one that preserved the connection between travellers and their immediate environments, gave way to travel by car, a privatised and atomised experience that deprived travellers of the varied sensations that the land, air and weather they passed through could offer them, and cut them off from interaction with fellow-travellers.

Today, with over thirty-three million cars on the roads of Britain, fitness-seekers are as likely to walk or run on the spot inside a gym than risk their health and safety outside on city streets. The gym, 'a wildlife preserve for bodily exertion' in Rebecca Solnit's phrase, is a

Cover of Rambles and walking tours around the Cambrian coast
by Hugh E. Page, 1936

(*National Library of Wales*)

replica of the real world: a place not to work, but to work out, to 'pump iron' instead of pumping water, to turn a pretend treadmill rather than a real, penal one.

The triumph of industry and of the new forms of transport, though, was never complete. Workers have frequently claimed the streets as their own, especially at times of conflict and crisis, and all kinds of walkers have insisted that they have a right to occupy both urban and rural space, for everyday and recreational purposes.

Walking has fought back in other ways. From the later nineteenth century there have been movements to promote walking for the recreation and health of workers and their families, especially in industrial towns where living conditions could be crowded and unhealthy. When the new town-dwellers of the nineteenth century found their access to countryside and fresh air much reduced, efforts were made to provide parks, promenades and other spaces for them to take exercise and recreation. At the same time, in the countryside, societies campaigned to preserve public footpaths, and to extend access to land.

After the Second World War long distance paths were established, culminating in 2012 in the Wales Coast Path, which made Wales the first country in the world to allow walkers access to its entire coastline. Today walkers and cyclists continue to protect their rights, and their rights of way, fiercely. In cities, the building of new cycle and pedestrian lanes, and movements to encourage neighbourhood-based services, and measures to slow cars and prevent them using residential streets as through routes, have begun to challenge the hegemony of the motor vehicle and restore cities to pedestrians.

Chapter 1: Hunters, invaders and pilgrims

In the beginning, we walked. Walking marked us apart from other mammals. We walked out of Africa, through the Levant, and across Asia and then Europe. Almost a million years ago our Neanderthal cousins first arrived on foot in what is now Britain. They didn't stay, but once the ice retreated and the sea level fell again – there was no 'English Channel', and the Dogger Bank was a dry plain, 'Doggerland' – humans repeated their trek, and eventually we stayed for good. It took many years to learn how to cross large expanses of water safely: Ireland for long stayed uninhabited.

In the beginning, then, it was by walking that we first found homes in the places we live in today.

Walking before history

In Wales there were hills and mountains, and a different climate, but these were no barriers to the new pedestrians. Neanderthals had already left their earliest traces in a cave near St Asaph around 230,000 years ago. The new humans began to settle in Wales about 31,000 BCE – mainly around the fringes of the land, since the interior was thickly wooded. We found homes where we could, in caves or other shelters. To survive we foraged for food in easy reach, and hunted what animals we could corner in the immediate area. Growing crops and tending domestic animals, on a settled patch of ground, came much later in this 'age of stone'. To start with we were on the move, always in search of new sources of food. In short, we spent most of our time walking.

Today it's impossible to recover the experience of those prehistoric walkers and their followers in the ages of bronze and iron. Their language and the record of it are lost to us. What we do have are a few direct signs of their walking: human footprints.

One day in February 2012 a retired geologist, Denis Bates, was walking on the beach at Y Borth in Ceredigion. Strong tides and winter storms often reshape this part of the coastline, stripping it of sand and exposing the blackened stubs of trees, remains of an ancient woodland that grew here when the sea was further off. Denis came across marks embedded in the peaty surface. They turned out to be footprints, left in the salt marsh thousands of years ago. Some were those of adults, but one belonged to a four-year old child, its toes clearly visible. Other prints were left by animals: cattle, a sheep or goat, and possibly a bear. In the same area were found traces of postholes and a wattle walkway made out of coppiced timber and laid across the waterlogged land. What exactly the owners of the feet were doing here is obscure. What's clear is that humans had long impressed their control over this part of the coast. Earlier, stone age flints and an auroch's bone had come to light in the same place. All this human activity was later engulfed and hidden when the sea level rose, giving rise perhaps to the legend of Cantre'r Gwaelod, the old kingdom in Cardigan Bay that was washed away when the guardian of the flood defences fell asleep and the sea rushed in.[1]

At Goldcliff on the edge of the Gwent Levels over 300 prehistoric footprints have been found embedded in the silts exposed by the very lowest tides of the Severn estuary. Their owners, who lived in the Mesolithic era, were of almost all ages. The average height of the adults was five and a half feet. Nearly everyone walked barefoot, most at a steady walking pace. Children, some as young as four years old, formed a large part of the group. They didn't seem to be at play, but were hard at work on the wetlands, walking together purposefully to and from a fishing or hunting site, or settlement sites that have been found in the area. Fish played a large part in the diet, and the remains of a fish-trap were found.[2]

All along the intertidal coast of the Gwent and Wentloog Levels, at Magor Pill, Redwick, Uskmouth, Peterstone and Rumney, and at other sites around the edge of Wales, barefoot prints of prehistoric men, women and children have emerged from the silty clay. For anyone who happens upon a child's footprint from 7,000 years ago, the vast span of time separating the beachcomber and the child suddenly falls away, and for a brief moment the two of them come face to face in shared humanity. No other traces of our prehistoric

Footprints in tidal mud, Uskmouth,
c4,200 BCE
(*photo Amgueddfa Cymru – National Museum Wales*)

ancestors – their tools or houses or forts or even bones – have the same power to bring a modern walker so close to prehistoric people. As Robert Macfarlane writes, Mesolithic footprints 'are among the earliest texts, from a period of history devoid of recorded narrative'.[3]

Groups of early humans in Wales were small. Their food came from hunting and foraging: settled agriculture still lay in the future. Walking was an essential way of finding food, and of moving camp from one location to another. Most people lived on or within reach of the sea. The sea and the larger rivers helped provide food, but they also made travel easier. Forests meant that long-distance land travel was slow and laborious, but people could transport themselves and their goods along rivers or the coast conveniently, and usually safely, by boat.

A revolution occurred in the Neolithic or New Stone Age: a shift to a settled pattern of life based on lowland agriculture. In Wales settlements were small and isolated, but ownership of land became important, and surpluses of food and other goods led to a more interconnected society. The sea was still a crucial means of travel, but on land uses of walking extended, from local hunting and foraging to longer distance trading and exchange. Farming, most of it pastoral, meant the clearance of woodland, and maybe walking became easier in some lowland areas that had been impenetrable before.

Tools became important, and the means of making them. In the middle and late Neolithic period what could be called the first large industrial plant in Wales began, at Graig Lwyd above Penmaenmawr. It produced polished stone axes in large numbers, from the igneous rock on the mountain headland. These enjoyed a near monopoly of use in north Wales and were exported to many places in mid and northern England. A worn prehistoric trackway can be seen today, starting from the site of the stone factory and leading eastwards to the river Conwy, a route that workers used to take consignments of the axes to the nearest port. Who made this journey we don't know: were there specialist traders, or were batches of the axes passed on from hand to hand? We don't know, either, what goods travelled in exchange in the other direction.

Around 1,600 to 1,400 years ago, in the 'Copper Age', another large industry arose in the same area. Workers dug and smelted copper from the mines of the Great Orme near Llandudno, probably the largest copper producer of its time in Europe. In the form of tools and weapons the copper found its way to many parts of southern Britain, as well as Brittany and as far afield as Sweden.[4] Much of it was carried by boat on rivers, like the Severn, and by sea. But some must have been walked for long distances, along ridgeways and other paths now lost to us. Later, Welsh copper was added to Cornish tin to make a harder metal, bronze. Again, metals travelled long distances, by water and where necessary by land.

Trading wasn't the only reason for long-distance walking. What we would now call cultural links also depended on travel across hundreds of miles. The best-known example is the transport of the 'bluestones' from the Preseli Hills in Pembrokeshire to Stonehenge in Wiltshire, a distance of almost 180 miles. We now know where the stones were quarried, between about 3,400 and 3,200 BCE: from Carn Goedog and Craig Rhos-y-felin, on the north side of the range. The dates are earlier than the building of Stonehenge, and the bluestones may have been used in a local stone circle for about a hundred years before being moved to Wiltshire. They may have been transported north and shipped along the coast. More likely, they went all the way to Stonehenge by land. Oxen may have been used to pull the stones, or maybe a team of carriers walked with each one loaded on a wooden 'pallet'.[5]

Migration was another type of long-distance walking. Archaeologists specialising in extracting and analysing ancient DNA (aDNA), the genetic signatures left by human bodies, now know that on at least two occasions, at the start of the Neolithic period and again in the early Bronze Age, large numbers of people migrated from the Continent to settle in Britain, bringing with them their own cultures and technologies.[6]

Though little recognisable remains of them today, it's likely that well-used tracks existed, even in the stone and bronze ages, to link communities that were far apart from one another. They acted as channels of trade, religion and ideas, just as much as the sea and rivers. We know nothing directly about the ideas of prehistoric people, but the cultural choices they made are reflected in the nature of their monuments. For example, the large Neolithic chambered tombs of the Talgarth area of Breconshire and the Vale of Glamorgan belong to the same regionally distinctive family of monuments as stone tombs in the Cotswolds – evidence of cultural influence operating along a land route. Most of the traffic along these early tracks would have been on foot: there's no evidence of domesticated horses being ridden until well into the Bronze Age.

In the Bronze Age influence brought along routes from the east into Wales intensified. Circular burial monuments, new kind of pottery, and the new metal technologies of copper and then bronze arrived. Improvement in the climate and increases in population encouraged people to settle on previously ignored upland areas. This is probably when feet began to wear established tracks along the hills – *cefnffyrdd* or 'ridgeways'. Many of them, like the 'Golden Road' on the Preseli Hills, are still in use by modern recreational walkers. Making these tracks was made easier because people were beginning to clear larger areas of inland woodland for pastoral agriculture, timber and charcoal. Many Bronze Age ritual monuments are on surprisingly high ground, and it's likely that people had to walk long distances to them from their homes on lower ground. Sometimes it's possible to guess the lines of tracks connecting concentrations of upland Bronze Age burial sites and stone circles – along the Kerry ridgeway in Montgomeryshire, in Cwm Cadlan near Penderyn, and two routes leading from the Severn valley and over the Berwyn range, one towards Anglesey and the other ending at Llanbedr, Merioneth.[7]

Bronze gave way to a harder metal, iron, from the seventh century BCE. Weapons became common, and heavily-defended villages or refuges ('hillforts'), some of them large, replaced the earlier scattered open settlements.

Bronze Age cairns above Cwm Cadlan, Powys
(photo Andrew Green)

The changes may or may not reflect an 'invasion' by new peoples, but society certainly became more complex and the economy more varied. Groups of peoples were amalgamated into the larger 'tribes' recorded by later Roman writers: the territory of the Silures, for example, occupied most of the central and eastern parts of south Wales. Organised warfare may have become more common, and defensive measures against it. In the later phases of the Iron Age the climate improved, populations recovered and farming flourished in the more fertile areas.

Walking still dominated land transport. Some of the defended enclosures have embanked tracks, wide enough for animals, leading up to them; they once linked with others. Occasionally archaeologists come across specially constructed tracks. At Goldcliff about twenty paths have come to light in the intertidal area, placed across the boggy ground of what are now the Gwent Levels. Some were made from tossing brushwood into place, others used big timbers, brushwood and planking. They may have been used to aid fishing or other activities, and may even have led to a ferry across the Severn estuary. In Swansea Bay are traces of another Iron Age brushwood track.[8]

Direct links with England and Europe were just as close as before. Trade in commodities like pottery and salt, and sometimes more exotic products, was long-distance. New, so-called 'Celtic' styles of art and decoration spread from the south and east through Wales. Some of this interaction was by sea, but most was by land. By now there was another common means of transporting people and goods: the horse.

Horses were used in conflict. The mounted warrior was a man of real significance. In France and parts of northern England horses were used to draw war chariots, a key mark of high status. Warriors were sometimes buried together with their chariots, and chariots and horses feature on some Iron Age coins. In 2019 two iron tyres and a sword were found by a metal detectorist in Pembrokeshire – the first evidence for a chariot to come from Wales. The existence of chariots and other, more mundane wheeled vehicles implies that at least some Iron Age routes in Wales resembled roads rather than tracks.[9]

Romans and post-Romans

With the arrival of the Romans in Wales we're on surer archaeological ground, and start to have the benefit of documentary evidence. Roman soldiers first marched into Wales in 48 CE as part of the plan to conquer Britain and subdue those who resisted their domination. The Romans met most resistance from two groups, the Ordovices in the north and the Silures in the south. The Roman advance was slow and sporadic, and it wasn't until the end of the seventies that Agricola, the governor of Britain, completed the conquest.

To overcome and control Wales the Romans relied, as they did elsewhere, on a network of fortresses and smaller forts, planted at strategically important locations and manned by legionary and auxiliary troops. The fortresses sat at the north and south 'entrances' to Wales, at Chester and Usk (later Caerleon). The forts – over thirty of them – were more numerous than usual. What made this system so effective was that these strongholds were linked by a network of new 'high-speed', 'all-weather' roads. They were carefully engineered. One section of road near Whitland was excavated in the 1990s. The ground here was peat marsh, and the military engineers first laid down a base of branches. They covered these with a foundation of quarried stone and a top layer of shale chips and waterworn cobbles, cambered so that rainwater drained into ditches on each side. The road surface, or *agger*, was about 4m wide. Later, the road was repaired, probably by civilians.[10]

Once roads were built, troops could be moved quickly, in attack or defence, from one place to another. It was many years before the network was complete. Mountainous country and the need to bridge frequent rivers made road-building difficult. Long, straight stretches, which made Roman roads so distinctive elsewhere, were less ubiquitous in Wales. And in upland areas the roadbuilders had to compromise their normal standards. It can be difficult to trace the routes of the roads, and often they have to be inferred from the positions of the nearest forts.

One surviving Roman road that's unusually clear can be followed north of Ystradfellte. It linked the forts of Coelbren and Brecon Gaer. At Blaen Llia a modern forestry track branches off the minor road running down Cwm Llia. Close by is a rectangular marching camp, a temporary stronghold the Romans used in the conquest phase of their occupation: probably the troops stayed here when building the road. The track, which follows the course of the Roman road, heads south-west through a forestry plantation. After an initial bend the road takes a straight line, upwards and then steeply down towards the ford over Afon Nedd Fechan, along a well-preserved cobbled stretch, about 8-10m wide.

At the core of the Roman army were the foot-soldiers of the legions. Each legionary was well (and heavily) equipped, with dagger, sword, spear, long shield and other equipment, like a trenching tool for building camps or roads. He wore *caligae*, or military boots of

Shoes from the Roman fortress of Usk
(photo Amgueddfa Cymru – National Museum Wales)

leather, with hobnails underneath to grip the road well (two soles with hobnails attached were found in a grave at Usk). He'd have been expected to cover at least twelve miles a day. Most forts lay within a day's march of one another. A surviving 'road-map' called the Antonine Intinerary, which might date from around 200 CE, lists some of the routes and places in Wales.

Moving soldiers and their supplies was the main use of the roads when the Romans first built them, but after they'd 'pacified' the population military garrisons were reduced. Many of the forts were abandoned or reduced in size. Roads were used for many civilian purposes, by merchants, messengers, itinerant workers and many others. Outside some of the forts and towns were buildings called *mansiones*, which offered official travellers, including 'postal workers' employed by the official mail service (the *cursus publicus*), overnight accommodation and stabling for horses.

Road travellers were helped in their wayfinding by milestones erected along the way. Strangely, to our way of thinking, the inscriptions on them seldom included mileage and destination, but they all recorded the name of the emperor on the throne when the stone was set up. About twenty milestones have been found in Wales. Many were erected along the north coast road from Caerhun to Segontium (Caernarfon), and on the south coast road near the fort of Nidum (Neath). Most date from the second half of the third century, when there seems to have been a programme to rebuild the roads. The milestones give us no information about who was responsible for building or maintaining the roads.

The marching feet began to falter at the beginning of the fifth century. Before then Roman Britain had been under attack from the sea to the west and east, but now all central military forces were withdrawn, and Britons were left to defend and govern themselves. What was going to become Wales was split into many parts. Some well-Romanised communities in the south-east probably continued and maintained themselves. In south-west Wales peoples from south-east Ireland arrived and settled. Areas gradually formed themselves into what later became the early Welsh kingdoms. Christian missionaries, the early 'saints', came, some by boat, and set up churches and monasteries.

It's tempting to think that this breaking apart must have isolated communities, restricting travel between them. But many of the Roman roads remained in use after the legions had left. About half way along the Ystradfellte section of Roman road, as you emerge from the forest, you suddenly come across Maen Madoc, an elegant stone around 2.7m high, standing by the roadside. It carries a carved inscription in Latin, 'Dervacus, son of Justus, lies here'. Dervacus was a local chieftain who lived in the sixth or seventh century, long after the end of the Roman occupation. Clearly local people were still living in the area, and walking along this road, in the early Middle Ages.[11]

Roman road and Maen Madoc, Ystradfellte

(*photo Andrew Green*)

Maen Madoc was not the only memorial stone set up after the Romans left that was sited close to a road. There's a cluster of early Christian stones from Margam, sited near the main south coast road used in Roman times.[12]

The Welsh who used the old Roman roads in the early Middle Ages had a name for them: *sarnau*. Several stretches, including the western road between Carmarthen and Caernarfon and the road linking Neath, Brecon and Caerhun, were named Sarn Elen, or Helen's Way. Later, some interpreted the name as 'track of the legion' (lleng), but the dominant tradition linked it with the wife of the late Roman emperor Magnus Maximus or Macsen Wledig. 'Macsen Wledig's dream', a tale written down in the thirteenth century but with a long oral prehistory, tells Macsen's story. Having seen a beautiful woman in a dream he orders messengers to search throughout the empire for her. They track her down in Aber Saint, or Caernarfon. As her price for marrying Macsen she asks for three forts to be built for her at Caernarfon, Carmarthen and Caerleon.

After that Elen decides to build great roads from one fort to the other across the Island of Britain. Because of that they're called Ffyrdd Elen Luyddog (Roads of Elen of the Hosts), since she came from the Island of Britain and the men of the Island of Britain would never have assembled those large armies for anyone but her.[13]

Other Mabinogion stories give an insight into how far people travelled across land in the early Middle Ages. Often the context is hunting. In the first 'branch' of the Mabinogi, Pwyll, prince of Dyfed, leads his hunt so far that he reaches Annwfn, the otherworld. Twrch Trwyth, the wild boar and anti-hero in 'Culhwch and Olwen', treks across the whole breadth of south Wales in his murderous career, from Porth Clais on the Pembrokeshire coast to the Severn estuary, pursued by Arthur and his band. His course tends to follow upland routes.

Other great walkers were the saints and monks of the early Welsh church. The earliest account of a British saint's life is that of St Samson, which was possibly written in Cornwall around the year 700. Its anonymous author has a talent for telling a good story.

Samson's father is from Dyfed, his mother from Gwent, and they take him as a child to St Illtud's famous school in the monastery of Llantwit Major. From there, with Illtud's blessing, he travels to the monastery on Caldey Island, off the south coast of Pembrokeshire. Messengers from his father make the long journey to the island to say that his father is dying, and urge him to come. Samson sets out, walking with a companion and a horse and cart. Braving 'a vast forest', the two are astonished to hear 'a frightful, shrieking cry from some awful creature near them on their right'. The sounds come from an old woman with shaggy hair, red clothes and a bloody trident, with which she stabs Samson's companion, almost to death. His companion has 'just a remnant of the breath of life' still in him. With the help of a prayer and artificial resuscitation he succeeds in restoring him to life. They continue their journey, and on the third day reach the home of Samson's father. The return journey is eventful, too: the group encounters a fire-spitting serpent capable of hurling lumps of earth, who is eventually overcome by Samson's steadfast faith.

After a spell in Ireland Samson returns to Wales and adopts the life of a hermit, in a forest cave near the River Severn. From there he's called to a synod, and walks there, reluctantly, to be ordained bishop, presumably in the year 521. But God calls him to wander again, and he leaves, with his holy vessels and books in a cart, for Cornwall and then Dol, in Brittany, where he dies.[14]

Samson was exceptional, in his ascetic lifestyle and also in the range of his travelling on foot. Most saints remained highly local. Only a few, like Dewi, Padarn and Illtud, were well-known outside a limited area.

There's another, strange source from the tenth century, that gives some impression of the experience of winter walking across Wales in the early medieval period. Normally called the 'Colloquy' or *De raris fabulis* (On uncommon tales), it's a school textbook, probably written in Wales. Its intention was to help readers improve their grasp of Latin through conversations (the author offers explanations of some words in Welsh, English and Cornish). One passage reads:

... light a fire for us and built it quickly, because I'm weak and tired from the labour of the journey, from the walking and the very long and filthy way; marshes and shit are everywhere here, and it's a very difficult and hard journey ... Get out of bed, my friends, and wake up from your usual sleep; strap on your belts and in the morning let's set out on the road: the road's long and the day's short. One person asks you which way we should go, and another says, 'I'm in the know, follow me, because I know the road and its short cuts, there's no need to ask anyone'.[15]

On long journeys the traveller needed to rely on the hospitality of strangers. Another Colloquy passage runs:

Now listen, priests, grant us help, by your soul! Give us food, drink, clothing and shoes! And then show us the right way, that will lead us to the next town or villa, or to St Peter's sacred church.[16]

Gerald of Wales

These are imaginary walks, and we have to wait another two centuries for a documentary account of a long journey, the only extended medieval narrative of walking in Wales. In the spring of the year 1188 the writer Gerald of Wales (Giraldus Cambrensis in Latin or Gerallt Gymro in Welsh), who was then about forty years old and Archdeacon of Brecon, set out on a circuit of Wales. He was accompanying Baldwin, Norman Archbishop of Canterbury, on a preaching tour intended to persuade people to join Henry II's Third Crusade. The Crusade's aim was to free Jerusalem from Salah al-Din Yusuf ibn Ayyub (Saladin), who had captured it the previous autumn.

Baldwin may have had another reason, to stamp his authority on the church in Wales. He was the first Archbishop of Canterbury to visit all four Welsh cathedrals. Gerald praises him for daring to 'undertake the task of travelling through our rough, remote and inaccessible countryside.' Baldwin might have felt some trepidation.

After all, his king had written that the Welsh were 'a wild people who cannot be tamed.'

Gerald, one quarter Welsh by birth, was born in Manorbier, in south Pembrokeshire. His feeling for Wales was genuine, as was his personal ambition. His consistent aim was to see St Davids recognised as the archbishopric of Wales, and himself installed as Archbishop. But he seems to have found it easy to make enemies, and his plan was a failure. Culturally, he was thoroughly Norman. His role on the journey is unclear. He wasn't an interpreter – he seems to have had little Welsh – and preached only on occasion. Perhaps, like Baldwin, he too had another rationale: to ingratiate himself with the Archbishop, and advance his own career. His Latin narrative of the trip, *The itinerary through Wales*, says little about its route, or even about its success, but it's full of incidental detail about the stories, traditions and miracles he encountered on the way.[17]

The travellers left Hereford, probably on 4 March 1188. From there the route took them through Radnor, Brecon, Abergavenny, Newport, Cardiff, Swansea, Carmarthen, Haverfordwest, St Davids, Cardigan, Lampeter, Llanbadarn Fawr, Tywyn, Caernarfon, Bangor, Anglesey, Basingwerk, Chester, Oswestry, Shrewsbury and back to Hereford. The distance to Chester was around 760 miles, which took over forty days of travel – an average of around 18 miles a day – nearer to walking than to riding pace. The party had horses to carry the luggage and presumably the most important travellers, such as Baldwin and Gerald, were on horseback, but others in the entourage must have travelled alongside them on foot.

The trip was well-advertised, because Baldwin was met at New Radnor, almost as soon as he entered Wales, by Rhys ap Gruffydd, 'the Lord Rhys', the dominant figure in independent south Wales at the time. Rhys was on good terms with Henry II, and probably had a hand in arranging the tour.

The first real challenge for the group was the journey across the Black Mountains from Brecon to Abergavenny. Gerald's anxiety is obvious: 'the natives of these parts are much given to implacable quarrels and never-ending disputes. They spend their time fighting each other and shed their blood freely in internecine feuds.' His talk of 'savage acts of violence' was no exaggeration.

The group continued southwards, through Usk and Caerleon to Newport, before turning west to Cardiff, along 'the coast-road which runs round the south of Wales' – maybe the old Roman road. Mass was celebrated in the cathedral at Llandaf. Then through Ewenny and the monastery at Margam towards the river Afan, where they were 'delayed for some time by the ebbing of the water'. With 'Morgan the eldest son of Caradog, as our guide and leader', they reached the next major obstacle, the estuary of the river Neath:

> As we approached the Neath, which is the most dangerous and difficult of access of all the rivers of south Wales, on account of its quicksands, which immediately engulf anything placed upon them, one of our pack-horses, the only one possessed by the writer of these lines, was sucked down into the abyss ... In the end it was pulled out with some difficulty, thanks to the efforts made by our servants, who risked their lives in doing so, and not without some damage done to my books and baggage. It was true that we had Morgan, the prince of these parts, as our guide, but we reached the river only after considerable danger and quite a few upsets. Against the advice of our leader, our fear of the unusual surface made us hurry across the quicksands.[18]

Gerald of Wales, stained glass, St James's Church, Manorbier
(photo Andrew Green)

At Swansea Baldwin and his party stayed in the castle, before crossing the river Loughor and moving north to pass over the Tywi by boat to reach Carmarthen.

Gerald notes that south Pembrokeshire was full of colonists from Flanders, settled there by Henry I, and that there was no love lost between them and the indigenous Welsh. Manobier, 'the most pleasant place by far' in Wales, receives a hymn of praise, and, equally predictably, Gerald spends many pages on St Davids. At Cardigan the group was welcomed (again) by Rhys ap Gruffydd, and many 'take the cross'.

Then on through Lampeter, Strata Florida, Llanddewi Brefi and Llanbadarn Fawr. Crossing the Dyfi the travellers found themselves in north Wales. Rhys ap Gruffudd said farewell, and they accelerated their pace. This was less hospitable country, geographically and socially. Merioneth, Gerald says, is 'the rudest and the roughest of all the Welsh districts':

> The mountains are very high, and narrow ridges and a great number of very sharp peaks all jumbled together in confusion. If the shepherds who shout to each other and exchange comments from those lofty summits should ever decide to meet, it would take them almost the whole day to climb down and up again.[19]

Crossing the Dysynni and Artro rivers and the great expanse of Traeth Mawr, the group reached Llŷn and noticed Ynys Enlli (Bardsey Island), the home of 'some extremely devout monks'.

Around Caernarfon Baldwin and his entourage entered a valley where the going was hard, with many steep slopes:

> We dismounted from our horses and proceeded on foot, in intention at least rehearsing what we thought we would experience when we went on our pilgrimage to Jerusalem. We walked the whole length of the valley, and we were very tired by the time we reached the farther end.[20]

The archbishop sat down to rest on an uprooted oak tree and listened to the song of an unidentified bird nearby. When someone remarked that it could hardly be a nightingale, which was unknown in this area, he replied, 'If it never comes to Wales the nightingale is a very sensible bird. We are not quite so wise, for not only have we come here but we have traversed the whole country'. This would be a sentiment shared by many English visitors to Wales in the centuries to follow, and expressed in a variety of ways, from distaste to disgust.

Things got no better for the poor Archbishop during the rest of the trip. The group crossed the Menai Strait from Bangor to Anglesey, and held one meeting there, near the seashore, before returning immediately.

At this point in his narrative Gerald includes a digression on the mountains of Eryri (Snowdonia) to the south, which 'seem to rear their lofty summits right up to the clouds'. For him and his companions this was unknown territory, a remote land of wonder and myth. He mentions two lakes, one with a floating island, the other containing eels, trout and perch, but all of them possessing only one eye. This view of the mountains, a combination of ignorance, terror and superstition, prevailed for centuries to come among visitors to north Wales.

By now you sense that Baldwin had seen enough of Wales. He moved swiftly east from Conwy, through Rhuddlan, St Asaph and Basingwerk to Chester. He and his band took just less than three days to cover over fifty miles, so all them by now must have been on horseback.

Gerald says very little about the roads Baldwin and his band travelled along in Wales. Apart from the episode of the Neath quicksands he mentions no dangers or difficulties they encountered. There must have been plenty. Gerald does mention the welcomes the party received when they arrived at different destinations. In another of his works, *The description of Wales*, he writes of the Welsh,

> They very much enjoy welcoming others to their homes. When you travel there is no question of your asking for accommodation or of their offering it: you just march into a house and hand over your weapons to the person in charge.[21]

Even the routes of the roads they took are seldom certain. It's often assumed that medieval travellers followed Roman or earlier tracks where they could, but that very few new roads were built throughout the Middle Ages, and few new bridges (Gerald says he crossed the river Usk by ford and the rivers Neath, Tywi, Dyfi and Mawddach by boat, but mentions no bridges). It's not easy today to judge how true these assumptions are.

It does seem that armies made new roads when they needed to. We hear of large number of trees being felled in Wales by English armies, under Henry II, Henry III and especially Edward I, to help speed the progress of troops along new roads, and to keep them safe from Welsh ambush. Between April and August 1277 up to 1,800 specialist workmen, recruited from England, were employed to cut a route from Chester to Deganwy. A cordon of around 200 feet was cleared on either side of the road – between 1,000 and 2,000 acres of woodland. The contemporary poet Gruffudd ab yr Ynad Coch lamented, 'don't you see the oaks crashing into one another?'[22]

Monasteries were also associated with road travel. Those at Whitland and Strata Florida were ordered to mend roads on two occasions, in 1278 and 1280, and Basingwerk Abbey was told to cut trees down to keep roads open and clear. Roads linking religious houses appear to have been important for long-distance travel. In 1238 leaders from all over Wales were summoned to Strata Florida Abbey to swear allegiance to Dafydd, son of Llywelyn the Great. The Abbey was a central location, and was presumably not too difficult to get to.

Archaeological evidence for roads of this period also comes from Strata Florida. Roads spread from the Abbey in all directions. One led east across the Cambrian Mountains for twenty-three miles to its sister foundation, Abbey Cwm-hir (a fit person could walk this distance in a day), with a spur to a third Cistercian abbey, Strata Marcella. This route was later called the Monks' Trod and has been described as 'the best-preserved medieval road in Britain'. The road was up to six metres wide, had been surfaced in places, and was well engineered, with terraces dug into the hill slope using a 'cut and fill' technique. Tradition records the name of another road from the Abbey, Lôn Lacs, which led to the Monks' coastal estate at Aber-arth. Strata Florida had been re-founded by Rhys ap Gruffudd in 1184, and

Monks' Trod, below Carn Ricet, Powys
(*photo Anthony Griffiths, from* Elenydd: ancient heartland of the Cambrian mountains)

it may have been he who built the roads to link not only the monasteries and their granges but also the different parts of the territory he ruled.[23]

It seems that monks were used to walking long distances. In 1195 the monks of Abbey Cwm-hir, who had stolen their abbot's horses after he refused to allow them to drink beer, were ordered to walk all the way to Clairvaux in north-eastern France, the Cistercians' headquarters, to receive their punishment.[24]

There's a tantalising document called the 'Gough Map' that on first sight should tell us more about medieval roads. Named after Richard Gough, an eighteenth-century antiquary, it's the earliest 'road map' of Britain to survive. It seems to show the routes of roads connecting places, and the distances between each place. But it's unclear when or why it was made, or how to interpret the routes and distances. One theory is that the two 'roads' shown in Wales, which fail to take the natural courses one would expect, show the routes that were critical to Edward I during his wars of conquest. The northern one links the new castles in his 'ring of iron'. But in truth the Map tells us little with certainty about the number, course or state of Welsh roads.

It's possible, then, that rather more care was taken to build and maintain Welsh roads in the Middle Ages than we can see from the historical and archaeological record. There would be good reason for it, because long-distance walking and riding were common. Soldiers, messengers, monks, traders, minstrels, outlaws and many others would have thronged the roads. Cattle and sheep were moved between winter and summer pastures (*hendre* and *hafod*), and later on to market. Poets, whose works survive in considerable numbers, often walked long distances in search of patrons. In the fifteenth century Lewys Glyn Cothi travelled all over Wales, and Guto'r Glyn was used to moving from house to house (*clera*) to entertain patrons with his poems. Madog Dwygraig was proud that he could travel in unknown parts of Wales without a guide. In a poem called 'The soul's conversation with the body', composed about 1380, Iolo Goch gives a description of the kind of journey through Wales that was not uncommon for wandering poets in search of patrons. He starts from his home in Denbighshire and walks along the Marches, through Carmarthenshire to Kidwelly and Whitland, before turning north through Cardiganshire and returning home. The poem praises the hospitality of those who gave him shelter and food. 'Ar hyd y byd rhodio bûm', he says: 'I wandered all over the world'.[25]

Pilgrims

There was one group of travellers who had a special reason for taking to the road for a lengthy period: pilgrims. Pilgrimage was a common custom in Wales, and there were many sacred sites that attracted people, from within Wales and beyond. Pilgrimage was a spiritual activity, a form of religious devotion. To be a pilgrim was a declaration of your profound faith as a Christian, a sign of humility and of imitation of the example of Christ himself.[26]

Pilgrimage called for a high degree of physical exertion from the individuals or groups who made the journey from their home to a place many miles, or even many countries, away. The English word 'pilgrim' and the Welsh 'pererin' come from the Latin 'peregrinus', a foreigner or stranger, and all but very local pilgrims deliberately exiled themselves, strangers in unfamiliar territory, that may be wild or even dangerous. To come as close as possible physically to a sacred site – the relics of a saint, or an ancient rood, or a holy well – gave pilgrims an additional, spiritual access to the sacred power itself, and its ability to affect their lives (or afterlives) for the better. The journey, however local, involved a transition from the material, familiar world towards a glimpse of another, better life.

Religious devotion, though, was often blended, for medieval pilgrims, with other interests, or self-interests. Probably the commonest was to seek a cure for an ailment or a disability through the intercession of the saint whose shrine you aimed to visit. Or maybe to give thanks to the saint for a successful recovery. St Dyfnog, whose church was in Llanrhaeadr-yng-Nghinmeirch in Denbighshire, was the general practitioner of medieval saints, able to help with all kinds of complaints:

> Pob cul afiach, pob clefyd,
> Pob gwan o bedwar ban byd,
> Pob efrydd rhwym (afrwydd rhus),
> Pob nifer, pob anafus.

> Every sick bag of bones, every disease,
> Every invalid from the world over,
> Every cripple, bandaged tight,
> Every crowd, every casualty.[27]

These are words of Dafydd ap Llywelyn ap Madog, one of several poets who wrote about pilgrimage and shrines. Some, like Dafydd, acted as virtual publicity agents for pilgrimage sites.

St Winefred's Well at Holywell was one of the pre-eminent pilgrimage sites in Wales, and indeed Britain, at the end of the Middle Ages, and is still visited today by those suffering from illness or disability and hopeful of relief. The poet Tudur Aled made large claims for the cures a dip in the waters could bring about: blindness, lameness, skin disease, mental illness, infertility, paralysis, deafness and dumbness, and even death itself could all be overcome.[28] The well attracted many wealthy Normans. In 1115 Richard, Earl of Chester made the journey there 'for his great merit and ghostly [spiritual] advantage'. Later, kings of England came: Richard II in 1398, Henry IV in 1403 and Henry V in 1416. It's likely that they had political motives, in turbulent times: pilgrimage was, in part, propaganda. Henry Tudor may have called there on his way to victory at Bosworth, and his mother, Margaret Beaufort, was responsible for building a new, Italian-style chapel beside the well between 1490 and 1500.[29]

St Winefred's Well, Holywell, engraving by
R. Wilkinson, c1790, from an original etching by Francis Place, 1699
(*Wellcome Collection*)

Kings and other elite visitors would have arrived at pilgrimage sites on horseback and with an entourage. But pilgrimage was an activity for people in all ranks of society, and most pilgrims travelled on foot. The time and effort needed to walk the journey were an important part of the experience, especially if the pilgrim was driven by another motivation, to atone for past sins. The classic, international pilgrimages, to Jerusalem, Rome or Santiago de Compostela, were very lengthy and, for most ordinary people, out of the question. Journeys to Welsh destinations were much more practicable, and could be presented as just as acceptable. According to one account, in the 1120s Pope Callixtus II 'encouraged English pilgrims to go to St Davids rather than Rome, because of the length of the journey; those who went twice to St Davids should have the same privileges in the way of benediction as those who went once to Rome.' Most of the pilgrims seem to have been men: there's little evidence for women making pilgrimages to shrines in Wales (a few are recorded as travelling to continental sites).[30]

In time, specific pilgrim routes became established. Madeleine Gray and others have reconstructed one route, from the Cistercian abbey of Llantarnam to Pen-rhys in the Rhondda valley, a site dedicated to the Virgin Mary and, like St Winefride's Well, one of the most popular pilgrim destinations in the fifteenth century. Some of the route lay on land owned by Llantarnam Abbey, and pilgrims could find accommodation in or near its granges and chapels, as well as in inns or other houses. Fit walkers might manage the distance, about forty miles, in two or three days, but sick pilgrims would have taken longer. Many, especially those seeking cures, would have walked in groups for mutual support and safety.[31]

Most pilgrims would have made the journey in summer or early autumn, to take advantage of drier weather and, if possible, to coincide with the three main festivals of the Virgin Mary, the Feast of Visitation (3 July), the Assumption (15 August) and the Nativity (8 September).

When they reached Pen-rhys, after a strenuous climb uphill, pilgrims found, in a forest clearing, a well, a chapel, a wooden painted and gilded image of the Virgin Mary, probably a hospital, and other buildings, all prepared to receive visitors. They'd remain there till the following morning. An all-night vigil was followed by services and a bathe in the holy water. The site expected each pilgrim to give an offering: money, large candles or other payment for its services. Another source of income was the selling of 'indulgences', which set the sinner free from punishment in Purgatory, in whole or in part. In 1398 the Pope granted the abbot of Llantarnam the right to sell indulgences to Pen-rhys pilgrims. These donations and sales helped pay towards the upkeep and extension of the sanctuary buildings and ornaments.

Pen-rhys had the advantage of 'publicists', local Glamorgan poets who advertised the benefits of a trip to the shrine, and may have received payment from the shrine for doing so. The work of six of them survive. Llywelyn ap Hywel ab Ieuan ap Gronw of Miskin, who was active between 1460 and 1480, sang of the Virgin:

> Dwyn enaid pob dyn uniawn
> A wna, a chorff, yn iachiawn.
> Rhoi clywed a dywedyd,
> Y mae i fyddar a mud.
> Aed dall i gyfy â hon,
> O'i phlegid caiff olygon.

> She causes the body and soul
> of every righteous man to become very healthy.
> She gives [the power of] hearing and speech
> to the deaf and dumb.
> A blind man goes to commune with her,
> and, as a result, gains [his] sight.[32]

A second, Gwilym Tew, describes Pen-rhys as 'a glade on the nose of the forest, Eucharist bread and holy water', a shrine that attracted 'people who worked with their hands'. He too writes of hopes for a cure, and of his offering:

> Af i Ben-rhys yn fy un crys, rhag ofn y cryd,
> ac ar fy nglin, oed pererin, dapr o wryd.

> I will go to Pen-rhys
> in my one shirt, in fear of fever,
> and on my knee,
> at the age to be a pilgrim,
> a candle, a fathom long.[33]

From Llantarnam (or Llandaf) to Pen-rhys was a fairly short journey, but other pilgrim trails in Wales were longer and harder work for the walker. An established route ran parallel to the north Wales coast towards another, much more difficult destination, Ynys Enlli (Bardsey Island), two miles off the western tip of Llŷn.[34] The island's fame arose from the tradition that 20,000 saints were buried there.

Among early saints reputedly buried on the island were St Dyfrig and St Deiniol. It's likely there was an early monastery there, in the tradition of the early Christian saints of the Near East, who sought out remote, desert locations as far they could get from secular society. By the thirteenth century an Augustinian monastery had been established, perhaps by Llywelyn ap Iorwerth. Soon Ynys Enlli was famous as a place of pilgrimage, well beyond Wales. In July 1284, Edward I, fresh from his victories over the Welsh, stayed for three days on the island.

The journey to Enlli was long and hard, but popular. In the late Middle Ages, churches along the pilgrimage route, like Gresford, Clynnog Fawr and Llanengan, important shrines in themselves, were extended and provided with new features. Many of the funds used to do this no doubt came from passing pilgrims. All along the way was a network of smaller sacred sites, easily 'readable', even by the walker wholly unfamiliar with the terrain: churches, chapels, and wells, many of them holy and known for their healing powers, where pilgrims could rest, bathe and fill their bottles. Farms, chapels and other places were geared to provide accommodation.

In Llŷn the walking became harder and more mountainous, until pilgrims reached Aberdaron, on the tip of the peninsula. Here they could pay homage in St Hywyn's church, or at several chapels and wells nearby. Then, as long as the weather was fine – bad weather could cut the island off for days or even weeks at a time – they'd take a small boat to Ynys Enlli, across one of the most dangerous passages of water off the coast of Wales.

Poets warned of the perils of the crossing. Bleddyn Fardd wrote of 'white waves that make loud the holy land of Enlli', Meilyr Brydydd of 'a wilderness of unperishable glory' and Enlli's purifying isolation (he wished to be buried there). Another poet, Rhys Llwyd ap Rhys ap Rhicert, tells of a sea journey from Aberystwyth to Ynys Enlli and back. On the return journey the pilgrims were lucky to survive. At one point, when waves threatened to swamp the boat, the captain considered throwing some of his passengers overboard.[35]

Such sea journeys weren't uncommon. Around the coasts of Wales, at Tenby and in Swansea Bay, pilgrim badges and ampulae, small shell-shaped flasks of holy water, have been found. It's thought they were thrown overboard from boats returning from shrines by pilgrims in thanks for their safe passage.

Pilgrim badge from Pembrokeshire
(photo Amgueddfa Cymru –
National Museum Wales)

Less difficult to reach than Ynys Enlli but still remote in its way was Pennant Melangell at the foot of the Berwyn Mountains in northern Montgomeryshire. Here was a shrine to St Melangell, the patron saint of hares. According to tradition, recorded in the fifteenth century *History* of the saint, she came to Wales from Ireland to escape an arranged marriage, and settled to a solitary life of devotion. One day a local prince, Brochwel, arrived to hunt a hare with his hounds. Melangell hid the terrified hare under her dress, and the dogs retreated, howling in fear. Impressed by Melangell's devotion and care, Brochwel gave her land as a sanctified refuge. Here she established a community with other women and lived for a further thirty-seven years.[36]

Melangell's grave became a site of devotion, and in the twelfth century a new shrine was built over her bones in Cwm Pennant, probably by Rhirid Flaidd, the local ruler. It stands, in reconstructed form, in the chancel of the church, the earliest Romanesque shrine of its kind, it's thought, in northern Europe. The relic-holder is supported on an arcade of columns, and above it is a gabled roof.

It was the prospect of coming close to the relics of Melangell that drew pilgrims from afar. Touching and kissing the bodily remains of a saint – even crawling underneath the relics – brought them as close they could get to the saint in heaven, and to God. For most people Pennant Melangell was a long way to walk. It was remote from towns, in deep woodland near the head of the Tanat valley. Few poets mention the site, and we know little about who its pilgrims were. It may be that they included women, attracted to a female saint. The shrine's reputation as a safe refuge from oppression and violence may also have added to its appeal.

Pennant Melangell offers one example of a 'proxy pilgrim'. When Morgan Herbert, then living in Worcestershire, made his will in 1526, he made provision for his servant, Howell Gethyn, to make a pilgrimage, wearing his master's 'gown of black cloth', to five sites, including Pennant Melangell, and to make an offering in each, for the benefit of Morgan Herbert's soul. Presumably visiting five shrines gave it five times the chance of a good passage. We've no record of whether (or how) Howell walked the long miles to visit the shrines.[37]

Another destination for pilgrims that could also mean a long walk, especially for those coming from England, was the journey to St Davids. One route linked St Davids with the other pre-eminent site, St Winefride's Well, a distance of over 150 miles. Its route can be traced in *Britannia*, a post-medieval 'road map' and one of the earliest printed strip maps, published by John Ogilby in 1675, which notes the hills (both up and down) in the walker's path. A playful poem by Dafydd ap Gwilym imagines a different route, from Anglesey to St Davids, a journey taken by a 'nun' as penitence for disappointing the author in love. He hopes she overcomes the barriers in her way. Most of them are rivers and estuaries, the perennial headache of coastal walkers:

Gydne gwin, gad, naw gwaneg
Dysynni, i dir Dewi deg.
A dwfnyw tonnau Dyfi,
Dŵr rhyn, yn ei herbyn hi.
Rheidol, gad er d'anrhydded
Heol i fun hael o fedd.

Ystwyth, ym mhwyth, gad ym hon,
Dreistew ddwfr, dros dy ddwyfron.

Dysynni of the nine waves,
let the wine–coloured girl on her way to David's fair land.
Deep too are the waves of Dyfi,
freezing water, against her.
Rheidol, for the sake of your good name,
give passage to a girl generous with mead.
Ystwyth, deep violent water,
in recompense let her over your breast for me.[38]

Pope Callixtus's ruling that two trips to St Davids equalled one pilgrimage to Rome – and therefore worthy of a 'plenary' indulgence, or release from punishment for sins – guaranteed St Davids a steady stream of walkers in the late Middle Ages.

St Davids was part of the 'indulgence industry', but it also had prestige as the home of St David's relics, after they were 'discovered' in the 1270s, and as a royal destination. William I, Henry II and Edward II all visited. And it had had a large cathedral, where the pilgrim could take part in services.

In the sixteenth century, pilgrimage, with its ritual and devotion at shrines, was one of many Catholic practices that came under suspicion, and then suppression, by the new protestants. Henry VIII's treatment of Pen-rhys, a Marian shrine, was extreme. Thomas Cromwell ordered the statue of Mary there to be removed, on 26 September 1538, 'as secretly as may be', after nightfall, possibly to avoid protest. The image was taken to London and burnt at Smithfield, in an orgy of iconoclasm. Hugh Latimer, Bishop of Worcester, eager to root out 'idolatry and many kinds of superstition' had written in June to Cromwell about the statue of Our Lady of Worcester:

...she hath been the devil's instrument to bring many (I fear) to eternal fire: now she herself, with her old sister of Walsingham, her young sister of Ipswich, with her other two sisters of Dongcaster and Penryesse [Pen-rhys], would make a jolly muster in Smithfield; they would not be all day in burning.[39]

The same happened in Llandderfel in Merioneth, in the same year. Cromwell gave the task of destroying the wooden statue of St Derfel (Derfel Gadarn), another object of pilgrimage, to Ellis Price of Plas Iolyn. Price reported to Cromwell that 'the people have so great confidence, hope and trust that they come daily a pilgrimage unto him'. Five or six hundred pilgrims had made offerings on that year's feast day, 5 April. The people of the area protested – no doubt they were all too aware of the economic value of the pilgrims to the area – and even offered Price a large sum, £40, if the government relented. But the image was taken off to London and burnt at Smithfield. Price spared the wooden stag that sat as the base of Derfyl's statue: its torso lies in the church today, a rare survival. The fire was used to burn to death a Catholic, John Forest, who refused to acknowledge the King as head of the church, so fulfilling a prophecy that Derfel's image would one day burn down a forest.

With the Reformation the age of pilgrimage was almost at an end. Most shrines ceased to attract large numbers of pilgrims. But St Winefride's Well survived. Elizabeth I threatened to close it, but it continued as a destination. James II paid an official visit there in 1686, and it also survived the Civil Wars and the Interregnum. In some remote parts of Wales the old ways continued. In 1567 Nicholas Robinson, Bishop of Bangor, complained to William Cecil about the survival of the 'dregges of superstition':

> ... I have found since I came to this country images and altars standing in churches undefaced, lewd and indecent vigils and watches observed, much pilgrimage going, many candles set up to the honour of saints, some reliquaries yet carried about, and all the countries full of beads and knots, beside diverse other monuments of wilful serving God.[40]

Images of Welsh pilgrims are rare. In St Illtud's Church in Llanelltyd near Dolgellau is a highly unusual stone pillar. Carved into its end is the outline of a single human foot, and a Latin inscription, which probably dates from the twelfth century. It reads, 'On the top of this stone is the footprint of Cynwrig; he himself is bound [by oath] before setting out for unknown parts.' The word for 'unknown parts' is 'peregre', the root word of 'pilgrim', and it's likely that Cynwrig was a pilgrim, anxious perhaps to make public his commitment to make a long walk to a distant destination.[41]

In another church, Llandyfodwg (Glynogwr), lies a stone relief effigy of a complete pilgrim. He holds a staff and carries a satchel. With him are badges of his mission, including two crosses, a scallop shell and crossed keys, the symbol of St Peter. He may have died near here on his way to a pilgrimage site, like Pen-rhys or St Davids. His name could have been Dafydd Fychane; if so, the monument may date to around 1450.[42]

The Reformation may have suppressed the custom of walking to distant shrines, but Cynwrig and Dafydd Fychane have had many followers in the centuries since. Destinations may have changed, and the reasons for walking to them, but recent years have seen a pilgrimage revival, discussed in Chapter 8.

Pilgrim memorial in St Tyfodwg's Church, Glynogwr

(*photo Andrew Green*)

Chapter 2: Drovers, loners and tourists

Under the Tudor monarchs and their successors Wales gradually ceased to be a 'medieval' country and started to become a 'modern' one. Sporadic armed conflict gave way to longer periods of peace. The population of Wales increased and so did economic activity, including mining and manufacturing. Towns began to grow and external trade to flourish. Henry VIII's Acts of Union of 1536 and 1543 assimilated Wales into England's systems of government and justice, and economic, social and cultural links with England all developed.

Roads

In other ways little changed. Most people seldom moved out of their local areas. Movement of people and goods was still slow. Until the turnpike trusts began their work in the second half of the eighteenth century, roads were mostly unimproved, so that long-distance travel remained difficult. After the Highways Act of 1555 individual parishes were supposed to maintain and improve their own roads according to the 'statute labour' or 'corvée' system, under the supervision of officers called 'surveyors of highways'. They had the power to compel all able-bodied residents to contribute six days' unpaid labour each year to roads. But few took the job seriously. In Wales a day that a parishioner was supposed to devote to road works was known colloquially as 'diwrnod i'r brenin', 'a day for the King', a phrase that came to be a proverb for idleness and frivolity. In the mid-eighteenth-century Valentine Morris of Piercefield, asked in the House of Commons what roads there were in Monmouthshire, is said to have replied 'None'. In response to a second question, 'How then do you travel?', he answered, 'In ditches'.[1]

Until quite late in the eighteenth century, if you wanted to travel long distances over land in Wales, or from Wales to England, you generally had only two choices: on horseback – the roads were seldom good enough to support wheeled traffic like coaches – or by foot. And for poorer people the choice was made for you. You had to walk.

Walking was how almost all working people in Wales got around, on their way to the fields, the quarries or mines, the nearest village or town, the coasts and rivers, the fairs, and further afield when that was unavoidable. Walking as an activity was so universal, so taken for granted, that we have hardly any accounts of journeys on foot before the eighteenth century, and none by working people (many of whom, of course, were unable to write). The vast majority of walking trips were local. Women often walked barefoot, up to the middle of the nineteenth century, a fact that surprised and often shocked visitors to Wales. But some people made a living from walking longer distances. The best-known group of them was the drovers.

The drovers

Droving cattle (and sheep and other animals) was an example of the increasing interdependence of the economies of Wales and England. Welsh cattle were highly prized. Cattle were specially appreciated for their meat by hungry members of the upper and middling classes of England. They were bred and fed initially in west and north Wales, before being herded over well-worn drove routes across the mountains and hills of Wales and then along lowland English roads, to be fattened in the English Midlands, Essex or Kent, and later sold in the large fairs and markets, like Barnet and Smithfield near London.[2]

Droving called for special skills and resources. Cattle had to be sought locally and paid for, assembled into large groups and shoed at recognised centres, and then escorted eastwards for hundreds of miles, often over difficult terrain and in bad weather. At market the drovers sold their beasts for the best prices they could command, before making the long return journey to Wales.

When droving to England began is unclear. It was certainly well under way as an organised activity by the fifteenth century. Around the middle of the century the poet Guto'r Glyn wrote a humorous poem entitled 'Porthmona' (Droving), in which the poet pictures himself driving sheep belonging to his noble patron 'Sir Benet', parson of Corwen, to the English Midlands:

Euthum innau i borthmona,
waethwaeth farsiandïaeth da.
Yr oedd ym ar ryw ddamwain
wŷr ar hur i yrru'r rhain,
deuwr yn eu llamdwyaw
a'r prydydd yn drydydd draw.
I Rug ac i Gefn yr Ais
ac i Warwig y gyrrais;
ac i Loegr drwy bob coegryd,
o bwll i bant i bell byd.

Myself, off I went droving
though the trade was fast going to pot.
I'd hired men on hand to drive the beasts,
two of them in the lead, and there, in no. 3 position,
yours sincerely, the poet.
To Rug, and Cefn yr Ais,
and Warwick I drove them,
to England, through every miserable ford,
every bog and trough to the end of the world.[3]

Things go from bad to worse for them. The lambs get stuck in hedges and ditches. Floods drown many of them. The market price is depressed. The drovers roam the Midlands ('sixty towns as far as Coventry') in vain. They walk to other parts of England in search of a better price: Lichfield, Stafford and York, where the locals 'mock our language'. Guto ends by making no profit at all ('I'm a wretchedly bad drover') – unlike, he says with some envy, his fellow-poet and drover Tudur Penllyn, who sold his sheep back home in Ardudwy.

Tudur Penllyn reacts to this reference with a poem in response, praising 'Sir Benet', as did Guto, and casting doubt on Guto's story of complete failure. Far from losing Benet's lambs in 'a flood full of wool' in the north of England, he suggests, Guto in fact made a fat profit on them:

Maent yn fyw, mintai ŵyn falch,
mae gwlân, defnydd rhag annwyd,
brethyn llawn brithwyn llwyd;
mae 'mhell, ei dröell a dry,
a'i gribwraig yn Lloegr obry.

They're alive, that happy troop of lambs!
There's wool enough to ward off cold,
wool cloth, flecked with white and grey.
He's far away, with his spinning wheel awhirl,
and his combing-woman, down there in England.[4]

Tudur warns Sir Benet that Guto is likely to ask his patron whether he can give him more lambs to sell in England. He'd be wise to refuse.

In a third poem Guto makes a counter-response to Tudur. He insists that his story is true. He really did, through ill-luck, lose every one of the two hundred lambs Sir Benet had entrusted to him. Tudur, with his long grey hair and big feet, is a slanderer, and pitiless, since he has lambs galore while he, Guto, has none.

Did Guto really drive sheep to England? It's been argued that his story is imaginary, invented as the focus of the playful literary competition between Guto and Tudur. The theme of the three poems, after all, is the unreliability of narrative. But the details of Guto's poem have the concreteness of real experience, and in another, unconnected poem he implies that he really did have a droving past. Tudur Penllyn was certainly a farmer, with experience of droving. Whatever the literal truth, the two poets and their patron share a common familiarity with the drover's life. They knew that it was financially precarious, physically exhausting and sometimes dangerous.

As it happens, Guto and Tudur are the first and almost the last of the Welsh drovers who speak in their own words at any length. As so often, a whole class of workers is almost entirely mute, in this case over a period of four centuries. There are few biographies or autobiographies, no diaries and few stories, just occasional sets of financial accounts. A few drovers achieved fame, but for other achievements: Dafydd Jones of Caeo (1711–77) may have been a drover before he was converted to religion and became a noted hymn-writer. His verse to a cobbler suggests long hours of walking:

Rhowch imi bar o dapau,
Rhai tewon, nid rhai tenau,
a ddalio i fyn'd o fan i fan,
yn wydnon dan fy ngwadnau.

Give me a pair of bindings,
thick ones, not thin ones,
that will take me from place to place,
tough under my soles.[5]

Otherwise, the life of the drovers has to be pieced together from scattered mentions in legal documents, descriptions by visitors and other writers, and from fieldwork on drove routes.

Droving was an important part of the economy of Wales by the seventeenth century. In 1644 John Williams, Archbishop of York, wrote a letter to Prince Rupert, after the start of the Civil War, asking for protection for the Welsh cattle trade, describing it as 'the Spanish fleet of north Wales, which brings hither that little gold and silver we have'. But the heyday of the trade was the eighteenth century and the first half of the nineteenth century, when droves of many hundreds of cattle would make their way across the mountains to England. In the 1720s Daniel Defoe noted that 'the whole county of Cardigan is so full of cattle that 'tis said to be the nursery, the breeding-place for the whole kingdom of England.'

The first task of the dealer or drover was to collect cattle locally, either from fairs or from individual farms, usually in the autumn. Owners of cattle were sometimes paid direct, so the purchaser needed to have funds at hand, though credit was often used. Enough money in hand was needed to pay the expenses of transporting cattle over a long period. This suggests that most buyers were not poor, and from the late eighteenth century specialist dealers emerged, like Roderick Roderick of Porth-y-rhyd and the Jonathan family of Dihewyd, who collected animals over a large part of Wales. Drovers were adept at getting a good bargain.

Assembling cattle for the spring journey to England was often no easy matter. Animals bought in Anglesey had to be escorted across the waters of the Menai Strait. Arthur Aikin, an English tourist, observed their passage in 1776:

> They are urged in a body by loud shoutings and blows into the water, and as they swim well and fast, usually make their way for the opposite shore: the whole troop proceeds pretty regularly till it arrives within about an hundred and fifty yards of the landing place, when, meeting with a very rapid current formed by the tide, eddying, and rushing with great violence between the rocks that encroach far into the channel, the herd is thrown into the utmost confusion. Some of the boldest and strongest push directly across, and presently reach the land; the more timorous immediately turn round, and endeavour to gain the place from which they set off; but the greater part, borne down by the force of the stream, are carried towards Beaumaris bay, and frequently float to a great distance before they are able to reach the Caernarvonshire shore.[6]

Cattle were brought together in centres close to the mountain crossings. An important centre in mid-Wales was Tregaron, a focus for cattle bought in Cardiganshire and north Carmarthenshire. In 1827 the town had twelve inns, many catering to the cattle trade. Before setting off, the feet of the cattle had to be shod, to avoid lameness on the hard roads ahead. There were several blacksmiths in the town (six in 1850) to provide for the cattle trade, with enclosures close by to keep cattle safe: one of them lay behind the Talbot Hotel. Nailing shoes was a tricky operation, requiring skill and strength to 'throw' or fell each beast (most were three or four years old) and attach to each hoof the 'ciw', an iron shoe consisting of two separate plates. In case shoes needed to be replaced en route, spare ciws were carried, covered in butter to avoid rusting, and on large droves a smith would accompany the herd.

By now the chief drover had hired between four and eight drove hands to escort the cattle (between a hundred and four hundred might make up a single drove). Rhys Morgan of Tregaron, who was still droving at the end of the nineteenth century, usually employed a dozen men. Ordinary drovers would receive pay of about 2s a day, topped up with a lump sum to meet the costs of their return to Wales.

Almost all drovers were men. An exception was Jane Evans of Ty'n y Waun, Caeo. She was a pig farmer, and would no doubt be used to driving her pigs long distances. Later she set out to join Florence Nightingale in the Crimean War, and she's commemorated by a memorial and bust inside Pumsaint Chapel. Other women would have come along, migrating to southern England for the season to work in agriculture and market gardening. Sometimes the drovers were joined by other travellers, like apprentices on their way to London. They could take advantage of safety in numbers, as well as the drovers' company and their knowledge of the route.

Pont Scethin, Merioneth

(*photo Andrew Green*)

Many upland drovers' roads can still be traced today. One of the best is the lonely track from Cors-y-gedol near Dyffryn Ardudwy via Pont Scethin to the Mawddach estuary at Y Bontddu.[7] The route from Tregaron led over the Cambrian Mountains to Abergwesyn and Beulah, and through Radnorshire into England. It avoided harder-surfaced roads, and, after 1750, some of the turnpike roads, and therefore the costs of having to pay charges at their gates. It also had sources of fresh water, essential for any long journey. The drove began at dawn. The pace was slow, around two miles an hour – the cattle were allowed to stop periodically to graze by the side of the road – and a day's journey would cover between twelve miles and twenty miles. To reach Warwickshire would take a total of sixteen days. The master drover might be on horseback, so that he could ride forward to arrange accommodation for the night. The other drovers walked with the cattle, keeping them on the move and preventing them from straying (the fourteen-mile mountain section was difficult and unfenced). The drovers were helped by dogs. In south Wales these were corgis. It was said in Ardudwy that dogs could find their own way home once the cattle had reached their destination, and often arrived back before their owners. The drove would stop for the night at an inn or farm, preferably with an enclosure for the cattle. Many inns, usually called the 'Drovers Arms', specialised in catering for the trade. Inns in remote areas could sometimes be identified by spying from afar one or more Scots pine trees planted nearby. The exterior wall of an old inn in Stockbridge, Hampshire still carries the words 'Gwair tymherus, porfa flasus, cwrw da a gwal cysurus' (well-seasoned hay, tasty pasture, good beer and a comfortable bed). The chief drover had the luxury of a bed indoors, but the other men slept outside with their cattle. The cost of overnight stays added considerably to the chief drover's expenses.

The passage of a large cattle drove along a public road was hard to ignore. First came the noise. To announce their arrival drovers would make the distinctive cry of 'Heiptro Ho'. John Jones, 'Jac Glan y Gors', is said to have travelled to London as a drover. In his satirical ballad *Dic Siôn Dafydd*, he has Dic joining a drove to London:

Dic Siôn Dafydd: illustration from John Jones, Dic Siôn Dafydd, *undated*
(*National Library of Wales*)

O'r diwedd Dic a ddaeth i Lunden,
a'i drwyn fewn llathen at gynffon llo,
ar hyd y ffordd, a'i bastwn onnen,
yr oedd e'n gweiddi, 'Hai! Ptrow ho!'

At length Dic went to London,
his nose a yard from a calf's backside;
and on the way, with his stick of ash,
he shouted, 'Hi! Ptro ho!'[8]

As an English eyewitness recalled, 'it was something entirely out of the common, neither shouting, calling, crying, singing, halloing or anything else, but a noise in itself, apparently made to carry, and capable of arresting the countryside'.[9] Soon the neighbourhood would be engulfed with cattle and tramping men for twenty minutes or more. Locals moved swiftly aside, and owners of cattle hurried to secure their own animals.

At the end of the journey lay another hard task: finding the right bargain at one of the many cattle fairs and markets, so that a profit could be made once all the drover's expenses had been taken into account. In this process fluency in the English language was essential. Here the cattle would change hands, and spend the summer or autumn being fattened in grass pastures. For the Welsh drovers Barnet was the most important of the fairs close to London. An account from 1856 gives a flavour, from an English perspective, of the impact of these 'barbarous' invaders:

> Imagine some hundreds of bullocks like an immense forest of horns, propelled hurriedly towards you amid the hideous and uproarious shouting of a set of semi-barbarous drovers who value a restive bullock far beyond the life of a human being, driving their mad and noisy herds over every person they meet if not fortunate enough to get out of their way; closely followed by a drove of unbroken wild Welsh ponies, fresh from their native hills, all of them loose and unrestrained as the oxen that precede them; kicking, rearing, biting each other amid the unintelligible anathemas of their inhuman attendants ... the noisy 'hurrahs' of lots of 'un-English speaking' Welshmen, who may have just sold some of their native bovine stock whilst they are to be seen throwing up their long-worn shapeless hats high in the air, as a type of Taffy's delight, uttering at the same time a tirade of gibberish which no one can understand but themselves.[10]

Having sold their cattle, the drovers faced the long journey home. The head drover could ride back, but the others had no choice but to walk all or most of the way. But they did not travel empty-handed. They brought back money (drovers were responsible for making rural communities familiar with a money economy). They'd bring with them the latest news from London and beyond, as reported in newspapers and broadsheets. Since news travelled slowly before the age of good roads and railways, the drovers were often the earliest messengers to west and north Wales of important events. It was said that it was drovers who brought the first report of the battle of Waterloo in 1815. They also transported pamphlets and books. Guto'r

Glyn, Tudur Penllyn and Dafydd Jones of Caeo were not the only drovers who were highly literate and cultured. One of the best-known poets of the seventeenth century, Edward Morus of Perthi Llwydion, often made the journey between north Wales and Essex. Morus, an autodidact, was a master of strict- and free-metre Welsh verse, and would alternate his summer droving with winter visits to Gloddaith and other gentry houses in north Wales, singing the praises of Thomas Mostyn and other patrons. In the eighteenth century the names of drovers often appear in the lists of subscribers to Welsh publications.

Drovers were also entrusted with the transport, in both directions, of legal and administrative documents, letters, taxes like ship money, and other financial payments. In April 1735 William Bulkeley of Anglesey talks in his diary of sending money to his son in London via 'Meyrig the Drover'.[11] The occasional drover turned out to be dishonest. In 1637 Richard Lloyd wrote that his nephew had 'entrusted a drover with the return of £400, in payment whereof the drover has disappointed him, whereby he is in danger of being committed before the Lords'.[12] But in general those who gave valuables to drovers must have had a high level of confidence in them. A newspaper report in 1850 said, 'Yet are many of these Welsh dealers clever, respectable men, who employ considerable capital of their own, and are trusted with a good deal of capital by others; many of them, I am told, make large purchases upon credit, and are generally found trustworthy'.[13]

Droving was always a hard way to make a living. An obvious problem was the sheer physical labour and hardship. The Pembrokeshire writer George Owen wrote in 1603 that there were over 3,000 young people employed in herding cattle in the county:

[they] are put to this idle education when they are first come to be ten or twelve years of age and turned to the open fields to follow their cattle, when they are forced to endure the heat of the sun in his greatest extremity to parch and burn their faces, hands, legs, feet and breasts in such sort as they seem more like tawny

Moors than people of this land. And then with the cold, frost, snow, hail and wind they are so tormented, having the skin of their legs, hands, face and feet all in chinks and chaps ... that, poor fools, they may well hold opinion with the papists that there is a purgatory ...[14]

Drovers protected themselves as best they could against the weather. Sometimes their employers paid for clothes, which included a broad-brimmed hat, a long smock, trousers and knee socks, and then leggings on top. Even if the weather was warm, drovers could expect to get wet often, especially when fording rivers.

There were other hazards. Transporting large quantities of cash was dangerous. Drovers could be targets for thieves and robbers, especially if they were thought to be carrying money. In 1825 a pig-drover from Corntown on his way to Neath market was stopped by two men near Ewenny, knocked down, and robbed of notes worth £56. In 1833 another pig-drover, Thomas Morris, had sold his pigs in Chepstow when he was knocked down and robbed by three men on the mountain between Aberdare and Caerphilly. London was a particularly dangerous place. In Kingston fair in 1812 Mr Roberts lost £800 in a robbery.

Travel was safer once drovers could rely on the banks set up in Wales to cater for their trade. By using the Black Ox Bank, set up by the drover David Jones in Llandovery in 1799 or the Aberystwyth and Tregaron Bank, established around 1810 and known as Banc y Ddafad Ddu, in tandem with London banks, they could avoid carrying much money themselves.[15]

Drovers could still be the victims of swindlers. Barnet fair was plagued by cheats ('thimble-riggers') – though they could be beaten:

A Welsh drover fell among the thimble-riggers at Barnet fair, and was considerably fleeced. He, however, had his revenge in the following fashion. Quitting the town with his drove, he espied one of his plunderers in the road; with the assistance of a brother drover or two, he made capture of him, fastened him, Mazeppalike, astride one of their wildest unbroken colts, started the animal off at a rough trot, and after a ride of four or five miles, the fellow, galled, jaded, and three parts dead, was glad to purchase his release from further torment, by disgorging his ill-gotten pelf.[16]

For some people, sympathy with the drovers facing such dangers failed to outweigh dislike for their own sharp practices. In his biting satire *Gweledigaethau y bardd cwsg* (Visions of the sleeping bard), published in 1703, Ellis Wynne places drovers in a special zone of his imagined Hell. Here they are themselves driven along by their persecutors. They're told by one of them, 'Lie down here. You might have been afraid of thieves on a London street before, but you yourselves were the worst kind of highwaymen, living on the road and on robbery, and killing poor families.'[17] Wynne exaggerates for satiric effect, but many people were suspicious of drovers – strange, loud, rough, wandering men who came roaring through their communities with their cattle, and who had a reputation for untrustworthiness. Many authors make references to the drunkenness of drovers.

Rhys Prichard of Llandovery, in his poem 'Cyngor i'r porthmon' (advice to the drover), written around 1630, could list several vices to which they were prone: dishonesty and sharp practice, profiteering, drunkenness and abuse of the poor.[18] Prichard's final warning is about bankruptcy. This was one of the most serious dangers of the drover's life. He often found it hard to recover the purchase cost of his animals. Market conditions could worsen; cattle disease was common; he could be robbed or fleeced; impatient creditors might foreclose. A law of 1706 forbade drovers from declaring themselves bankrupt, but it was ineffective, and reports in nineteenth century newspapers of drovers going through court bankruptcy proceedings are common.

What brought a gradual end to the drovers was the coming of the railways to rural Wales from the 1850s. By the mid-1870s most cattle could be herded to a station for easy, swift and comparatively cheap transit by rail to England, and it was no longer necessary to walk them eastwards. The last long-distance drove of Welsh sheep was thought to be between Tregaron and Harrow in 1900, though flocks of sheep were still being moved on foot within Wales into the 1930s.[19]

Itinerants

But drovers were not the only workers who walked long distances for a living during this period. For example, itinerant traders carried printed material, often on foot, to all parts of Wales: books, but also broadsides and chapbooks, newspapers and periodicals, annuals and almanacks, in both Welsh and English. Literacy increased in Wales in the second half of the eighteenth century and beyond, thanks largely to the circulating and Sunday schools, and there was a ready market for reading. Bookshops were few, and readers relied for their supplies on the arrival in towns and villages of individual hawkers. A catalogue of 1822 lists fifteen itinerant booksellers, including two women, Gwenni Ellis and Sarah Thomas.[20]

It wasn't an easy way to make a living. As one writer commented, booksellers 'were used to disappointment; it was a tiring business, carrying books through storm and heat, from quarry to quarry, from house to house ... living freely in the open air, and knowing that they were doing good – their work was work to gladden the heart, even if, at times, it could break it'.[21]

Only a few names of early travelling booksellers are known. William Hope of Mostyn, 'Y Bardd Byddar' (the Deaf Poet), who published a poetry anthology in 1765, was probably an itinerant bookseller,[22] and Thomas Williams of Llanrwst (c.1782–1855).

More is known about one of the last walking booksellers, Richard Jones (1848–1915). Born in Aberangell, he was prevented by poor health and poverty from becoming a minister, as he wished, and turned to bookselling. He'd start from his base in Machynlleth, and later Cemais Road, with stock he acquired from publishers like Thomas Gee in Denbigh and Hughes and Sons of Wrexham. He wandered the roads of Merioneth and Montgomeryshire, attending fairs in centres like Dinas Mawddwy, and travelling hundreds of miles a year, his back bent with Welsh books and magazines. Much of his stock was religious, but he also carried literature for children, like *Trysorfa'r plant* and *Cymru'r plant*. Children called him 'Dyn y Llyfrau', the Books Man; he'd also acknowledge the name 'pilgrim'. He made a point of reading all that he sold, so that he could recommend items to readers with conviction. When he died, it was said that 'seeing his bag would spark a child's curiosity, and buying a book was a way to open the mind's eye of many a boy and girl'.[23]

Richard Robert Jones was not an itinerant bookseller, but he was an inveterate and bookish wanderer on foot. He was born, the son of a carpenter, in Aberdaron in 1779 and became known later as 'Dic Aberdaron'. He had no formal education. He learnt to read Welsh from his mother, and later English. He'd a remarkable gift for languages, for by the age of twenty, with the help of friends and books, he'd mastered Latin, Greek and Hebrew. His aptitude for practical work was non-existent, he could never keep at a job for long, and he suffered beatings from his frustrated father. Today he might be termed a 'savant', but that label hardly captures his singularity.

Richard Robert Jones *the wonderful Linguist.*
born at Aberdaron, Caernarvonshire now living in Liverpool
Drawn Engraved & Published by A.R Burt, Miniature painter Chester. May 30. 187

Richard Robert Jones, 'Dic Aberdaron',
engraving by A.R. Burt, 1823
(*National Library of Wales*)

About five years later Dic broke with his family and left home with his books. He was penniless and had to sell some of them, but was befriended by William Cleaver, Bishop of Bangor, who gave him books and work, and then by Rev. John Williams at Treffos, Anglesey, where he learned French (he later added Italian). In 1807 he went to London and then Dover, 'furnished with a small packet on his back, a long pole in his hand, round which was rolled a map of the roads, and his few remaining books deposited in the various foldings of his dress'. Here he extended his knowledge of Hebrew, and began learning Chaldean and Syriac, before returning to Wales in 1810. In Bangor he earned money by working on the Hebrew words in a Latin dictionary, and continued to work on dictionaries and grammars. His interest in languages was strictly linguistic, and he'd little interest in the content of his texts. From 1821 he concentrated on his own work, a dictionary of Welsh, Latin and Hebrew, but after finishing it he could find no one to publish it.

In 1822 one of his patrons, William Roscoe, published a memoir of Dic, 'whose destitute situation requires the benevolent aid of those who may be disposed to afford him their assistance':

> His person and dress at this time were extremely singular: to an immense shock of black hair he united a bushy beard of the same colour. His clothing consisted of several coarse and ragged vestments, the spaces between which were filled with books, surrounding him in successive layers, so that he was literally a walking library.[24]

Dic spent the rest of his life without employment, wandering in search of subscriptions from his base in Liverpool, 'where he may be seen at times walking with a book under his arm without noticing or speaking to any one'. He was often accompanied by cats, of whom he was very fond, and he'd blow on a ram's horn, 'which he did in such a manner as might have entitled him to rank with those who, in elder times, overthrew the walls of Jericho, and rendered him no inconsiderable nuisance to the neighbourhood'. In 1838 he turned up unannounced in the house of the poet Eben Fardd:

> I was coming into my own house to have a bite to eat, one fine warm summer day, when who did I see sitting on a chair inside the house but Dic Aberdaron, busy chewing on a penny white loaf,

which he pushed into his mouth bit by bit, with some difficulty, it seemed, because his beard, like a thick bush, almost covered its opening. Our conversation began with Cornelius Agrippa, king of the magicians, as Dic called him ...[25]

Dic died in St Asaph in 1843 and was buried there. An englyn by Ellis Owen was carved on his gravestone. It remembers him as a 'dictionary of every province. / Death took away his fifteen languages, / now, below, he has no language at all'. Later poets also found a place for him. T.H. Parry-Williams called him a 'fool with languages ... licking up one after the other / a lump of learning, he hobbled from place to place / his library tower tied round his body.' R.S. Thomas, in a counter-poem, was more generous. For him, Dic was a 'radiant soul, shrugging / the type's ignorance / off, he hastens towards / us, to the future / we inhabit and must / welcome him to.'

Dic Aberdaron was a celebrity of sorts in his lifetime, and there are several contemporary portraits of him. Most individual tramps and beggars attracted little or no attention, except when they featured in legal records. This was because, from Tudor times, they often came under official persecution. A series of statutes passed between 1530 and 1597 imposed penalties for vagrancy. Performers – 'vagraunt and idle persons, naming theim selfes mynstrelles, rithmers and barthes' – were especially targeted. This was in part because their work could easily be interpreted as sedition, especially in unsettled times. In 1547 a wandering poet, piper and fiddler called Robin Clidro was prosecuted with others in a Flintshire court. Some of his verses survive, and show how his bawdiness and satire might have got him into trouble. In 1612 Siôn Lewys Môn, a 'crowder' or crwth player, was one of a group of 'idell persons, loyterers and nightewalkers' in Denbighshire.[26]

A tramp we know much more about was Thomas Williams, 'Capelulo'. His autobiography, published in 1854, gives a rare, detailed and frank glimpse into the life of a wanderer along the roads of Wales in the first half of the nineteenth century.[27]

Williams was born in Llanrwst, one of eleven children. His father was a hatter and his mother a baker. He soon left school, without learning to read, and tried to find occasional work. His nickname was 'Tom Ddrwg' (Bad Tom) and he was always getting into scrapes and suffering injuries. He soon developed a liking for drink. He joined the army and saw service in the Napoleonic wars and then in South Africa, South America and India. Eventually he was discharged, without a pension, and worked and begged his way home from Plymouth, by canal to Newport and on foot via Merthyr and central Wales, arriving at Llanrwst, barely recognised by his family, shortly before his father died. He took occasional jobs – roadbuilding, droving cattle to London and doing errands for gentry – and also raised money by begging, as he walked from town to town and village to village all through north and mid Wales.

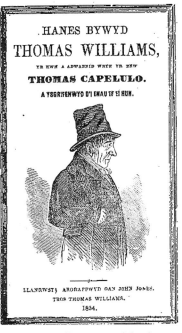

Thomas Williams, 'Capelulo', from Hanes bywyd Thomas Williams, 1854

Much of his income, he freely confessed, he squandered on drink in taverns. His drinking bouts resulted in him losing money through theft and deception, and a spell in police cells and court. He won a reputation for accepting bets in taverns to run naked through towns at night. While selling books in Bangor he met a woman whom he married, but she cynically abandoned him immediately, making away with all his money and furniture. At one point he shared his journey and his begging with an Irishwoman ('no one knew we were not man and wife'). He was not averse to deception himself. In desperation he sold his trousers, and walked from Llanrwst to Capel Curig and on to Dyffryn Mymbyr in the hope that someone would take pity on his condition. Once, in the middle of the day, he had sex while blind drunk with a 'bad woman': a group of children gathered round them, and 'Mr Williams yr Exciseman' had to separate the two with a whip.

Aware that drink would kill him, Thomas eventually pledged to give up alcohol, and after a final heroic bout of drinking in every one of the pubs of his home town, he kept his promise, refusing all offers of a drink when begging or in exchange for the books he sold.

The theme of the sinner saved by religious conversion was common enough in texts of this period. Their narrators had an interest in exaggerating their former debauchery in order to magnify their new state of grace. But even granting Thomas Williams some licence in the detail of his stories, he paints a convincing picture of the harsh life of down-and-outs on the roads of Wales.

The life of the tramp was all the harsher on account of prejudice and hostility shown them by the more fortunate. In 1871 a letter to the editor of the *Newtown and Welshpool Express* complained that

> ... the district is swarming with tramps of the very worst stamp. Five have just passed in a troop and here are two more forming a rear guard. The latter have just called, asking for bread. On being refused, one of them started to argue with my sister on the ways of Providence ... What is to be done towards scouring the country of these vagabonds? The most effectual way by far would be for every man to take physical force and use violence, driving every tramp out of the country and allow the police officers to refer to some other source for promotion.[28]

The editor agreed, claiming that the county was 'completely overrun with hordes of these fellows which swarm about the country at this time of the year'. One answer to the 'vagrancy problem' was the workhouse. Life in the workhouse at Narberth in Pembrokeshire was so dire that vagrants there would tear up their clothes in an effort to be sent to prison, where conditions were better.[29]

By the eighteenth century there were other long-distance walkers on the road who were anything but wanderers. These were men with a mission – a religious mission to convert and save human souls, through 'exhortation' or preaching and setting up local groups of 'methodists'. The most energetic of these was Howell Harris, who in his earlier years travelled on average 6,000 miles a year through Wales and England – mostly on horseback, although he also walked. His stamina was impressive, his personal hygiene less so. In a letter in 1748 he wrote, 'I have now visited in that time [nine weeks] 10 counties & travaild mostly 150 miles every week, & discoursed twice every day and sometimes three & four times a day: & this last journey I have not taken off my cloaths for 7 nights ...'[30] Another enthusiast, and friend of Harris, Edmund Jones, walked 400 miles in north Wales in 1782, when he was almost eighty, preaching twice daily.[31] Even if they had a home chapel, such Methodists and other nonconformists, like Owen Davies, Miles Edwards, Isaac Price and Thomas Oliver, were in part itinerant and travelled long distances each year.

Visitors

Most visitors to Wales before the eighteenth century came with a specific mission. Some were in search of the antiquities of the country. John Leland (c.1503–1552) developed an obsession for listing and rescuing manuscript books from the libraries of monasteries about to be shut down by Henry VIII, and appointed himself as a national 'antiquarius'. Later he made long tours of England and Wales, recording in notebooks the places and ancient monuments he found. Between 1536 and 1539 he spent time in Wales, travelling mostly on horseback, and made observations on what he saw.

Others were intent on finding plants. Unlike Leland, they needed to use their legs to do their work. One of them was Thomas Johnson, a London apothecary and gardener who pioneered field botany and the cataloguing of medicinal plants. In his short life Johnson published several books, including, in 1641, a supplement to his *Mercurius botanicus*, in which he listed the plants he'd found while on expeditions on foot in Eryri. He's the first person whose name we know who climbed to the summit of Yr Wyddfa (Snowdon), on

3 August 1639. After staying with his friend Thomas Glynn (or Glynne), himself an active botanist, at his home, Glynllifon, he set out, probably from Llyn Cwellyn. His party included an unnamed local 'lad' as guide, and Edward Morgan, another gifted Welsh botanist, as translator. He gives a vivid description of the climb, emphasising the danger of the ascent, the 'terror' of the mountain, and the phlegmatic spirit of the botanists:

> The initial ascent was difficult, but after that the place opened to a plateau. It was broader but its sides were just as steep, with, on the left, huge cliffs, and on the right, a difficult slope. So, at length, after climbing for three miles, we conquered the very peak of the mountain, covered in thick clouds. Here the path was very narrow, and as we climbed we felt terrified by the cliffs on either side, with their rough rocks, and the Stygian bogs scattered here and there, the biggest of which the locals call 'the Devil's House'. But when we came to a point on the ridge beyond which we could not go, we sat down amid the clouds. First, we put into order the plants we had collected at such peril between the rocks and cliffs, and then we ate the food we had brought with us.[32]

The list of plants Johnson found on the climb is impressively long, and may indicate that the 'young lad' he employed was well acquainted with the mountain flora of Eryri, and exactly where to find them.

Johnson's example induced other botanists to visit Eryri, including John Ray, one of the most eminent naturalists of his time, who climbed Yr Wyddfa in 1658 and again with two botanist friends in 1662. Ray also paid Thomas Willisel, previously a foot-soldier in Cromwell's New Model Army and possibly the first working-class botanist in Britain, to collect specimens in the area. According to Ray, he 'is indefatigable, & could endure any hardship, & live as well upon oatcake & whig as another man upon flesh and wine, & ramble over hills & mountains & woods & plains'.[33]

A friend and correspondent of Ray, and also of Edward Morgan, was Edward Llwyd (or Lhuyd). Llwyd, from Llanforda near Oswestry, was Keeper of the Ashmolean Museum from 1690 to his early death in 1709, and a key part of the flowering of scientific thought in the late seventeenth century, which depended on empirical observation and analytical reasoning, supported by an international network of scholars exchanging frequent letters. He was a polymath, combining interests in natural history, palaeontology, archaeology and the history of language. Today he's considered the father of Celtic linguistics and one of the most able scholars Wales has produced.

Llwyd visited Wales on many occasions, but his longest and most intensive tour, mainly on foot, took place between May 1697 and April 1701, in the company of three young Welsh research assistants and preceded by a 'moving library' of reference books, microscopes and other aids. After two years of travelling in all parts of Wales, the party continued to Ireland, the Highlands of Scotland, Cornwall and Brittany, before the final return to Oxford.

Throughout his travels he sent letters to his correspondents. Postal services were unreliable. Sometimes his messages went astray: he speculated that suspicious local people might be intercepting them. The surviving letters show the breadth of his interests: stones and fossils, monuments and inscriptions, plants and flowers, and Welsh manuscripts of all kinds.[34] Little is said in the letters about how the research team operated from day to day while in Wales, but William Pryce, a Cornish antiquary who met Llwyd during his tour of Cornwall in August 1700, preserves a glimpse of him in action, and the dangers he faced from suspicious locals:

Mr. Lhuyd came into the country at a time, when all the people were under a sort of panick, and in terrible apprehension of thieves, and house-breakers; and travelling with his three companions (with knap-sacks on their shoulders) on foot, for the better searching for simples, viewing, and taking draughts of everything remarkable, and for that reason prying into every hole and corner, raised a strange jealousy in people already so much alarmed ... At Helston, as Mr Lhuyd was poring up and down, and making many enquiries about Gentlemen's seats, &c. he (with his companions) was taken up for a thief, and carried before a Justice of the Peace.[35]

People travelling on foot who showed a very close interest in their surroundings were apt to excite suspicion and sometimes hostility among the local inhabitants. In Pembrokeshire in 1698 Llwyd wrote that the country people 'were very jealous of us, and suspected us to be employ'd by the Parliament in order to some farther Taxes, & in some places for Jacobit spies'. In 1701, during their tour of Brittany, he and one of his assistants were arrested as suspected spies, their books and papers 'ty'd up in a napkin' and confiscated. The men were held in the castle in Brest for two weeks before being released and deported.

Llwyd's 'prying' and 'poring' took him to all kinds of locations – gentry houses, churches, coasts and cliffs, islands, mountains, lakes, rivers and quarries. Many of them could only have been reached on foot. He thought nothing of climbing high in the mountains to search out new botanical specimens – he found the very rare 'Snowdon lily' (once called, in his honour, *Lloydia serotina*) on the steep upper slopes of Yr Wyddfa – or to scale mountain summits taking scientific measurements. 'Next summer come twelvemonth', he wrote in 1696, 'I intend to try the Barometer and Thermometer on the top of Snowdon and Cader Idris, and to take their perpendicular height.' (John Caswell had already made such measurements, on both mountains, in 1682, and Edmund Halley would repeat the feat on Yr Wyddfa, what he called a 'horrid spot of hills', in 1697.) Llwyd climbed Glyder Fach and left a graphic description of the violent cluster of knife-like rocks called Castell y Gwynt on its summit. He spent much time chasing after inscriptions and manuscripts, but he'd also pay close attention to vernacular knowledge, especially in the case of place-names: 'As for Caer Vorwyn I can not see why an illiterat shepheard may not be beliv'd in such a case as soon as a Bishop; for the names of mountanous and desert places are better known to those of his profession than men of learning.'[36]

Llwyd's four-year field trip, covering over three thousand miles, called for a strong determination, and a strong constitution. 'Since my coming to Wales', he wrote in September 1696, 'I have been generally upon the ramble in the day time and in company at night'. Luckily, his health remained good. Later, however, when he was in north Wales, a persistent cough developed into asthma, and his health grew worse. In 1709, in Oxford, he caught a chill, developed pleurisy, and died. He'd succeeded in publishing only the first, linguistic volume in his projected series of large-scale books, *Archaeologia Britannica*, the results of his many years wandering and studying the Celtic lands. Most of his unpublished manuscript notes were later lost or destroyed.

No one repeated what Llwyd had done in Wales. During the eighteenth and early nineteenth centuries natural historians, historians and antiquarians continued to study Wales through travel and fieldwork, but few of them worked on the same scale or with the same intensity as he did.

Samuel Brewer, who had met Llwyd, was an example of an unusually persistent amateur botanist. He came to Wales in 1726 with the noted botanist J.J. Dellenius, and later stayed in north Wales for a year. He climbed Yr Wyddfa thirteen times and the Glyderau seven times in search of botanical specimens, especially mosses, and seems to have been fearless in his mountain climbing, since he dismissed his guide, Richard Parry, who was unwilling to follow him to the inaccessible places he sought.[37]

A later archaeologist who was unusually dedicated to scouring the countryside for antiquities, in the Edward Llwyd tradition, was John Skinner, the rector of the church of Camerton, Somerset. He spent years researching antiquities of all kinds in his local area and throughout England and Wales, recording his findings in around 150 diaries. He was a complex character, described by Virginia Woolf as 'tormented and querulous ... harsh, peremptory, apprehensive, and without hope'. In December 1802 he set out for Anglesey, determined to visit as many monuments as he could. He abandoned his horse at the Moel-y-don ferry and continued across the island on foot, guided by local people. Amateur but obsessive, he walked incessantly, tracking down churches, inscribed stones, chambered tombs, hut circles and local superstitions, making notes and sketches as he went. He was interested in current developments, too, including discussions on Thomas Telford's first plans to build a bridge across the Menai Strait, copper mining at Parys Mountain, and the local impact of Methodists:

> A dreary walk of two miles over the sands to Aberffraw was rendered still more disagreeable by an incessant and heavy rain and we had no small degree of anxiety the whole of our walk lest we should be still more unfortunate in not gaining admittance at the public house as we understood that a number of Westleans with Mr. Charles at their head were to have a meeting the following day in the village.[38]

Skinner was vexed by rain and strong winds, wretched accommodation and poor food, and the apparent theft of his walking stick, but by the time he recrossed the Strait he'd walked 168 miles in ten days. He returned to Wales for other tours in the 1830s, but put an end to his own life in 1839.

In the later seventeenth and early eighteenth centuries visitors with more general interests began to come from England and elsewhere, and wrote about their experiences of extensive travelling through the country. John Taylor, an eccentric Londoner known as the 'Water Poet', published an account, in verse and prose, of his 'painfull circuit' of Wales in 1652, when he was 74 years old: 'a short relation of a long journey', as his title page says, 'performed by the riding, going, crawling, running, and writing of John Taylor'.[39] Taylor rode his 'dumb Dun Beast' from town to town, throwing himself on the hospitality of country gentlemen, and complaining about the poor roads, incomprehensible language and expensive guides. But Taylor was curious about Wales, and added a sympathetic brief history of the country up to the death of Llywelyn ap Gruffudd.

Other travellers were frankly contemptuous in their view of

Wales. In 1682 William Richards published his *Wallography*. Though it claims to be the record of a walking tour in Wales, it's unclear whether Richards ever set foot there. His satire, sometimes funny, sometimes crude, set a pattern for many later English writers on Wales:

> The country is mountainous, and yields pretty handsome clambering for goats, and hath variety of precipice to break ones neck; which a man may sooner do than fill his belly, the soil being barren, and an excellent place to breed a famine in.[40]

The Welsh were quarrelsome and addicted to stealing ('every thing sticks to their pitchy fingers'), and their language was incomprehensible and primitive:

> Their native gibberish is usually pratled throughout the whole Taphydome, except in their market towns, whose inhabitants being a little rais'd, and (as it were) pufft up into bubbles above the ordinary scum, do begin to despise it.[41]

Some claim that Richards was a clever ironist, parodying English attitudes to Wales.[42] The same could not be said of the anonymous author of *A trip to North-Wales: being a description of that country and people*, published in 1701. 'The country', wrote the author, 'looks like the fag end of the Creation; the very rubbish of Noah's flood', and its language was 'inarticulate and guttural, and sounds more like the gobling of geese, or turkeys, than the speech of rational creatures'.[43]

Tourists

From around 1770, salesmen, tramps, preachers and others roaming the roads and lanes of Wales began to encounter another kind of traveller: middle-class English men – and a few women, and visitors from continental Europe – driven not by the necessity of making a living, or in search of specimens, but by curiosity and adventurousness. They were on 'tours' of the country, and eventually they became known as 'tourists' (the first use of the word in Britain occurs in a 1772 review of Thomas Pennant's Scottish tour). Their main interest was in the landscape of Wales, which attracted them because it was so different from what they were used to at home, and many of them wrote diaries and published narratives of their adventures. We know of over 1,200 accounts by tourists, in manuscript and print; the largest number dates to the period 1790 to 1840.[44]

By far the most influential published work of this kind, though by no means the first, was Thomas Pennant's *Tours in Wales*, first published in parts between 1778 and 1784. Pennant, who lived at his family estate at Downing Hall, Flintshire, was a distinguished naturalist, antiquarian and historian, with a deep understanding of, and feeling for, his country. He toured mainly in north Wales, often with John Lloyd, the Welsh-speaking vicar of Caerwys, and an artist, Moses Griffith, who supplied illustrations to his books. Later tourists who were unable or unwilling to visit the places he described would often quote his words, confident in their accuracy. Pennant usually travelled on horseback, although he was also a confident mountain

Cadair Idris, watercolour by Moses Griffiths, from Thomas Pennant's Tours in Wales, *1783, extra-illustrated version*

(*National Library of Wales*)

walker, climbing Yr Wyddfa twice, once at night. His composite description of climbing is topographically accurate, highly detailed in its observation and emotionally expressive, as in this picture of swirling mists on the slopes, easily recognisable by walkers caught in such conditions today:

> A vast mist enveloped the whole circuit of the mountain. The prospect down was horrible. It gave an idea of numbers of abysses, concealed by a thick smoke, furiously circulating around us. Very often a gust of wind formed an opening in the clouds, which gave a fine and distinct vista of lake and valley. Sometimes they opened only in one place; at others, in many at once, exhibiting a most strange and perplexing sight of water, fields, rocks, or chasms, in fifty different places. They then closed at once, and left us involved in darkness: in a small space, they would separate again, and fly in wild eddies round the middle of the mountains, and expose, in parts, both tops and bases clear to our view.[45]

What prompted many people to visit Wales, and particularly one small corner of it, in the final decades of the century was the growth of the British 'picturesque' movement. Its key moment was the publication in 1782 of William Gilpin's illustrated book *Observations on the River Wye*. Gilpin's aim was to 'examine the face of a country by the rules of picturesque beauty', and his innovation was to look at a landscape, in his case the Wye valley downstream from Ross-on-Wye, as if it were a well-composed picture. He valued irregularity and roughness in both landscape and its image, and the lower Wye, with its meanders and steeply wooded banks, provided a suitably domesticated version of his ideal. Dozens of visitors later came on the 'Wye tour', often drifting downriver in special boats and stopping on the way to sketch, paint and picnic. A new picturesque landscape was even created for them at Piercefield, near Chepstow. It seems that few of these aesthetes, however, made the Wye Tour on foot.[46]

Wales also featured in another, rather earlier aesthetic

movement, pioneered in Britain by Edmund Burke, that prized the 'sublime' in nature (and, as with the picturesque, in art and literature). The 'sublime', Burke maintained, impressed spectators by instilling fear, horror and other strong emotions in them, and held them in an elevated state of astonishment. The classic 'sublime' landform was the mountain, and the influence of Burke's ideas began to change the way in which visitors viewed, for example, the peaks of Eryri. Again, most visitors were content to take their exquisite pleasure in the terrors of the Welsh mountains from below. But there were exceptions. In July 1756 George Lyttelton, an aristocratic politician, poet and artistic patron, climbed Moel Hebog. His account reflects faithfully the principles of the sublime and how it operates on the mind:

> The hill we stood upon was perfectly clear, the way we came up a pretty easy ascent; but before us was a precipice of many hundred yards; and below a vale, which, though not cultivated, has much savage beauty; the sides were steep, and fringed with low wood ... But the mountains of Snowdon, covered with darkness and thick clouds, called to my memory the fall of Mount Sinai, with the laws delivered from it, and filled my mind with religious awe.[47]

This kind of response to mountain walking became common, even hackneyed. In 1770 an anonymous writer experienced similar feelings of awe after climbing Yr Wyddfa. On the descent a storm overtook the writer, evoking from him a Satanic quotation from Milton's *Paradise regain'd*, and his own echo of Milton's language, 'The thunder reverberated from rock to rock, and the whole artillery of heaven seemed to be at once discharged.'[48] The mountain often evoked poetic quotation, and God, in the minds of later writers. Charles Bucke wrote confidently that 'the man, who climbs Snowdon as an atheist, feels, as it were, ere he descends, an ardent desire to fall down and worship its Creator!'[49]

Almost all visitors who toured Wales before the last decade of the eighteenth century did so on horseback (or later by carriage). Few departed from the main roads, and fewer still were bold enough to explore the country on foot. As a result, those who did choose to walk excited comment. Karl Philipp Moritz, a German visiting England in 1782, reported, when walking from Richmond to Windsor, that 'a traveller on foot in this country seems to be considered as a sort of wild man, or an out-of-the-way being, who is stared at, pitied, suspected, and shunned by every body that meets him.' Another Continental traveller, Armand-Louis-Bon Maudet, Comte de Penhouët, published an account of his walk through south Wales in June 1796. As a Breton he felt less uncomfortable: 'I lose in some degree the denomination of foreigner, as Bretagne was formerly peopled by the inhabitants of this country.'[50]

Tourists could understand that slower meant better. Here is the diarist John Byng, who toured north Wales in summer 1784:

It is impossible to explore this country, but on horseback; as from Dolgelle, we have travell'd nothing but narrow paths; and it is also necessary to be furnish'd with usefull legs, and sound lungs: to suppose that Wales can be seen from a carriage is a grand mistake; for every one knows that the most curious things are the most conceal'd, and inaccessible?[51]

But Byng himself seldom trusted his 'useful legs' to walking trips of any length, and refused to be led up Yr Wyddfa, or to the top of Cadair Idris, even by the legendary guide Robin Edwards. Byng was a natural conservative, and his view of mountains, as frightening objects to be avoided if at all possible, remained that of earlier generations.

Within a few years, though, pedestrian tourism was becoming common. A rather later walker, Robert Newell, listed the reasons it appealed to some travellers:

It is the safest, and most suited to every variety of road; it will often enable you to take a shorter track, and visit scenes (the finest perhaps) not otherwise accessible; it is healthy, and, with a little practice, easy; it is economical: a pedestrian is content with almost any accommodations; he, of all travellers, wants but little ... And last, though not least, it is perfectly independent.[52]

Visitors who chose to come to Wales on foot had dissociated walking from its previous reputation as the reserve of the poor, and embraced it for its positive attributes. Newell's contention that walking was the safest mode of transport may reflect the danger of falling from horses or falling out of carriages. For more adventurous travellers it was independence that appealed most: independence not only in how to travel, but also freedom from social constraints like family ties and expected ways of behaving.

One of the very first pedestrian visitors was George Plumptre, a Cambridge undergraduate, who arrived with a companion in 1792 for a tour of north Wales. They brought a knapsack, which they carried in turns, containing clothes, shoes and other items, including a book, a tin drinking can and a map of north Wales. The cost of hiring horses and fear of injury persuaded them to trust to their feet, and they set off 'gay as larks, resolved not to let anything be a difficulty to us.' So pleased was Plumptre with the experience that he came back for other walking tours in 1797 and 1799.[53]

Iolo Morganwg

Before turning to other visitors on foot, we should meet one of the most remarkable walking Welshmen, of this or any other period. He was one of the most extraordinary cultural figures of his day, recognisable by many who passed him. Many years after his death an old friend, Elijah Waring, recalled his appearance (he also drew a sketch of him):

About thirty years ago, there was often seen, on the highways and bye-ways of Glamorganshire, an elderly pedestrian, of rather low stature, wearing his long grey hair flowing over his high coat-collar, which, by constant antagonism, had pushed up his hat-brim into a quaint angle of elevation behind. His countenance was marked by a combination of quiet intelligence, and quick sensitiveness; the features angular, the lines deep, and the grey eye benevolent but highly excitable. He was clad in rustic garb; the coat blue, with goodly brass buttons, and the nether integuments good homely corduroy. He wore buckles in his shoes, and a pair of remarkably stout well-set legs, were vouchers for the great peripatetic powers he was well known to possess. A pair of canvas wallets were slung over his shoulders, one depending in front, the other behind.

Iolo Morganwg, drawing by Elijah Waring, etched by Robert Cruikshank, 1850
(*National Library of Wales*)

These contained a change of linen, and a few books and papers connected with his favourite pursuits. He generally read as he walked, 'with spectacles on nose,' and a pencil in his hand, serving him to make notes as they suggested themselves. A tall staff, which he grasped at about the level of his ear, completed his travelling equipment; and he was accustomed to assign as a reason for this mode of using it, that it tended to expand the pectoral muscles, and thus, in some degree, relieve a pulmonary malady inherent in his constitution.[54]

This was Edward Williams, known to most people as Iolo Morganwg. His self-description, 'rattleskull genius', sums up the brilliance, multiplicity and restlessness of his intellect. Born in the Vale of Glamorgan in 1747, Iolo received no formal education. He was by trade a journeyman stonemason, but also a farmer and builder, pioneering Unitarian, gardener, poet, vegetarian, antiquarian, cultural inventor, myth-maker and forger, fair trade retailer, copier of manuscripts, political radical, patriot and pamphleteer. He's known today as the founder of the modern Gorsedd. Iolo spent periods in London as well as Wales, and was an inveterate walker.

He preferred walking to riding. 'My manner of travelling', he wrote, 'is always on foot. I cannot ride above 4 or 5 miles at farthest. My father & mother had all their lives a horse, but I never rode him.' In addition to this aversion to horses, he was never well-off, and walking gave him the chance to meet others and observe carefully everything around him.[55] Finally, he may have regarded walking as a democratic or even rebellious form of transport in comparison with more class-based alternatives.

As he went along, 'with all my ears open', he'd make notes in pencil in his notebook, about people and their language, antiquities, the natural world, agricultural practices and much else. He also spent years travelling to private libraries to copy Welsh manuscripts, as his contribution to a compilation of medieval Welsh literature, *The Myvyrian archaiology of Wales*. He continued walking into old age: 'in spite of my lame foot, in spite of my asthma, in spite of my villainous cough that struggles to get loose, I persist in walking.' In 1795 he walked from his home in Flemingston to Bristol and back, a distance of ninety-four miles, in thirty-six hours.

Seven years later, in May 1802, Iolo set out on much longer, month-long journey, which he recorded in pencil in a notebook, from London to his home.[56] His walk took him through Oxfordshire, Warwickshire and Shropshire and along the border counties of Wales. His notebook is a strange rattle-bag of tumbling thoughts: comments on soil, crops, hedges and other agricultural details jangle alongside extended rants against political enemies, notes on churches and prehistoric antiquities, an expert mason's commentary on the use of architectural stone, anecdotes about the manners and language of the people he meets, philosophical musings, and unexpectedly tender personal reflections. There are also some jokes. At the point where Gloucestershire, Worcestershire and Warwickshire meet, 'a matron-like woman very gravely told me, I might make water in the three counties all at the same time.'

It wouldn't be too fanciful to imagine the notebook as a real-time read-out of the multitudinous thoughts passing through Iolo's fertile mind, thoughts prompted in part by the rhythms of his walking.

The notebook was private and never intended for publication. It can be read, though, not just as a series of jottings but as a biting critique of the typical tour narrative. The English traveller might admire Welsh scenery, but, more often than not, he laments the poverty of the country, both town and country, condemns dirty inns and poor food, puzzles at the strange manners of the Welsh, and mocks their incomprehensible language. Iolo turns the tables. He treats the counties of England he passes through in exactly the same patronising and captious way as the English tourists habitually treat Wales. Much of England displeases him. Oxford is a 'factory for parsons', full of 'young toffs', and its shire is a 'land of dirt', Birmingham 'is for a place of its oppulence, nor well built', Coalbrookdale is a disappointment, compared with Merthyr Tydfil, and in Shrewsbury 'the stench of the town has operated several times as a powerful emetic to me.' Inns stink, and food is too expensive. Iolo complains that as a pedestrian he receives worse treatment in inns than 'a scoundrel in a carriage, or well mounted on a costly horse.' He finds Midlands dialects amusing, and parodies the speech of an 'English rustic' when asked for directions: 'two moil, whoy it may be so, but I'll be angd if Oi knowd, tho Oi was born and bred theeur.'

By contrast, once he's back in Wales, Iolo is relieved to find the land more attractive, the food and lodgings improved, and the people generally more pleasant and hospitable. Near Meifod he stays for a week with Walter Davies, 'Gwallter Mechain', whom he was helping to prepare a report on the state of agriculture in south Wales, and along the way he visits, among others, Mr Wayman, the farmer of Griffin Ffloyd, Mr Morgan the wool-stapler of Knighton, and Mr Powel the orchardist of Glasbury.

Iolo departs from the English tour-writers in other respects. They're virtually all wealthy and upper or middle class, whereas he's firmly working class. And while they bring with them the conformist assumptions of their class, Iolo has a radical and deep-felt repugnance for those in power – politicians, judges, churchmen, gentry and others – who support injustice and oppression. At several points in the notebook this disgust explodes off the page. In Shrewsbury, he laments bitterly that the gaol is 'used as a Bastille to chastise those who dare tell truth', and now houses his fellow radical 'poor Thomas Spence', jailed for seditious libel. In Presteigne, home of the Great Sessions and Quarter Sessions, he launches into a violent condemnation of unjust judges.

While some of the English tourists often recognise the pride the Welsh feel for their country, they're content to observe it. Iolo, on the other hand, is frank about the depth of his attachment to Wales, and sees no contradiction between his patriotism and the universalist view, shared with other radicals, that he's a 'citizen of the world'. On approaching the border, he writes,

> To say that my soul brightens up at a sight of my native country will be termed nationality, prejudice, weakness, silliness, but why so? What is a man that does not love that country that it is most peculiarly his own, and in that, the spot that gave him birth. Why just such another brute as he that loves not his own father or mother more than those of his neighbours, or of strangers, a man that has no warmth of affection for the particular can never have for the general; who loves not his own parent will never, can never love man. Who loves not his native home will never in a proper sense be a Citizen of the World.[57]

Iolo was fifty-five years old when he came to the end of his walk home from London. Meanwhile, a new generation of much younger, Romantic walkers was already beginning to explore Wales on foot. They were to transform the way Wales was experienced by visitors.

Chapter 3: Romantics, climbers and artists

Samuel Taylor Coleridge

One of the first of the new, Romantic pedestrians was a young Cambridge student, Samuel Taylor Coleridge. His university career had been troubled. He arrived at Jesus College in autumn 1791, and, although his academic talent was obvious and he won prizes, he spent much of his time partying, politicking, writing poetry, and flirting with Mary Evans, the daughter of family friends in London. In December 1793, in a fit of despair, he joined the army under the pseudonym Silas Tomkyn Comberbache. He wasn't a natural soldier, to say the least, and the episode was disastrous. The regiment finally 'let him go', recording in its roll, 'discharged S.T. Comberbache, insane; 10 April 1794'. Returning to Cambridge, he accepted the penalties the University imposed on him. But his interests now lay elsewhere. His new life, he decided, would begin with a walking tour of Wales.[1]

Why did Coleridge choose Wales, and why did he choose to walk? Tours of the country were now a common pursuit for English visitors, especially since it was close by, and because continental travel had been made difficult by the upheavals of the French Revolution (which excited Coleridge). But there were other

Samuel Taylor Coleridge, oil painting by Peter Vandyke, c1795
(*National Library of Wales*)

83

reasons, connected with the early stirrings of that other revolution, Romanticism.

Coleridge didn't meet William Wordsworth until early autumn 1795, though William's younger brother, Christopher, was a Cambridge friend, and the two poets were familiar with each other's published works (Wordsworth had published his early walking poem 'An evening walk' in 1793). Wordsworth already knew parts of Wales well. In 1791 he went to Denbighshire to stay with his friend Robert Jones at Plas-yn-Llan, Llangynhafal, and spent four months on a walking tour of north Wales. He climbed Yr Wyddfa at night to see the sun rise from the summit, an experience that provides the climactic moment in his later, long autobiographical poem 'The prelude'.

Wordsworth revisited Plas-yn-Llan in 1792 and 1793, and then, in June 1793, after a tempestuous period in France, he walked alone up the Wye valley. In his poem 'Lines written a few miles above Tintern Abbey' he recalled that transcendent experience five years later, after a second visit to the Wye in summer 1798, this time with his sister Dorothy.

Coleridge set off on foot from Cambridge on 15 June 1794 in the company of a fellow-undergraduate, Joseph Hucks.[2] According to Coleridge, Hucks was 'a man of cultivated, tho' not vigorous understanding', a verdict confirmed by reading his account of the tour, which he published in 1795 as *A pedestrian tour through north Wales in a series of letters*. In his book, he omits most anecdote and human interest, and fails to mention Coleridge by name. A few of the letters Coleridge wrote while in Wales, to Robert Southey and Henry Martin, survive to supply some of the brio and vigour lacking in Hucks's book.[3] He wrote in a letter to Robert Southey, 'I have bought a little blank book, and portable ink horn – as I journey onward, I ever and anon pluck the wild flowers of poesy.' Unfortunately, the notebook doesn't survive.[4]

The two friends first stop off at Oxford, where they're introduced to Robert Southey. A twenty-year old student, Southey was already known as a prolific poet and as a political firebrand and republican.

Coleridge and Southey spend nearly three weeks in earnest political discussion, developing the idea they called 'pantisocracy', a new kind of self-governing society based on equality and the sharing of property.

Coleridge and Hucks, their minds aflame with political idealism, finally leave Oxford in July. Their decision to make the journey on foot is entirely deliberate, a statement of rebellion against the usual mode of travel expected of young gentlemen. In walking they renounce their middle-class backgrounds and ally themselves with the workers of Wales:

> We are so completely metamorphosed that I much doubt whether you would recognise us through our disguise; we carry our clothes, &c. in a wallet or knapsack, from which we have not hitherto experienced the slightest inconvenience: as for all ideas of appearance and gentility, they are entirely out of the question—our object is to see, not to be seen; and if I thought I had one acquaintance who would be ashamed of me and my knapsack, seated by the fire side of an honest Welsh peasant, in a country village, I should not only make myself perfectly easy on my own account, but should be induced to pity and despise him for his weakness.[5]

By the time they reach Conwy Hucks says that the walkers present 'a very formidable appearance', with their trousers, knapsacks and sticks. Sometimes they excite ridicule, at other times alarm, especially among children, who assume they're Frenchmen. Country people take them for army recruits. Coleridge is carrying a curious walking stick he has bought in Cambridge, decorated with an eagle's head, the owner's portrait, and the 'line of beauty in very ugly carving'.

It's hot, tiring weather for walking. Coleridge writes that 'the roads, white and dazzling, seemed to undulate with heat – and the country, bare and unhedged, presenting nothing but stone fences, dreary to the eye and scorching to the touch.' A poem he writes on this part of the journey, 'Perspiration: a travelling eclogue', repeats these details, and emphasises the political inflection of pedestrian travel, with its opening cameo of upper-class coach-riding:

> The dust flies smothering, as on clattring wheels
> Loath'd aristocracy careers along.
> The distant track quick vibrates to the eye,
> And white and dazzling undulates with heat.[6]

This may be the first instance of walking being seen as an act of resistance to power, a sentiment that only became a familiar one in the twentieth century, after walking had become a minority means of locomotion. It emerged, significantly, at a time when the powerful and affluent had found a means of transport that set them distinctively apart from most other travellers.

Hucks has a more dignified self-image of the two walkers. 'Behold us, then, more like two pilgrims performing a journey to the tomb of some wonder-working saint, than men travelling for their pleasure and amusement'. He's aware of the 'foreignness' of Wales, 'so dissimilar in every respect to England', but his view of the journey ahead is no different from that of the usual tourist in Wales:

> Surrounded on all sides by cloud-capd mountains; arrived amongst people, to whose language I am a perfect stranger, and whose manners and customs are as eccentric as they are singular, every circumstance attracts attention, and every object excites admiration.[7]

They travel through Gloucester to Ross-on-Wye, where they stay in the King's Arms. Coleridge scratches on a window shutter of the inn some republican verses in praise of the philanthropist John Kyrle, the 'Man of Ross'. He renews his attack on the arrogance of aristocratic power: 'richer than miser o'er his countless hoards, nobler than kings, or king-polluted lords'. They head north, through Hereford, Leominster and Bishop's Castle, and enter Wales near Montgomery. On the way from Welshpool they get lost, despite being assured that the road was 'as straight as an arrow'. They ask for directions from an 'honest Cambrian of respectable appearance' called Owen ap Jones ap Evans, who directs them to the Goat Inn at Llanfyllin. Here they're disappointed by the dry bread and bad cheese, but Coleridge diverts himself by getting involved in a political row:

> … I preached pantisocracy and aspheterism [a Coleridge coinage meaning 'communism'] with so much success that two great huge fellows, of butcher-like appearance, danced about the room in enthusiastic agitation – and one of them of his own accord called for a large glass of brandy, and drank it off to this, his own toast – 'God save the King. And may he be the last.'[8]

From Llanfyllin they walk to Llangynog. Coleridge calls it 'a village most romantically situated', though Hucks is less impressed: 'surrounded on all sides by barren and sandy hills'. In the morning they climb over the Berwyn mountains. For Coleridge they're 'most wild and romantic', and bring out his poetic impulse: 'there are immense and rugged clefts in the mountains, which in winter must form cataracts most tremendous… I climbed up a precipice on which was a large thorn-tree, and slept by the side of one of them near two hours.' The heat is oppressive. They take frequent stops beside rocks to consume, in Coleridge's words 'draughts of water cold as ice, and clear as infant diamonds in their embryo dew'.

As they descend the mountains towards Bala in the afternoon, the sun, reflected on the surface of the river Dee below, shines 'with unsufferable brightness'. Hucks, untouched by Coleridge's early Romantic awakenings, finds the mountains around Bala 'grand and sublime, but not interesting'. Coleridge, by contrast, celebrates them in a new poem, 'Bala Hill': 'with many a weary step at length I gain / thy summit, Bala! and the cool breeze plays / cheerily around my brow.' In the inn at Bala Coleridge falls into conversation with a 'Welsh democrat', who shakes his hand warmly 'with flesh-bruising ardor'. Soon he incites another political punch-up:

Shortly after, into the same room a well drest clergyman and four others – among whom (the landlady whispers me) was a Justice of the Peace and the doctor of the parish – I was asked for a gentleman – I gave General Washington – The parson said in a low voice – (Republicans!) – After which the medical man said – damn toasts! I gives a sentiment – May all republicans be guillotined! Up starts the Welsh democrat. May all republicans be *gulloteen'd* – and then you will be the first! Thereon rogue, villain, traitor flew thick in each other's faces as a hailstorm – This is nothing in Wales – they *make calling one another liars* etc. – necessary vent-holes to the sulphurious fumes of the temper![9]

Hucks gives a slightly different account of the incident, in which his friend is innocent of any provocation and the two prudently withdraw from the scene when the din becomes too loud.

Later they meet two Cambridge student friends, John Brooke (or Brookes) and Thomas Berdmore. Coleridge calls them 'rival pedestrians [who] were vigorously pursuing their tour – in a *post chaise*! We laughed famously. Their only excuse was that Berdmore had been ill.' Brooke and Berdmore stay with them, apparently, for most of the rest of the tour.

At Wrexham Coleridge has a serious shock. While at the church he catches sight of Elizabeth, the sister of his London sweetheart, Mary Evans. They're on holiday, staying with their Welsh grandmother. He hasn't seen Mary since joining the army, and is uncertain whether she'd rejected him. Elizabeth turns white and Coleridge flees back to his lodgings. From the window of the inn he sees Elizabeth and Mary passing by outside. They each start, and utter a short cry, and, as Hucks reports, walk past four or five times, trying to catch another sight of him. But Coleridge feels ill, almost faints and retires to bed. For a whole day he's unable to eat or sleep. Distance, though, soon puts the affair into perspective, and he recovers soon enough to write an elegant short poem in Latin ending with words, 'vale ah! formosa Maria!' (farewell, beautiful Mary!), and later a poem, 'The sigh', that again mentions her by name.

The party passes through St Asaph, and at Holywell visits St Winefride's Well, a magnet for pilgrims since the middle ages, but also now a tourist attraction. Coleridge takes 'an excellent cold bath'. At the beach near Abergele Hucks notices a strange custom, one 'that has an air of great indelicacy to the stranger': men and women of the lower orders bathe together naked, without the usual precautions of machines or dresses. The fastidious Hucks quickly retires from the scene, while Coleridge assures Henry Martin in a letter that the bathers 'live together in the greatest purity'. Hucks seems happier in Conwy, where in the church he searches out the tombstone of one of his ancestors, William Hookes, famous for fathering forty-one children.

The group arrives at Aber, after walking along the new, greatly improved road round Penmaenmawr, and settles at the rather expensive inn. Next morning they decide to climb to the summit of Penmaenmawr and book lunch in the inn for two o'clock. But the day doesn't go well. They insist on walking without a guide and choose the steepest, most difficult route of ascent, consistent with Coleridge's belief that 'every man [is] his own path-maker – skip & jump – where rushes frow, a man may go.'[10] Despite 'a vast number of unexpected obstructions', they struggle to the summit, but they're overcome with exhaustion and tormented by thirst. Preparing to descend, they happen to overturn a large flat stone, and discover a small spring. Many years later Coleridge pointed out that this incident inspired a stanza in *The rime of the ancient mariner*:

I took the thought of 'grinning for joy' in that poem from a friend's remark to me, when we had climbed to the top of Plinlimmon [he means Penmaenmawr] and were nearly dead with thirst. We could not speak from the constriction, till we found a little puddle under a stone. He said to me – 'You grinned like an idiot'. He had done the same.[11]

With throats unslaked, with black lips baked,
Agape they heard me call:

Gramercy! they for joy did grin,
And all at once their breath drew in,
As they were drinking all.[12]

On the way down the walkers become separated. Dusk falls. Hucks calls out the name of his friends, but is met with silence, apart from the distant barking of a dog. He begins to imagine phantoms: the spirit of the mountain, or armed bandits. But he manages to stumble back to the inn, along with the others, at about nine o'clock.

On the following day the friends make an even more dangerous trip, taking 'lostness' to a near-fatal extreme. They decide to walk across Traeth Lafan and wade across the Menai Strait at the lowest ebb of the tide. They set off in bare feet, with initial guidance from a local clergyman, but are engulfed in fog before they're half way across. They become separated and lose contact. Finally, when all seems lost, they hear the voices of the ferrymen, who rescue them and take them to the Anglesey shore.

The friends decided to climb Yr Wyddfa. They rise at four o'clock in the morning. The weather isn't promising, but Coleridge and most of the others decide to set out, if only to do some botanising. They take the route now known as the 'Snowdon Ranger' path. Hucks excuses himself: his cold is worse. The party returns at four o'clock, tired and disappointed. Clouds shroud the mountain, and though they reach the summit they can see nothing. From Beddgelert they walk to Tan-y-bwlch, but in trying to reach Harlech they wander into impossibly boggy land. Hucks complains that the country people are ignorant about their own roads, and have little idea of distance: what they promise will be five miles and 'a pretty good step' can turn out to be ten miles. At Harlech Coleridge and Hucks find no one to open the castle and show them round, so they scale the walls. This excites the attention of the townsfolk, who gather around them, taking them to be 'free-booters.' The friends explain themselves and the locals, paid off with some money, retreat to the pub to spend it.

After a night in the Golden Lion in Dolgellau, 'a large and dirty town', Coleridge and his companions set out to climb Cadair Idris.

Cadair Idris

(*photo Andrew Green*)

They hire a guide and load him with provisions: ham, fowl, bread, cheese and brandy. Though the weather is fine below, clouds again envelop the peak. Hucks stares down the precipice from Pen-y-gadair, which calls to his mind Milton's famous description of dark Chaos and the gates of Hell. The guide leads them to the bed of the giant Idris, and rebukes them for laughing at his superstition. Their next stop is Tywyn, where Hucks complains of damp sheets on his bed in the inn. 'Lard, sir', replies the maid, 'it be impossible, for they have been a slept in four or five times within this last week.'

From Tywyn they travel on a ferry across the Dyfi estuary, and on to Aberystwyth, 'a very respectable bathing place' and to Devil's Bridge to see the Mynach falls, which were beginning to attract visitors after Thomas Johnes of Hafod built accommodation there in 1792–93. Tregaron, reports Hucks, is a 'miserable hole', and the friends have to break a window to let air into their room. Wisely, they use a guide to help them cross the 'lonely and trackless' Cambrian mountains. It rains heavily all day and for twenty miles they meet not a soul. At Llandovery on 2 August Hucks says goodbye to the others and returns home via Brecon, Abergavenny and the Wye valley. He pleads urgent business, but you suspect he was finding Coleridge's pace and energy too exhausting.

Without Hucks's narrative we lose sight of Coleridge after Llandovery. He too passed through the Wye valley and on 5 August crossed on the ferry from Chepstow to Bristol, where he'd stay for some months, lecturing, planning pantisocracy, and meeting Sara Fricker, who would become his wife. He'd come again to Wales, though not on a walking tour. In April 1795 he returned to the Wye valley with Southey and the Fricker sisters, and in August 1798, with the Wordsworths, he visited their friend, the radical republican and atheist John Thelwall, who was sheltering from political persecution in Llyswen, near Brecon.

Thelwall was himself a committed walker. In 1797 he walked from London to Nether Stowey in Somerset to join Coleridge there. He'd used an earlier series of walks in southern England as the basis for *The peripatetic*, an experimental work in verse and prose published in 1793, which combines elements of the novel, travel narrative, political tract and satire: 'I pursue my meditations on foot, and can find occasion for philosophical reflection wherever yon fretted vault (the philosopher's best canopy) extends its glorious covering'.[13]

The 1794 walking tour of Wales left important marks on Coleridge. It seeded his love of long walking, which he practised constantly over the next ten years. He hadn't been long in Bristol before he was off walking again, with Southey in the Mendip Hills, Cheddar Gorge and the edge of the Quantock Hills – hills that, when he revisited them with the Wordsworths in 1797, led to the creation of his best-known poems, *The rime of the ancient mariner* and *Kubla Khan*. Walking in Wales, he discovered, gave him direct access to a natural world, in landscape and in close-up, that ignited his imagination and sparked his poetry. Love of nature was paralleled by romantic love, or the pain of it. And Wales taught him that even the most exalted states of mind or heroic status can be punctured simply by laughing at the self – part of his own distinctive version of Romanticism. In Wales he found the first big challenge to his immense physical energy – he'd walked about 500 miles in a month – and a means of satisfying his boundless curiosity.[14]

For a time Coleridge was interested in literature in Welsh – to the extent of making an English version, in July 1794 or soon afterwards, of one of the traditional Welsh verses known as *hen benillion*:

Dod dy law, on'd wyt yn coelio,
Dan fy mron, a gwilia 'mriwio;
Ti gei glywed, os gwrandewi,
Sŵn y galon fach yn torri.

Probably Coleridge used a translation first published by Edward Jones in 1784. His own version lacks the economy of the original, and perhaps carries a hidden reference to the affair with Mary Evans:

If while my passion I impart,
    You deem my words untrue,
O place your hand upon my heart
    Feel how it throbs for *you*!

Ah no! reject the thoughtless claim
    In pity to your Lover!
That thrilling touch would aid the flame
    It wishes to discover.[15]

In 1803 Coleridge was talking about devoting six months to learning Welsh and Irish. But, like many of his ambitions, the plan was never fulfilled.[16]

More Romantic walkers

Two years after Hucks and Coleridge, in 1796, a young man called Charles Shephard made a walking tour of Wales. He lacked

Coleridge's vigour and optimism, and indeed he warned his readers against walking:

> ... the roads are rendered so supple and cloggy by the rain, that it is almost impossible to proceed; and when, perhaps, you have dragged on at the rate of about a mile an hour, you are frequently unable to meet with any accommodation, at least with such an accommodation as a traveller, and particularly a genteel one, would desire; consequently, you are reduced to the sad extremity of either sleeping in a filthy bed, or of proceeding to the next place, however wearied.[17]

Even if you can find a decent inn, Shephard says, you can't be certain of a welcome, since innkeepers are suspicious of travellers on foot.[18]

A more sympathetic pedestrian was Richard Warner. He'd been a curate to William Gilpin in Boldre, and no doubt learned much from him about travelling in Wales. In August 1797, at the age of thirty-four, he set out on an eighteen-day walking tour of Wales, publishing his account in a book the following year.

Warner claims that the pedestrian's 'independent mode of travelling enables him to catch beauties in his walk through an Alpine country, which the incumbrance of a carriage, and even the indulgence of a horse, prevents another traveller from enjoying.' He argues against walking alone. He has a companion, Richard Cruttwell, referred to as 'C.', 'with whom one can interchange sentiment, and communicate observation'. The two give careful thought to what they need to take with them:

> A single change of raiment, and some other little articles for the comfort of the person, form all the necessary baggage of a foot-traveller... C., conceiving it might be best effected by the assistance of side-pockets, has had two receptacles of this kind, of considerable dimensions, added to his coat. My plan is a different one: a neglected *Spencer*, which, though somewhat threadbare and rusty, may still make a respectable figure in North

Wales, has, by the taylor's skill, been fitted up with a sportsman's pocket, that sweeps from one side to the other, and allows room sufficient for all the articles necessary to be carried. Accoutred in this manner, and provided with maps and a compass, which we understand are indispensably requisite amongst the mountains of Merioneth and Caernarvonshire, we left Bath this morning as the clock was striking five.[19]

Later Warner finds a better solution than specially tailored pockets, which, he admits, make him look like a common pedlar. In Cardiganshire he meets three pedestrian gentlemen, each of whom carried 'a handsome leathern bag, covered with neat net-work, which, being suspended from the right shoulder by a strap, hung under the left arm, in the manner of a shooting-bag'. He recommends carrying a 'small drinking horn', because although milk and other drinks are not hard to find on the way, 'yet the vessels from which we quaffed these potations were not always so clean as those we had been accustomed to use.'

Warner recommends taking a map. For the first time detailed and fairly accurate maps were now available that could help walkers find their way. In 1795 John Evans of Llwyn-y-groes, Llanymynech published by subscription nine sheets covering north Wales, at a scale of almost one inch to a mile, together with a single north Wales sheet. These maps, which he took twenty years to prepare, were praised for their accuracy and the quality of their printing by the engraver, Evans's neighbour and fellow map-maker Robert Baugh. They superseded an earlier map of north Wales published by Thomas Kitchin in 1764, and they held their own until the Ordnance Survey was set up and started work in Wales in the 1830s.

Warner and Cruttwell set a good pace, averaging over twenty miles a day. After crossing the Severn by boat they walk to Usk, then Brecon, Rhayader, Devil's Bridge, Machynlleth, Dolgellau, Beddgelert, Caernarfon and Conwy, before turning south, through Llangollen, Llanymynech and Montgomery, to end in Chepstow. Warner spends much time observing and talking to Welsh people – he has an eye for beautiful young women – and is struck by the harsh working and housing conditions on farms and in lead mines. As he walks on, he develops an affinity with the people and an appreciation of their history. He denounces Edward I and praises Owain Glyndŵr, and with the help of guides he climbs Cadair Idris and Yr Wyddfa.[20]

Warner was encouraged by his first tour of Wales to return in 1798. On this occasion he covered 783 miles in six weeks, with two friends, at an average of eighteen miles a day. At St Donat's he heard about a fellow-pedestrian who had passed through six weeks before. The suspicions of the locals were aroused by his appearance and his inquisitiveness, and he was taken for an Irish spy. Fears of a French invasion are still common in south Wales, in the wake of the abortive attack on Fishguard the year before. 'A fierce-looking fellow, with a pack at his back, a huge staff in his hand, and with several other singularities about him', the man had been spotted taking plans of the castle and asking a local woman for information. A crowd of seventy or eighty locals, armed with muskets, pitchforks and sticks, set out from Llantwit Major in search of him. They tracked him to the middle of a cornfield. The musketeers formed a line, took aim and felled him with a volley of shots – only to find they'd destroyed the local farmer's scarecrow. Warner notes laconically that the innocent pedestrian, unconscious of the hue and cry, had long since departed, and was 'quietly sauntering on to Pyle'.

Warner later claimed that his first published tour

... originated a taste, among the younger part of my countrymen, for pedestrian tours into the principality: so that, since its appearance, the number of genteel foot-travellers there, has, (as I have been informed) nearly equalled those, who have flown through its romantic and picturesque scenery, in the various vehicles of our country of everlasting migration, from the one-horse-chaise, to the barouche and four, with two out-riders. But, my 'Walk' did more than this, for it animated the old to resume the use of their legs; and inspired the fair sex, with a desire to emulate my exertions ...[21]

In the year after the publication of his first book, Warner reports, three 'spirited young women' set out with satchels on their backs and staffs in hand to walk from the Severn to Caernarfon, and would have completed the circuit had not one of them been taken ill. (Unfortunately, he says no more about them.)

By now English tourists and their accounts were so common that they provoked a reaction from Welsh writers. Richard Warner was the object of sharp criticism, along with other English authors of tours in Wales, in a biting review published in 1799 by Theophilus Jones.[22] Jones, best known for his history of Breconshire, attacked the writers for their lack of interest in the Welsh people and how they lived:

> Whether it be from the want of knowledge of the language, or from too transient an acquaintance with the inhabitants, it is remarkable, that, among all the tours into this country, which have met the public eye ... we have nothing like a resemblance of the men and manners of Wales ...[23]

Unsurprisingly, Jones saw tourists' lack of the Welsh language as a major handicap.

> The knowledge of the Welsh language is so absolutely necessary to a traveller among British antiquities that without it he cannot take three steps without the risk of breaking his neck.[24]

He ridicules Warner's choice to walk, 'this silly and ridiculous whim of converting pleasure into toil'. He blames 'folly and the inexperience of youth' for introducing pedestrianism, and 'fashion and caprice' for keeping it alive. Yet Jones's criticism of most of the tourists is that they rush through the country without taking the time to discover it thoroughly.

The walkers continued to arrive. Coleridge was followed in the autumn of 1802 by one of his avid admirers, Thomas de Quincey. De Quincey started out on a solitary, four-month walking tramp round the country as a release after running away from Manchester

Grammar School, where he had an unhappy time. He was an orphan and sixteen years old. He began the trip with an allowance from an uncle of a guinea a week, but when he failed to keep his family informed of his progress the money ceased. De Quincey walked between seventy and a hundred miles a week. For him travelling on foot was a necessity, not a choice, but he found that there was

> 'no disgrace attached in Wales, as too generally upon the great roads of England, to the pedestrian style of travelling. Indeed, the majority of those whom I met as fellow-tourists in the quiet little cottage-parlours of the Welsh posting-houses were pedestrian travellers'.[25]

De Quincey's account of his wandering in Wales, in his memoir *Confessions of an English opium eater*, forms a prelude to the drug-fuelled mental journeys he describes later in his book. He started by walking through Flintshire and Denbighshire, before lodging in Bangor. After quarrelling with a landlady there, he walked to Caernarfon, Dolgellau, Tan-y-bwlch, Harlech and Barmouth, and through Cardiganshire and Montgomeryshire. The tranquillity of the 'sweet sylvan routes' and the 'eternal motion of winds and rivers' of Wales, and the absence of 'huge Babylonian centres of commerce' appealed to de Quincey. 'Happier life I cannot imagine', he wrote, 'than this vagrancy, if the weather were but tolerable.' He claimed that he was never in complete health unless he walked between eight and fifteen miles a day. Nights he could spend outdoors, at least till October, and sometimes he used a hand-made canvas tent. He'd no need to fear wild animals, or 'Thugs'. Though his money was short, the cost of food and basic accommodation was modest: he found it was hard to spend more than three shillings in a week.

Once his money was exhausted, things became rather harder:

> I subsisted either on blackberries, hips, haws, &c., or on the casual hospitalities which I now and then received in return for such little services as I had an opportunity of rendering.[26]

Near Llanystumdwy he was taken in for three days by a young family of four sisters and three brothers. They spoke English and treated him hospitably. He wrote letters for them, including love letters for two of the sisters. But on the fourth day the parents returned. They'd been to Caernarfon for a Methodist meeting. The 'churlish faces' and repeated response of 'Dim Sassenach' of these 'two grave sexagenarian Welsh Methodists' made it clear to de Quincey that he was no longer welcome. He said goodbye to them, and borrowed enough money to exchange rural deprivation in Wales for poverty on the streets of London. In the *Confessions* de Quincey makes a point of counterposing the peace and hospitality of Wales with the harsh and impersonal world, the 'tumult and uproar', of the capital city.[27]

Nine years after de Quincey's adventures in Wales, another young Romantic writer, Percy Bysshe Shelley, came to Wales. While a first-year student at Oxford, he'd already published a novel and poems. Then, in February 1811, he issued anonymously an inflammatory pamphlet, 'The necessity of atheism', which led to his swift expulsion from the University and to difficulties with his family. To escape, Shelley walked in July all the way from Sussex to the Elan Valley in Radnorshire to stay with his uncle, Thomas Grove, the owner of Cwm Elan. He returned to the Elan Valley in April 1812, this time with his young bride, Harriet Westbrook. They intended to buy a house there, at Nantgwyllt, but no money was available and the couple went back to England. The landscape, though, left a strong impression. In his poem 'The retrospect: Cwm Elan, 1812', Shelley recalls, like Wordsworth, an earlier vision, of 'jagged peaks that frown sublime, mocking the blunted scythe of time'. By the end of the year he was living at Plas Tan-yr-allt near Tremadog, in a house owned by William Madocks, the founder of Porthmadog and Tremadog. He was unimpressed by the kind of society he found there. The locals returned Shelley's hostility. After what he claimed was a nocturnal break-in and gunfight in February 1813, he fled Wales and his unpaid debts within a week, and never returned.[28]

In November 1812 Shelley had met Thomas Love Peacock, the future author of *Headlong Hall* and other 'conversation novels'. The two became lifelong friends. Like Shelley, Peacock was a poet, an atheist and a keen walker in Wales. Two years earlier he visited Tremadog and took lodgings at Tan-y-bwlch, Maentwrog. He developed a strong and lasting affection for the landscape of Wales, which he called 'a terrestrial paradise', and for Welsh history and traditions. There he met a parson's daughter, Jane Gryffydh, whom he married, much later, in 1820. Leaving Tan-y-bwlch in April 1811, he walked eighteen miles to Dolgellau. On the next day he walked seven miles to Tal-y-Llyn and climbed Cadair Idris, accompanied by Edward Jones, the landlord of the Blue Lion Inn, Minffordd. Jones was a familiar figure to many tourists, as schoolmaster, stone carver, mountain guide and talker. Richard Warner met him in 1797 and wrote that his 'natural ingenuity has been sharpened into cunning by a long residence in England', a comment he resented. Peacock calls him 'an original character, who in the triple capacity of publican, schoolmaster, and guide to Cadair Idris, manages to keep the particles of his carcase in contact.' Down from the mountain, and after tea at Minffordd, Peacock walked on to Machynlleth (another nine miles) by moonlight, and, on the following day to Tywyn. After that, happy in mind and body, with his dog, a clean shirt and a copy of Tacitus, he intended to keep walking, through south Wales to his home in Surrey.[29]

As the years passed, more and more tourists came to Wales. Those who walked could sometimes choose to walk light, like Benjamin Malkin:

> The plan which I adopted was that of walking; but taking a servant on horseback, for the conveyance of books as well as necessaries, without which convenience almost every advantage of a pedestrian is lost, except economy, and that is completely frustrated by so expensive an addition.[30]

Daniel Carless Webb recommended his fellow-pedestrian to appear respectable by carrying a light green bag (rather than a blue one, which might suggest he was a lawyer). This would prevent him 'meeting with the disagreeables, incidental to pedestrians, by a rough reception from ignorant waiters, and surly innkeepers.' In it he should keep 'one shirt, one pair of stockings, two neckcloths, two pocket handkerchiefs, a pocket-compass, map, drinking-horn, paper, and implements for writing.'[31]

Even so, walking had its pains and rigours. They included, according to one tourist in 1819, 'galled feet, heavy rain, despicable roads, dark nights, bad accommodation, or what is worse, none at all'. Hospitality could be limited. One landlady in 1823 was 'old and stingy, and having no regard to the capacious appetites of us pedestrians'. Shoemakers in Wales, it was alleged, did not know how to repair boots. Then there was the problem of exhaustion. J.T. Barber wrote in 1803, 'I do not conceive, that a man enduring the fatigue of trudging day after day through miry roads, can maintain an exhilaration of spirits congenial with the beauties that surround him.'[32]

Walking tourism was a middle-class pursuit. A rare hint of working-class walkers occurs in the diary of Robert Ker Porter, a Scottish painter on a walking tour of north Wales in 1799 with an artist friend, Thomas Underwood. At Mallwyd they came across a group of fellow-walkers. Porter treats them with hauteur: 'on our return to the inn, there came a group of four pedestrians fatigued, famished and filthy. They seemed men very thick upwards and were bound for Birmingham – Underwood thought them buckle formers.' (Thousands of workers were employed in Birmingham in the eighteenth century to manufacture shoe buckles.)[33]

Women walking

Tourists were also overwhelmingly male. Of the 1,200 or so Welsh tours that were written up to 1900 only around two hundred were by women. But the women were often exceptional people. One of the first was Catherine Hutton. She was the daughter of a radical Unitarian, William Hutton (their house was burnt, along with Joseph Priestley's, by a reactionary mob in the Birmingham riots of 1791). She came to Wales eight times, and she was particularly adventurous, travelling in remoter parts on foot as well as on horseback.

In July 1796 Catherine was near Mallwyd:

The sublimity of these scenes shook my nerves. The only way in which I could contemplate these towering hills, woody glens, and rushing waters, was on my feet. We sent the servant on with the horses, and walked nearly four miles before we reached Mallwyd, chiefly in the rain; but enraptured at every step we took ...[34]

Catherine Hutton at the age of forty-three:
engraving by J.W. Cook, undated
(*Trustees of the British Museum*)

In August she was walking to Dolgellau, and met some local people travelling in the same direction. Catherine wrote with style and acute intelligence. Here her narrative keeps a careful, empathetic eye on the progress of her companions:

As we walked slowly up the mountain we were overtaken by a Welshman, on his poney, and a woman on foot, who was fully a match for him and his horse. It was a comfort to meet with our fellow creatures in so desolate the region, though we could not communicate our ideas to each other. The ideas of the woman, if we might judge by her words, were very copious, for her tongue was never at rest ... They accompanied us to Dolgelly, nearly six miles, keeping close to our horses heels; walking when we walked, and trotting when we trotted; the woman trudging barefooted; always talking, never out of breath or discovering the smallest symptom of fatigue.[35]

Catherine was curious about almost everything she saw on her journeys. She took a close interest in the Welsh people she met, and was sympathetic and well-informed about Welsh culture and the Welsh language, at one point explaining its orthography. She felt comfortable on foot, and insisted on not rushing through the country:

> Travellers at this rate cannot see Wales ... to find out all its beauties, a man must travel on foot; or at least on a Welsh Keffil. He must be acquainted with the Welsh gentry and clergy, and travel with a pass from one of their houses to another. So might he learn what was worth seeing, and where to find it.[36]

Just as remarkable was Elizabeth Smith. She was born near Durham in 1776. After her father, a banker, was bankrupted in 1795, she lived for a few years at Piercefield near Chepstow. Almost entirely self-taught, she learned at least ten languages, and wrote poetry, translations and other linguistic works. In July 1798, during a stay at Conwy, she climbed Yr Wyddfa – the first known ascent by a named woman tourist. Like Wordsworth and Coleridge, she wanted to see the sun rise from the summit. With her mother and aunt she set off at eleven o'clock, and two hours later called for their guide. The two other women, alarmed by the steep slopes ahead, decided to go no further, but with the (monoglot Welsh) guide Elizabeth pressed on. Each summit ahead appeared to be the last, but was not, until at last she found herself at the top of a thrilling 'abyss':

Elizabeth Smith, engraving by R.M. Meadows, after John George Wood, 1809
(British Museum)

I am standing indeed at the top of the abyss, but with a high rocky peak rising on each side of me, and descending very near perpendicularly into the lake at the bottom. I have taken a rough sketch of one of these peaks, with the lake in the deepest shadow; I am turning over my paper, (which the wind renders very difficult,) in order to draw another; – I look up, and see the upper part illuminated by a beautiful rose-coloured light, while the opposite part still casts a dark shade over its base, and conceals the sun itself from my view. If I were ready to jump into the pit with delight at first seeing it, my ecstasy was now still greater.[37]

Even more intrepid in her approach to Yr Wyddfa was a later walker, Ellen Weeton, a Lancashire woman of independent thought who worked as a governess. In June 1825, at the age of 48, she set off alone from the Snowdon Ranger to traverse the mountain via the summit. She was aware that a woman climbing alone and without a guide was unusual, but was determined not to be deflected, as she wrote in her journal:

The guide, seeing that I was out of the path ... called out to me, but I was quite deaf. He continued shouting, and I was forced to hear; he was telling me to keep in the copper path, &c. I knew the way perfectly well, for my map and my guide had been well studied at home.[38]

Defeated, the guide disappeared. Ellen imagines him descending, 'vexed ... that it should be seen that any body could ascend without him, – and a woman, too!' It seems from her description that she descended from the summit via Crib Goch, a difficult and often dangerous ridge:

Not far before me, the path wound along a most awful precipice. Now I *was* startled! for the first time ... there was no crossing lower down. I must either return home as I had come, or climb the only way there was ... Whilst crossing the ridge, perhaps 100 yds., perhaps 200, or even more, for I was too terrified to ascertain – the precipice on my right and left both, was too much for my head to bear; on my right, if I slipped ever so little, nothing could save me, and Oh! it looked like an eternity of falling; it seemed to my giddy head, half a mile down.[39]

Walking was Ellen's preferred mode of travelling. On an earlier occasion she'd planned 'a very wild scheme' to walk across the whole of Wales, moving from farmhouse to farmhouse in a chain, but thought better of the idea when she considered not only her lack of the Welsh language but also 'the many insults a female is liable to'. 'If I was but a man now!', she reflected bitterly, 'I could soon do it.'[40]

Ellen Weeton always preferred to walk on her own, so that 'my thoughts, as well as my feet, may ramble without restraint'. For her, walking was a particular and personal pleasure, and also a liberation from the drudgery, servility and abuse she suffered in her home life. Aaron Stock, the husband she married in 1814, had beaten her and robbed her of her daughter after their separation in 1822. To judge by her vivid account of it, her bold traverse of Yr Wyddfa gave her special joy and exaltation.

Mountain walkers and climbers

By the end of the eighteenth century mountain climbing was an established element of a tour of Wales for more energetic travellers. They could engage mountain guides, hire ponies for at least part of the ascent, and stay nearby in inns that catered in part for them. The inn at Capel Curig kept a visitor's book, and the volume for 1801 to 1836 contains many references to residents climbing Yr Wyddfa. Yr Wyddfa and Cadair Idris were by far the most frequently climbed mountains. Scaling the peaks of others, like the Glyderau, Tryfan and Pumlumon, for only for the most adventurous.

The earliest account of mountaineering in Wales is by William Bingley, yet another Anglican cleric. Bingley, born in Doncaster, travelled through north Wales in summer 1798, while still a

Cambridge undergraduate, and published his tour in 1800. He was a keen botanist and partly for that reason chose to travel mainly on foot:

> [The naturalist] is enabled to examine the country as he goes along; and when he sees occasion, he can also strike out of the road, amongst the mountains and morasses, in a manner completely independent of all those obstacles that inevitably attend the bringing of carriages or horses.[41]

Bingley had befriended an experienced climber, Peter Bayley Williams, the rector of Llanrug and Llanberis and a man steeped in Welsh history and literature. It was Williams who suggested 'the wild idea of attempting to climb apparently up the face of the precipice' of Clogwyn Du'r Arddu, on the north flank of Yr Wyddfa. Bingley was aware that Edward Llwyd and John Ray had found rare plants in this area. They began the climb, he says, 'without once reflecting on the many dangers that might attend it'. They were soon scrambling on their hands and knees on the rocks. Half way up, the going became tough, with larger masses of rock above them, but they agreed to continue. Williams, who was wearing strong nailed shoes, led the way over the next, difficult section. Behind him, on a leather belt fastened to his waist, he hauled up a small basket containing their provisions and botanical specimens. Then he fixed himself to a rock, took off his belt and gave the other end to Bingley, who succeeded in following.[42]

This ascent of Clogwyn Du'r Arddu is the earliest recorded account of an assisted rock climb in Britain. Yr Wyddfa was a favourite with Bingley, and he claimed to have climbed it seven times, via all the routes known to him.

The two friends also explored the Ogwen valley. During what turned out to be for Bingley 'by far the most laborious walk I have ever ventured upon in the course of one day', they tackled Tryfan, 'a most arduous undertaking'.

As more and more 'climbing tourists' arrived in Eryri, they created more work for local guides.[43] The names of over sixty of them, boys, men and women, are known. Few were professional and most worked part-time during the climbing season. Many built reputations for their expertise in route-finding, botany and other specialities. One of them, Richard Pugh, printed a poster in 1827 advertising his services as 'guide general to the tremendous mountain of Cader Idris'. He claimed to have provided a 'small cottage' at the summit for visitors to dine in without worrying about the weather, and also offered for hire 'cloaks, and other coverings of goat skins with the hair on'.

Another well-known guide was John Morton. In 1803 he leased an inn by the side of Llyn Cwellyn, and from there led walkers up Yr Wyddfa. In 1822 his charge for escorting a single person was seven shillings, a sum thought by one writer to be exorbitant. He called himself the 'Snowdon Ranger', a name also applied to the building and to the path. He was still working when George Borrow called at the inn in 1854.

Richard Pugh, mountain guide, and his hut on the summit of Cadair Idris: drawing from Eliza Rand's manuscript diary 'Tour of Wales and the Marches beginning on 22 August 1827'
(*Amgueddfa Cymru – National Museum Wales*)

Artist walkers

The walkers who travelled to Wales from the 1770s were influenced by what they'd read about Wales, especially by the tours of their predecessors. But they were also drawn by how artists had portrayed the beauties of the country. Hundreds of artists came to Wales. Landscape paintings, and especially the widely-circulated prints that derived from them, gave would-be tourists a taste of mountain and river scenery, castles, churches and ruined monasteries. Just as the tourists tended to follow established routes around the country, so the artists developed a repertory of standard subjects and associated 'views' of them.

An important forerunner of these artist-tourists was Francis Place, described as 'Britain's first native topographical artist'. He has a good claim to be considered the first on-the-spot landscape artist in Wales. In 1678 he journeyed through south Wales, as far as Pembroke, with William Lodge, a fellow-member of the 'York Virtuosi', a club of men interested in science, travel and the visual arts. They chose to travel on foot, and Place claimed that they'd covered 700 miles in seven weeks in south Wales and the West Country. He sketched on the spot, with pen and ink, on portable sketchbooks, working up the sketches later with watercolour washes. This wasn't a usual activity at the time, and he and Lodge were arrested in north Wales on suspicion of being Jesuit spies.[44]

From the mid-eighteenth century more artists arrived. Some were employed by local landowners to depict their own houses and estates. In 1770 Paul Sandby came to work for Sir Watkin Williams Wynne at Wynnstay on the Dee, and together they spent a fortnight touring north Wales (a large part of it owned by Sir Watkin). Three

Oystermouth: drawing by Francis Place, 1678
(*Amgueddfa Cymru – National Museum Wales*)

years later he toured south Wales with the botanist Sir Joseph Banks. His prints of the two tours, published in 1775 and 1776 using the new toned aquatint process, found a wide audience and sensitised many to Welsh scenery. Another employed artist was Moses Griffith, engaged by Thomas Pennant in 1769 to accompany him on his tours and illustrate what they found.

An artist who was very willing to leave the road behind and use his feet to find new viewpoints was J.M.W. Turner. Turner first came to Wales aged seventeen in 1792 and was so overwhelmed by what he found that he returned four times before 1800. Already the spirit of the first generation of Romantic writers was making itself felt. Departing from the well-mannered subjects and descriptive, topographical style of Sandby and Moses Griffith, Turner began to transform his Welsh scenes into an inner landscape of deep feeling and recollection. Castles, abbeys and derelict mills kept their place, but became infused with emotional colour.

Cadair Idris: a stream among rocks near the summit, drawing by J M W Turner, Hereford Court Sketchbook, 1798

(*Tate Gallery*)

Turner did something most earlier artists avoided: he took solitary walks into remote country and clambered up the slopes of mountains. Cadair Idris seems to have held a magnetic effect on him (he was aware of Richard Wilson's famous painting of Llyn Cau). In 1798 he climbed the mountain from the south. One sketch, on paper splotched with spots of rain, shows the stream of Nant Cadair falling steeply away, and another hints at Llyn Cau. In both sketches the walls of the mountain ahead form a dark, menacing arc.[45]

Turner was soon followed to Wales by other English artists. One of the finest and most sympathetic to the landscape of the mountains was the watercolourist Cornelius Varley. In 1805 he climbed Cadair Idris. Like Turner, he felt a special attraction to the mountain and drew a series of highly sensitive sketches of its northern face. He left a lyrical description of his ascent, including the sight of a 'Brocken spectre':

> The Sun surrounded by small bright & lofty clouds illum'd the whole heavens & was spreading his beams over a bright ocean of lower clouds... Thus night below & glorious sun shine above, then golden Vapour began to play on our Mountain, but on looking Eastward that end of the mountain was coverd by a luminous fog or Cloud on which we saw in perfection (what has been mysteriously described as the Spectre of the Brocken) a bright halo or ring of light with our distinct Shaddows within. We were on the highest brow of the mountain the shadow of which intercepted the lower part of the ring & on it stood our whole shadows. The head of my shadow was in the center of his ring & my shadow beside his. We threw up our hats & moved about. The shadow did the same ...[46]

Another walker-artist came from Wales itself. Around 1800 the publisher John Boydell suggested to Edward Pugh, a Ruthin painter living in London, that he might provide illustrations for a new tour of Wales. Boydell was concerned that artists from outside Wales, 'unacquainted with the language or the country', tended to repeat the

Edward Pugh, probable self-portrait with Miss Wowski, from Cambria depicta, *1816*

(National Library of Wales)

same stock Eryri scenes. Pugh, a Welsh-speaker who knew his country well, would do better. Both men died before the book, *Cambria depicta*, subtitled 'a tour through north Wales, illustrated with picturesque views by a native artist', was published in 1816.[47]

Pugh brings a new, informed and informal tone to 'depicting' Wales. He visits many of the usual sights, including countless gentry houses, and he often recommends picturesque viewpoints to the fellow-artist. But his narrative also includes many stories, folklore and customs, like peat-cutting and cattle-shoeing, and he records many chance conversations in Welsh and English with people he meets on the road.

His seventy illustrations depict views of scenery and architecture, but also contemporary Welsh people, including a reputed witch, Jane Williams ('Shane Bwt'), Mary Thomas 'the fasting woman', Bella the fortune teller and John Hughes, the 'infant Hercules'.

To collect his material Pugh walked a thousand miles or more throughout north Wales, probably between 1804 and 1806. He thinks nothing of diverting to climb hills and mountains on the way. He carries 'a light knapsack on my back, containing only what is barely necessary, an umbrella in my right hand, and under my left arm a small portfolio suspended to my right shoulder by a broad piece of tape'. He constantly keeps the reader aware of the experience of walking. The heat of the sun beats on his head and he dips his feet in a roadside stream. On Aran Fawddwy he sinks up to his knees in a bog, and near Penmachno he fords a river up to his elbows. He loses his dog, 'Miss Wowski', asleep in the gorse. He falls into conversation with a 'jolly grey-headed old man' about his two wives, and entertains men he meets with a tune on his new flageolet. He disturbs a group of sleeping fishwomen 'lying like so many porpoises basking in the sun'. He visits a colony of 'those indolent birds called puffins', stamps on a yard-long snake, and retreats from ferocious bulls. He hires boats to explore the coast of Anglesey, and is mistaken for a French spy while sketching in Flintshire.

Despite his deference to the upper classes and backward glances to the picturesque, Edward Pugh brings a new, recognisably modern voice to the walker's experience of Wales.

Later in the nineteenth century writers like George Borrow were to follow in his inquisitive footsteps.

Chapter 4: Rebels, workers and believers

Building roads

Roads and walking have a complex connection. For centuries most roads were little more than broad paths or tracks. Walkers, their main users, shared them equally with horses and other animals. But by stages from the late eighteenth century this democratic balance broke down. Wheels began to overtake feet and hooves. Roads fell into commercial ownership, and pedestrians were steadily marginalised, forced on to verges, pavements and ditches to make way for carts, carriages and eventually motor cars. Today that change is complete. Roads are now hostile places for walkers, who are constantly threatened by accidents and close shaves, poisoned air, fearfulness and a loss of mental equilibrium.

This process was accompanied by other, more cognitive changes. Improved roads and, from the mid-nineteenth century, the new railways altered perceptions of human speed. Walking pace no longer supplied the default setting for timing journeys. Instead, as machine-powered modes of transport extended and shrank time and distance, a travelling speed of around three or four miles an hour appeared inferior and impossibly slow. Walking long distances came to be seen as an activity for the poor and eccentric only: those unable to afford a coach or a train ticket or those with an irrational prejudice against the new modes of travel.

The change started with the turnpike trusts. During the eighteenth century, as the population rose and economic activity quickened, those in power began to see the poor condition of unmodernised roads as a brake on agricultural and industrial development. Their solution, outsourcing projects to local contractors, was one that mirrored the early development of capitalism. Typically, a group of local well-to-do people – gentlemen, landowners or industrialists – would form an alliance or trust. They'd then apply, through a private Act of Parliament, for a licence, held typically for 21 years, to improve, or build anew, a specific length of main road. They contributed or borrowed money to upgrade the road, and aimed to recoup their capital expenses by charging most road users a toll, the level of which was fixed by law. Tolls were paid at a 'pike' or fixed post set at the roadside, though the pikes were soon replaced by permanent tollgates. The charge varied according to the size of the vehicle, and there were some exemptions from payment, including pedestrians.

The turnpike system, established by statute in 1663, was slow to be adopted in Wales, where road traffic flows were lower than in England. The earliest trusts operated in the English borders, but by the 1790s much of the country was criss-crossed by roads run by dozens of turnpike trusts. In Carmarthenshire over 300 miles of roads were under their control by the end of the century. These included main routes, but also less obvious routes, like that between Llanllwni and Brechfa. The principal turnpike roads tended to go west-east, linking Wales and England – as did the new 'Irish' road Thomas Telford built between 1815 and 1826 to link Shrewsbury and Holyhead – the first civil engineering project ever funded by Parliament. As Iolo Morganwg remarked in 1805, 'every part of Wales has an easy and direct communication with London, but north and south Wales have no more intercourse than they have with the man in the moon' – a sentiment easily echoed today.[1]

The results of the work of the turnpike trusts were mixed. Certainly, roads were widened, straightened and resurfaced. New roads and bridges were built. Thomas Evans, writing in 1819, claimed that thanks to the trusts Wales had 1,000 miles of new or improved roads.[2] The Kidwelly Trust built a new bridge at Loughor, removing the need for travellers going west from Swansea to divert to Pontarddulais. In 1787 the Llandeilo Rwnws Bridge Trust, owned by a powerful Carmarthen politician, John Jones of Ystrad, opened a new bridge at Nantgaredig, so that lime could be transported from kilns in Llanddarog, south of the river Tywi, to be spread on fields to the north.

Often, though, roadbuilding methods were primitive. Mary Morgan, travelling to Milford Haven in 1791, described how roads were repaired near Hay-on-Wye:

Their custom is to throw down vast quantities of huge stones, as large as they come out of the quarry, the size of a man's head, and many of them four times as big. These are spread over the road in heaps, perhaps a mile distant from each other, covering a great many yards of it. You must either drive over them, or wait till the people, who are there with large hammers for the purpose, have broken them.[3]

In remoter parts of Wales the coming of turnpike roads made little difference to local people. Hugh Evans recalled how, in his childhood in 'Cwm Eithin' (Llangwm, Denbighshire) in the mid-nineteenth century,

The 'big coach' would run along the turnpike in the summer; but it was not for the people of Cwm Eithin, it would be carrying *byddigions* [bigwigs]. If one of the locals was seen on it, the gossip would last a week. They went everywhere on horseback, on carts and trolleys, or on their two feet ... they were great walkers.[4]

Many turnpike trusts were poorly managed. By the 1830s a third of them were in a precarious financial state. The collection of tolls was sub-contracted to agents, who naturally followed their own interests. And most trusts found that the income from tolls wasn't enough to allow them to recover their outlay.

Rebellions and risings

But for those who had to use the turnpike roads regularly the toll charges felt burdensome or even extortionate. Though trusts couldn't increase the amounts they charged, they faced no limit on the number of tollgates, and some trusts tried to increase their income by planting gates at frequent intervals. William Matthews, touring south Wales in 1786, wrote that 'a traveller, to be happy throughout, must stand reconciled to the paying twice within a few hundred yards', and in 1827 another tourist, Eliza Rand (or Read), passed through 83 tollgates in 17 days.[5] By the end of the 1830s, when farmers and rural workers were facing desperately hard times, the problem had become urgent. As the 'Rebecca riots' burst out, the focus of discontent, and sporadic violence, was the tollgates.

On 13 May 1839 the Whitland Trust's new tollgate at Efail-wen was destroyed and the toll-house set on fire. The Trust rebuilt the gate, but on the night of 6 June a crowd marched back, drove away the constables guarding it, destroyed the gate again and demolished the house. The men were disguised: their faces were blackened and some of them wore women's clothes. A third riot took place in daylight at Efail-wen on 17 July. Its leader was addressed as 'Becca'. Efail-wen saw the first appearance of 'Merched Rebecca' or the daughters of Rebecca, the Old Testament figure who was urged to 'let thy seed possess the gate of those which hate them'. Their attacks on tollgates resumed in summer 1840 and continued sporadically for three more years, often accompanied by letters, signed 'Becca & children', to men in authority threatening violent action.

Collective walking now carried a connotation of menace and violence. Across Carmarthenshire, Cardiganshire and Pembrokeshire men marched together to protest against injustice, and take action. On 19 June 1843, alerted by notices on church and chapel doors, people began to gather in Newchurch, north of Carmarthen. Magistrates got wind of the movement and an attempt was made to dissuade the crowd from marching, but the leaders insisted on their grievances, not only about tolls, but also about the poor law, tithes and church rates, and rents. Led by a band, around two thousand men came on foot, followed by about three hundred farmers on horseback. Their leader was disguised in women's clothes and wore horsehair ringlets. His followers carried staves, brooms 'with which to sweep away the foundations of the toll-houses and the workhouse', and placards, one of which read 'Cyfiawnder a charwyr cyfiawnder ydym ni oll' (justice, and lovers of justice all of us). They entered Carmarthen, wound their way through the town and presented their demands to magistrates at the Guildhall. Parts of the crowd were provoked into bursting into the workhouse, ejecting the residents, smashing furniture and throwing beds out of the windows. In the end dragoons had to be called to quell the riot. Some of the rioters were gaoled or bound over.[6]

Later in the year Rebecca's tactics changed. Attacks on tollgates gave way to a series of mass meetings to gather support for a range of demands. These too involved much walking, since they tended to be held in upland locations to avoid official interference, for example Llyn Llech Owain on Mynydd Mawr, which drew agricultural and industrial workers from the Tywi and Loughor valleys.

Rebecca was finally suppressed, but her labours were not wholly in vain. In response the government set up a commission to investigate the turnpike system in south Wales. As a result of its recommendations, the numerous trusts were consolidated within individual counties, tolls were standardised, and county road boards were set up. For a period, south Wales enjoyed a better road system than any other part of the country.

Rebecca belonged to an existing tradition of popular protest in Wales, most of which relied on workers using their feet to make their impact felt.

It was the new industrial workers, tightly connected by trade, class and geography, who were most likely to rebel, protesting against their conditions and calling for change. They had no trade unions yet, and little bargaining power, but if they worked together they had weapons: the ability to withdraw their labour, and even do damage to their workplaces. They also had their feet. Their employers and other authorities feared them most when they were on the move in large numbers. 'Collective bargaining by riot' is how one historian described the process.[7]

A tradition of protest grew among the iron workers of Merthyr Tydfil and other rapidly expanding towns at the heads of the Valleys. Strikes broke out in 1816, in the depression that followed the end of the Napoleonic wars, and iron workers from Merthyr and Tredegar visited iron works from Tredegar to Llangynidr, stopping production in each place. More strikes and actions followed in 1817. A common action was to organise marching groups to persuade or coerce other workers to join them. Marching was used often in what became known as the 'Scotch cattle' actions of 1820-35, in what the authorities fearfully called the 'Black Domain' of north-west Monmouthshire, when iron workers responded to high prices and cuts in pay by enforcing strike discipline. Strikers would attack the houses of scabs, agents and contractors. In Blackwood in 1833 men walked the streets, some carrying arms, wearing horns on their heads, calling on houses as they went.

A much more significant event was the 'Merthyr Rising' of 1831. Since 1800 Merthyr had developed as a centre of radical thought, from 1807 incorporated in the Cyfarthfa Philosophical Society, and many of its leading figures embraced the spirit of political reform.[8] But it was reductions in iron workers' wages and lay-offs, as well as grievances about the debtors' court, the Court of Requests, that sparked general discontent and protest. By 2 June 1831 a crowd had taken over Merthyr. Carrying flags labelled 'Reform', men marched through the town and visited over a hundred houses and shops, liberating goods taken by the Court and restoring them to their owners. A great crowd flooded to Cyfarthfa, stopped the ironworks, and marched on to put an end to production at other works. A red flag was waved – its first appearance in nineteenth century protest, and a clear sign of working-class solidarity against authority. There was no police force, and no soldiers were stationed in Merthyr, so troops were called in from outside. This meant more marching. A detachment arrived from Brecon, after a forced seven-hour march across Bannau Brycheiniog. In a violent confrontation soldiers opened fire and at least sixteen people lost their lives. Undeterred, the rioters continued to occupy most of Merthyr, and later pursued what was almost a guerrilla campaign against the troops, before they were finally defeated.

Eight years later came a still greater, more deliberate, rebellion, later known as the Newport Rising. It had its roots in the eastern Valleys. Coordinated mass marching was crucial to the intentions of its instigators. The movement for political change had now crystallised around the demands of the Chartists, who sought radical changes to the way Parliament worked. They found ready supporters in the already radicalised industrialised areas, where Chartists held peaceful processions of supporters walking the streets to demand change. The Rising, half demonstration, half insurrection, was stoked by grievances about pay and working conditions, and sparked by the prosecution and imprisonment in August 1839 of a Chartist leader, Henry Vincent. Local Chartists were also being detained in the Westgate Hotel in Newport. On the night of Sunday 3 November about 5,000 workers, many armed with guns, pikes, cudgels and knives, marched down the Sirhowy and Ebbw valleys in three columns, starting from Nant-y-glo, Blackwood and Pontypool. Their intention was to converge on Newport.

Chartist rising at Newport, 1839, design for Newport mosaic mural
by Kenneth Budd

(*Oliver Budd*)

Overnight the weather was poor, the coordination of the columns was bungled, and the campaign in the town on Monday was chaotic. A crowd gathered in front of the Westgate Hotel. Soldiers inside opened fire. At least twenty Chartists were killed, and many more wounded. The leaders were arrested and put on trial on charges of treason. Eight defendants were found guilty and condemned to death. After loud protests across the country the government commuted the sentences. Five were imprisoned and three were transported to Tasmania.

The Newport Rising was the last rebellion of its kind. In the second half of the nineteenth century people found less violent, more institutionalised ways of protesting and advancing their causes. Parliament was gradually reformed, political parties claimed to represent workers, trade unions emerged, and some worker protections were made into law. All the same, reformers continued to appeal for support, denounce the powerful, and win over their fellows by taking to the streets and roads, rather than confining themselves to council chambers and newspapers. Marching as a way of protesting against the status quo and building pressure for social change was still in its infancy.

Women workers walking

For almost all workers throughout the nineteenth century, personal movement, whether collective or individual, meant walking. Agricultural work, as in all previous centuries, entailed walking for hours in the fields every day. Some tasks, like transporting lime for use on fields, meant escorting horse-led carts for longer distances.

By the mid-century there were as many people employed in industry as in agriculture. The new industrial jobs also involved much walking, even though many workers, like colliers, tended to live close to their workplace.

Seasonal workers often made prodigious journeys on foot. Francis Kilvert noted in his diary that his old parishioner Hannah Whitney reported that 'when she lived by Whitney's brook, three Cardiganshire women used to pass by the house every March walking to London to weed gardens.'[9] These passers-by belonged to a whole class of women, 'merched y gerddi' (the garden girls). From at least the middle of the eighteenth century they'd travel each spring from central Cardiganshire, in the feet of the old drovers, to work in the commercial gardens and parks of London. Rural poverty intensified in the county in the first half of the nineteenth century, and families were always in need of additional income.

These women were strong, and accustomed to hard, burdened

Welsh market woman returning from Aberystwith over Constitution Hill,
engraving from The Leisure Hour, *September 1863*

(*National Library of Wales*)

walking. Many were already used to carrying up to sixty pounds of peat in baskets, strapped to their backs, from upland areas for sale on the Cardiganshire coast. For them walking two hundred miles to London wasn't the formidable obstacle it might seem today. It also held for them the promise of adventure, escape from the social disciplines of home, and possibly financial reward if luck ran their way. Catherine Davies of Llanddewi Brefi, it was reported, went to London, married a gentleman and inherited his wealth, part of which she used to found a school back home in Cardiganshire.

The walkers included women of all ages: farmers' wives and daughters, maidservants and occasional workers. Sometimes they took children with them. The journey would take about a week, mainly along the drovers' routes. Small bands of women would gather, typically in Tregaron, set out at midnight and cross the Cambrian

Mountains in time for breakfast at Abergwesyn. There they'd be joined by women coming from other directions. Then onward through Beulah, Builth and Erwood, and towards the border for the first overnight stay. The women could travel up to thirty miles a day. One source describes how they'd entertain themselves as they walked, and exchange banter and repartee with local lads at the roadside. They walked barefoot and carried their shoes strung round their necks, to avoid wearing them out too soon. Some carried bags of vegetables and fruit to sell on the way, and knitted stockings as they walked, to be sold for money to pay for their lodgings in London.[10]

When they arrived in London at the start of April they went immediately to look for work in the gardens. The Welsh faced competition from other women migrant workers from western England and Ireland, but possibly held an advantage because of their reputation for hard work and honesty. They also excited interest for their appearance. According to one star-struck Londoner in 1817,

> For beauty, symmetry and complexion they are not inferior to the nymphs of Arcadia and they far outvie the pallid specimens of Circassia! Their morals, too, are exemplary; and they often perform this labour to support aged parents, or to keep their own children from the workhouse![11]

As workers, women were preferred to men: they were paid less, but they were also trusted to handle produce more carefully. If work was plentiful they'd send home, and another wave of women would follow. Labour – sowing, weeding and harvesting – was constant, as one crop quickly followed another: peas, turnips, strawberries and much else. To keep soft fruits in good condition the women would carry them to markets in the city centre, a journey of up to 25 miles, balancing heavy baskets on their heads.

The women slept in barns or other comfortless accommodation offered by farmers. Their pay was low by London standards, but not in comparison with what they might have earned at home, if they earned anything at all.

The poet Daniel Davies, 'Daniel Ddu o Geredigion', wrote of them:

O na bawn i fel colomen
Ar Sant Paul yng nghanol Llunden,
I gael gweled merched Cymru,
Ar ei gliniau'n chwynnu'r gerddi.

Shame I'm not a pigeon, perched
in the middle of London on St Paul's
With my eye on the Welsh girls
Weeding the gardens on all fours.[12]

By September most of the women were ready to walk back to Wales,
except those moving on to the hop harvest in Kent, where they could
supplement their summer earnings. They might return with as much
as twelve pounds from all their work, a large sum in Ceredigion. Some

The strawberry trade: pottling, from Illustrated London News, *27 June 1846*
(*National Library of Wales*)

Cocklewomen, oil painting by William Meredith, 1843

(National Library of Wales)

of them were later employed in the commercial nurseries of the Teifi valley that supplied plants to Welsh estates for their gardens, orchards and plantations. The seasonal migration of women to London continued until around the middle of the nineteenth century, when industrial growth transformed the rural economy and Victorian assumptions about the role of women in economy and society took a tight grip. It would be many years before women again felt able to walk long distances together.[13]

Within Wales other special groups of women walked long distances, regularly and throughout the year. Cockle women would pick cockles on the tidal sands of the Burry Inlet off Pen-clawdd and other places on the north Gower coast. When they'd raked, sieved, washed, boiled and shelled enough cockles, on a Saturday they'd load baskets of them on the backs of donkeys and walk them barefoot across the peninsula to Swansea market. Once they'd sold the cockles they faced the journey home. They'd have walked a total of almost twenty miles in the day. The arrival of the railway in Pen-clawdd in 1867 shortened the journey and reduced the need to walk, but old traditions survived. In 1890 a male observer noted that the cockle woman

... still retains her homespun dress of variegated Welsh flannel, mostly red and black for the gown, and black and white, or grey, for the small shawl or 'turnover'. She is not ashamed to show her shapely legs in black stockings. Her arms are for the most part bare, and she wears on her head ... a little half bonnet, half hat not unlike in shape a single shell of the bivalve in which she trades, and hence called the 'cockle-shell'.[14]

Thomas Jenkins

Many other workers had jobs that often required them to travel away from home on foot. Thomas Jenkins, a Llandeilo cabinet-maker, amateur astronomer and inventor, kept a diary from 1826 to 1870.[15] It shows how, in his earlier years, he walked long distances to carry out commissions. He'd often walk to Carmarthen and back, a distance of 32 miles (to go by coach would have cost him two shillings). He thought nothing of walking across the hills to the Amman valley in the south and into Cardiganshire to the north. Walking was not all for work. On 11 July 1843 Jenkins travelled with a friend, D.B. Evans, with whom in January he'd founded the 'Llandilo Mechanics Mutual Instructing Institution', to the top of Trichrug: 'the air being clear we had the most delightful and extensive view of the county on all sides'. A year later he went on a 10-day walking tour to Pembroke Dock, to see warships being built, before completing a long circuit home through Cardigan, Aberaeron, Devil's Bridge and Lampeter. Summer 1839 included a formidable amount of walking. Between 4 July and 27 August Jenkins travelled a total of over 320 miles in Carmarthenshire and Cardiganshire, and his new wife Ann Evans, already pregnant, shared at least 60 of them as her 'honeymoon'.

In later years Jenkins's travel patterns changed. He began to use a bicycle (velocipedes became more common from the 1850s). On 21 December 1849 he built a passenger-carrying tricycle he called a 'homomotive', and the next day trialled it on the road to Carmarthen, achieving an average speed of over six miles an hour. The railway came to Llandeilo in 1857, linking the town to Llanelli, and the line to

Carmarthen followed in 1865. From 1857 the diary records increasing numbers of trips made by rail. Jenkins was able to travel further than ever before, but could also travel by rail over local routes he'd have walked in earlier years.

Slateworkers and leadminers

Thomas Jenkins was self-employed, but hard walking to start work was the lot of many who were employed by others, and not only seasonal workers. North Wales slate workers often had to trudge for miles before a long day's arduous and dangerous labour in the quarry – which itself was often preceded by a long mountain climb, like the huge zig-zag path up the slate tip at Oakeley Quarry, Blaenau Ffestiniog.[16] Once quarrying had been a small-scale activity. But from the 1780s new capitalists, like Richard Pennant, Lord Penrhyn, used their fortunes to purchase land, and buy out its owners. At its height the Penrhyn quarry employed almost 3,000 people. Like quarry workers elsewhere, they were almost all male, and monoglot Welsh speakers.[17]

Many slate workers lived in villages fairly close to the quarries: Bethesda, for example, in the case of Penrhyn. But others travelled from much further afield. The Dinorwig quarry employed men from sixty villages in Caernarvonshire and Anglesey, and the same was true of other quarries. Dr R.D. Evans, who gave evidence to a government enquiry into the Merionethshire mines in 1895, said of 'commuters' to the Blaenau Ffestiniog mines:

Men who, on a wet day such as this, walk from Tremadoc to Portmadoc, and then travel by the Festiniog Railway, cramped up in these so-called carriages, which are really no better than trucks, and who have afterwards to walk from the station to the top of the Oakeley, or the Cwmorthin, or the Votty and Bowydd Quarry, have really exhausted their muscular energy before they get to their day's work. Men who go through this fatigue every morning cannot possibly give a fair day's work for a fair day's wage. They also injure their health, for they take their breakfast early and are in a state of semi-starvation until they partake of their so-called dinner at mid-day, which principally consists of bread and butter and tea.[18]

Dr Evans reported that his quarrymen patients, who worked in dust all day long, often suffered from respiratory diseases. Other common problems were rheumatism, haemorrhoids, hernias, typhoid and tuberculosis. The usual diet of the workers was poor and lacked nourishment. Workers aged prematurely, and their average life spans were short. Accidents were common and could lead to serious injury or death, even for men not working at the stoneface. Between 1883 and 1892 116 men were killed in accidents.

Some of those living furthest away were 'barracks workers.' On Monday morning workers at the Dinorwig quarry who lived on Anglesey would rise at three o'clock and walk to the Menai ferry at Moel-y-don. This journey might take them an hour, if a quarryman lived in Brynsiencyn, but it could much longer if he lived in Llangefni or Llannerch-y-medd. After the crossing the men would walk to the station at Y Felinheli and catch the quarry train to Dinorwig, arriving at 6.15am. Then they'd walk up the mountain, leave their food supplies for the week in their *barics* (barracks), and begin their day's work. They left off work and departed for home on Saturday. Sunday was the only compete day in the week when they could be with their families.[19]

Anglesey Barracks, Dinorwig quarry
(*photo Hefin Owen*)

Twin rows of barracks, built of granite in the 1870s and known as Dre Newydd or Anglesey Barracks, survive today at the Dinorwig quarry (they were only abandoned in 1937). Earlier barracks had been located even higher up the mountain: the 'Aberdaron Gallery' was 600m above sea level. To rent a two-room cottage cost a shilling a month. The barracks were primitive in the extreme. They were overcrowded, poorly ventilated and drained, and unclean, so that infections spread quickly and were taken home by the workers. Six men could share a room, and often two or three men would share a bunk. The only light was candlelight or a paraffin lamp, and a single open fire was used for cooking and heating. Sanitary provision was usually lacking. Water supplies could be contaminated and there were no showers.

Morgan Richards, one of the founding members of the North Wales Quarrymen's Union, looked back to the 1830s, and summarised the experience of his quarryman father:

> I well remember the time when I was myself a child of bondage; when my father and neighbours, as well as myself, had to rise early, to walk five miles before six in the morning, and the same distance home after six in the evening; to work hard from six to six; to dine on cold coffee, or a cup of buttermilk, and a slice of bread and butter; and to support (as some of them had to do) a family of perhaps five, eight or ten children on wages averaging from 12s to 16s a week.[20]

Several quarries in Gwynedd supplied honestones, used to sharpen tools. One of them was Melynllyn, high on the flank of Carnedd Llewelyn. Each Monday morning in the 1880s the quarrymen climbed 1,800 feet from their homes, a distance of four miles, carrying linen bags full of food and night clothes. In their barracks they kept a peat fire burning, and their food in a cage out of reach of mice. In winter they woke to find their beards stiff with frost.[21]

The mountains of Eryri yielded copper as well as slate and stone. The 'Miners' Track', used by walkers today to reach the summit of Yr

Wyddfa from Pen-y-Pass, had its origin in a quite different route, taken by miners carrying copper from the Britannia mine on the shore of Llyn Llydaw. Before the road was built between Llanberis and Pen-y-Gwryd men would transport the ore up to Bwlch Glas on their backs – a feat hard to believe today – and transfer it to horse-drawn sleds along the route of what is now the Snowdon Ranger Path to Llyn Cwellyn.[22]

In mid-Wales lead miners endured the same harsh conditions as the miners of Eryri. Even into the twentieth century many of the men working the more remote mines of upland Cardiganshire had to made long walking journeys from their homes on Monday mornings to reach work. During the week they stayed in grim barracks beside mines at Bryn-yr-Afr, Cwmystwyth and Bwlch-glas. In 1854 George Borrow lost his way in the trackless country around the lead mines of Esgair Fraith and Esgair Hir, east of Tal-y-bont. In this 'cold, bleak spot', he was helped out by a 'captain' or mine manager, who arranged a guide to set him on the way south.[23]

Francis Kilvert

For some fortunate people walking was both an unavoidable part of performing a job and an unmixed pleasure. This was true of the diarist Francis Kilvert when he was curate of the parish of Clyro in Radnorshire between 1865 and 1872.

Francis Kilvert was the son of a Wiltshire vicar. After he left Oxford University he served as curate for his father before moving to Clyro as curate to the vicar there, Richard Lister Venables, who became a father-figure to him. Kilvert began to write his diary, it seems, on 1 January 1870, when he was almost thirty years old. It gives a detailed and sympathetic picture of Clyro and the hill country above it, and of the ordinary people of Radnorshire, who were still relatively isolated and attached to their traditional rural life. Between 800 and 900 people lived in the parish.

Kilvert loved Wales, and even believed he had Welsh blood in his veins. Radnorshire became a natural home for him. He felt an

St Michael's Church, Clyro

(*photo Andrew Green*)

instinctive sympathy and understanding for the people. The county was no longer Welsh-speaking in the main, but it retained its otherness, which he respected.

Kilvert was highly conscientious, shouldering most of the burden of pastoral work – he called it 'villaging' – among the parishioners, who were scattered over a wide, mainly upland area to the north. He set out on foot from home to visit them (there were over sixty such visits in 1870 alone).

He'd little choice but to walk. As a curate – an ordained priest but, in effect, a trainee vicar – he earned only around £60 a year. At Clyro he occasionally borrowed, but could never afford to own, a horse. He never mentions travelling by coach (though he went by train often enough, travelling second class). But walking was much more than a necessity. Kilvert was already a very keen walker. He'd been on a hiking tour of the Alps, and still used his old Swiss haversack. Even more important, it was only on foot that he was able to spend time in the countryside which he'd grown to love. His diary is above all a diary of movement, and it aims to capture the movement around him.[24]

'He is tall', wrote Venables when he first interviewed Kilvert, 'with a black beard and moustache'. The only surviving photographic portrait confirms this, and a cousin later described him as 'very sleek and glossy and gentle – rather like a nice Newfoundland dog.'[25] He was an easily recognisable figure, striding through the lanes and fields above Clyro, in all weathers. On 13 February 1870 the weather was 'fearful, violent deadly E. wind and the hardest frost we have had yet', but there was a service to be taken at the chapel:

Went to Bettws in the afternoon wrapped in two waistcoats, two coats, a muffler and a mackintosh, and was not at all too warm ... when I got to the Chapel my beard, moustaches and whiskers were so stiff with ice that I could hardly open my mouth and my beard was frozen to my mackintosh.[26]

A couple of weeks later the weather had improved. On 26 February Kilvert sketched a walking self-portrait:

A lovely warm morning so I set off to walk over the hills to Colva [five miles to the north], taking my luncheon in my pocket, half a dozen biscuits, two apples and a small flask of wine. Took also a pocket book and opera glasses ... Went on up the Green Lane. Very hot walking.[27]

Kilvert was a keen student of animals and plants, and the 'opera glasses' and notebook were essential equipment for observing and recording them. He preferred to walk on his own:

I had the satisfaction of managing to walk from Hay to Clyro by the fields without meeting a single person, always a great triumph to me and a subject for warm self congratulation for I have a peculiar dislike to meeting people, and a peculiar liking for a deserted road.[28]

> I like wandering about these lonely, waste and ruined places. There dwells among them a spirit of quiet and gentle melancholy more congenial and akin to my own spirit than full life and gaiety and noise.[29]

But Kilvert was no recluse. He mixed easily with his gentry and middle-class neighbours but also enjoyed the company of the working people in their cottages in the hills, and was anxious to do what he could to make their lives easier. His diary records many of the rural characters he came across on his 'villaging': John Morgan, a veteran of the Napoleonic wars, ancient Hannah Whitney of Rhosgoch, John Price, the hermit vicar of Llanbedr, poor demented Mrs Watkins.

Kilvert didn't confine his walking to the bounds of his parish. In the company of friends he'd explore places within easy reach, including the Golden Valley, Capel-y-ffin and Llangorse Lake. On these trips he clearly considered himself a traveller rather than a tourist, to judge from this diary extract from 5 April 1870 on a trip to Llanthony Abbey:

> What was our horror on entering the enclosure to see two tourists with staves and shoulder belts all complete postured among the ruins in an attitude of admiration, one of them discoursing learnedly to his gaping companion and pointing out objects of interest with his stick. If there is one thing more hateful than another it is being told what to admire and having objects pointed out to one with a stick. Of all noxious animals too the most noxious is a tourist. And of all tourists the most vulgar, illbred, offensive and loathsome is the British tourist.[30]

Occasionally he ventured further into Wales. In June 1871 he hired a guide, Robert Pugh, to take him up Cadair Idris from Dolgellau. His lengthy diary narrative, unusually for him, veers into a gothic register. 'Cader Idris', he wrote, 'is the stoniest, dreariest, most desolate mountain I was ever on … The mists and clouds began to sweep by us in white thin ghostly sheets as if some great dread Presences and

Powers were going past and we could only see the skirts of their white garments ... It was an awful place in a storm. I thought of Moses on Sinai.'[31]

They descended by the Foxes' Path, a brave choice even in good weather:

The path was all loose shale and stone and so steep that planting our alpenstocks from behind and leaning back upon them in Alpine fashion we glissaded with a general landslip, rush and rattle of shale and shingle down to the shore of the Foxes' Lake [Llyn y Gadair]. The parsley fern grew in sheets of brilliant green among the grey shale ... As we entered Dolgelly the old man said, 'You're a splendid walker, Sir', a compliment which procured him a glass of brandy and water.[32]

The mild Radnorshire hills offered a landscape much more to Kilvert's taste, where his feet could wander freely and his eye focus intently on nature close at hand.

His view of the natural world, if not pantheistic like William Wordsworth's, was close to reverential. A single enigmatic sentence which appears in the diary on 20 June 1871, 'an angel satyr walks these hills', hints at a primitive spiritual unity of individual and nature. Kilvert disapproved of hunting and shooting wild animals. On 13 November 1871 he watched the squire pass by with a shooting party and commented acidly, 'What a fine day it is. Let us go out and kill something.'[33] Ancient human remains, he thought, should also be respected rather than disturbed. When the Woolhope Club excavated a cairn at Twyn-y-beddau near Hay on 26 May 1871 and unearthed human bones, Kilvert was dismayed.[34]

He reacted with especially violent language to the destruction of trees. When trees were felled at Cwmgwanon in March 1872, he lamented:

Cwmgwanon Wood is being murdered. As I walked along the edge of the beautiful dingle and looked sadly down into the hollow, numbers of my old friends of seven years standing lay below on both banks of the brook prostrate and mutilated, a mournful scene of havoc, the road almost impassable for the limbs of the fallen giants ... The New Barn meadows are fearfully cut up by the timber carriages which are hauling away the fallen giants, ash and beech. The shouts of the timber haulers were ringing hollow and echoing through the wasted murdered dingle. My beautiful favourite Cwm is devastated and laid waste.[35]

There was a strong sensual side to Kilvert. He wrote often frankly about girls who took his eye, many of them surprisingly young – perhaps a reflection of the 'satyr' half of his nature. He hoped to marry one of them, Fanny Thomas, whom he called 'Daisy'. When her father refused to give his assent, on the grounds that he was a poor curate without prospects, Kilvert felt humiliated and depressed. He moved back to Wiltshire, then had a short spell in St Harmon, Radnorshire, before becoming vicar in Bredwardine, nine miles from Clyro in west Herefordshire, where he died of peritonitis at the age of thirty-eight. But it was the Clyro area that he always regarded as his happiest home.

Years later a cobbler in Rhayader, in conversation with the diarist's nephew, remembered Kilvert walking, 'bad weather or snowy roads', to St Harmon on Sundays from his home in Rhayader. 'Quiet gentleman, great black beard', he recalled, 'like a foreign gentleman, as my father used to say ... 'e was a great walker, sir. Many a pair of boots my father soled for Mr Kilbert.'[36]

Children walking

For Victorian children, walking to work had its equivalent, walking to school – especially after the 1870 Education Act and the school building movement that followed it. Often they too needed stout shoes or boots, because it wasn't uncommon for children to have to walk many miles to and from school, especially if they lived in the countryside.

In 1846 commissioners were sent by Parliament in London to investigate the state of schools in Wales. When their reports, the so-called 'Blue Books', were published in 1847, many in Wales were outraged by that they saw as a prejudiced and insulting account of Welsh morality and culture. The commissioners sometimes commented on the difficulties children had in getting to school. One of them complained, when visiting Llansadwrn, Carmarthenshire,

> Among the many bad roads I had to travel over in Wales I found this one of the very worst. It was raining heavily on the day of my visit, and in one part the road was crossed by a rapid stream, then two feet deep. There was only a plank-bridge across it. The other way is two or three miles round. By the direct way no child, on the day I saw it, could have safely come.[37]

In upland areas of Carmarthenshire and Pembrokeshire, the writer continued, schools, even if they existed, were often far away from children's homes: 'there can hardly be said to be road between them; mere tracks over stony and marshy hill-sides.' It was unsafe, he considered, for young children to walk the hill-road between Caeo and Pumsaint in bad weather. Many parish roads were little better than 'brook-channels'. In north Wales many pupils were accustomed to walking eight miles or more every day to get to school.

Before the 1870 Education Act many children never went to school. They spent much of their time outdoors, often helping to supplement the meagre incomes of their parents. Robert Thomas, 'Ap Fychan', later a well-known nonconformist preacher, was brought up in the early nineteenth century at Pennantlliw-bach near Llanuwchlyn, in a crowded house – he was one of ten children – and in absolute poverty. He remembered his mother in tears once because she couldn't afford to feed the family anything more than swedes and the water they were boiled in. Robert spent his time roaming the area on foot. He and his brothers and sisters would collect lichen from rocks, to be sold to dye clothes. They'd also gather rushes, and knit stockings, again for sale, and sometimes he'd walk, with his sister

Margaret and his brother Evan, around the 'upper parts of Meirion' and as far as Aberystwyth, begging for money and staying overnight in houses or barns. On these expeditions, as well as a bible and hymn book, they carried leather, nails, an awl, a needle and tailor's thread and a small hammer, so that they could repair their shoes and clothes on the journey. Robert was only eight years old. Later he was given a job as a shepherd boy before becoming an apprentice blacksmith.[38]

The best-known child walker in Wales in the nineteenth century was Mary (or Mari) Jones. Mary was fifteen years old and lived with her impoverished mother at a cottage called Tŷ'n-y-ddôl in Llanfihangel-y-Pennant at the head of the Dysynni valley. In 1800 she walked to Bala, 26 miles away, to acquire from Thomas Charles, the famous Methodist preacher and educationalist, her own bible. Charles, impressed by her pious determination, gave her one, and was inspired by her example to establish, four years later and with the help of others, the British and Foreign Bible Society, with the aim of publishing and distributing bibles all over the world.

That's the core of the story. But there are no contemporary records or accounts of Mary's heroic trip, or of her critical influence on Thomas Charles. The earliest detailed published source is a book published in Welsh by Robert Oliver Rees in 1879.[39] Rees explains that he obtained his knowledge of Mary

Mary Jones, engraving from Robert Oliver Rees,
Mary Jones, [1879]

Jones orally from two men, both now dead. He tells how Mary's parents, poor weavers by trade, are both pioneer Methodists. From the age of eight Mary attends Methodist meetings and becomes extremely pious. There's no bible in the house, but she walks every week to a house two miles away to read the nearest copy. For six years she saves her pennies until she has enough money to buy her own copy, the 'only thing she craves'. But there are none to be had in the neighbourhood. Her best hope, she's told, is Thomas Charles, who lives in Bala, far on the other side of Cadair Idris.

Mary sets off, very early on a summery spring morning, across the lower slopes of Cadair Idris. She borrows a 'wallet' to put her bible in, and her shoes, to be worn only when she reaches Bala. She travels barefoot. It's a perfect, cloudless day, and a warm breeze plays at her back, as if to say 'go forward in good heart, little Welsh lass'. It's late when she reaches Bala – too late for her to meet Thomas Charles. In the morning she succeeds in visiting him, and impresses him with her knowledge of the scriptures. All his bibles are gone, but he gives her one he's promised to someone else. Mary places it in her wallet, amid tears on both sides, and Charles vows to renew his efforts to place a bible in every home. Mary says farewell to him and walks home, again barefoot but with her bible safely stowed. For the rest of her life – she dies in 1864 at the age of 80 – she never tires of reading and re-reading her bible.

From the 1880s this and other mythologised versions of the Mary Jones story circulated widely, not only in Wales but across the world. First, the story made the leap from Welsh into English. In 1882 Mary E. Ropes produced a fictionalised version in English of Mary's story for children.[40] She coloured Mary's story with a late-Victorian sentimentality that touched many young readers.

Her book was republished over fifty times and translated into six languages. The Bible Society and the Methodists were keen to exploit Mary as an exemplar of a pious life, and her journey as a successful search for Christian salvation.

Walking barefoot was common enough among rural women in 1800, and Mary's walk was not as unusual as the legend suggests. Bala was a magnet for early Methodists in north Wales, thanks to the eminence of Thomas Charles, and many enthusiasts walked long distances to hear him preach. In 1792 John Elias, who later became celebrity preacher of fierce Calvinist principles, led a group of young people on foot forty miles from Llŷn, praying and singing hymns and psalms as they went.[41] By the end of the nineteenth century, however, barefoot walking was unusual and long-distance walking, especially by lone women, had become an abnormal activity.[42]

Tramping

On her route Mary might have met another kind of long-distance walker, the tramp. Mary's mission would have excited only admiration, but tramps were men (mostly) who tended to arouse suspicion. As wanderers they lay outside the social boundaries of settled communities, in the same way as Romanies, and in their begging they offended against the expectation that they should sustain themselves economically. Words referring to them – in English, vagabond, beggar, dosser and tramp, and in Welsh, *crwydryn*, *trempyn*, *treiglddyn* and *gwibiad* – were often used in an insulting way. Tramps also ran the risk of offending against the law. Anti-vagrancy legislation remained in force in the Victorian period.

By the middle of the nineteenth century the social composition of tramps was changing. Most now came from outside Wales, especially from Ireland in the wake of the famine of the late 1840s. This only added to the social disapproval felt for them by nonconformists, for whom respectability was a key virtue. Many accusations could be aimed at them: their appearance and dress were loathsome, they were unable to support themselves, and they had a tendency to viciousness and criminality. In the words of the historian David J.V. Jones, the tramp represented 'the most obvious antithesis of the Victorian trinity of work, respectability and religion'.[43]

In fact, the word 'tramp' covered many different kinds of people: unemployed labourers, workers with redundant skills, tradesmen and hawkers, gardeners and other itinerant workers, ballad sellers and musicians. Many factors could lead to life on the road: unemployment, crop failure, high rents and prices, inadequate poor relief and mental illness. Only some tramps conformed to the stereotype of the 'sturdy beggar', avoiding work, constantly soliciting for money, and prone to thieving and violence.

Vagrants were a particular problem for poor law guardians when they applied for relief. The manager of the Wrexham workhouse wrote in 1848 that 'vagrants, as a class, deserve but little pity, and ought rather to be under the cognizance of the police than the poor law officer.'[44] Elaborate work tests were set for them, and sometimes they'd be passed on to the police, who found them equally troublesome. Some ended up in prison, after receiving heavier sentences than local people convicted of similar offences. They sometimes preferred gaol to workhouse. The most notorious example was John Jones, 'Coch Bach y Bala' (1854–1913), who became a media celebrity and folk hero through the many attempts he made to escape from the north Wales gaols in which he was held for property crimes.

The main source of information about tramps in Wales is the world of officialdom and social control. But occasionally we hear from others with less prejudiced views of vagrants. On 3 July 1872 Francis Kilvert walked ten miles from Clyro to visit the 'little grey hut' or 'cabin' that was the home of a vicar, John Price, the 'Solitary of Llanbedr' near Painscastle. Price, born in Carmarthenshire and educated at Cambridge University, was a man of legendary self-denial. He became known as 'the tramp's chaplain'. He'd welcome passing vagrants to his church, and organised Sunday morning services specially for them. He donated a sixpence to each one who attended – word soon spread among the vagrants of the area – and provided oil stoves in the church to warm them in winter. The tramps, it was said, would use the stoves to cook food they'd brought, and then ate lunch in a barn nearby: he'd join them there, and listen to their stories.[45]

In *Cwm Eithin* Hugh Evans includes affectionate portraits of tramps who used to visit his rural north Wales valley in the mid-nineteenth century. He calls them not 'tramps' but 'bonheddwyr' (gentlemen) 'who can live without the need to work'. They included Jac y Pandy, Jac Lanfor, Wil Lonydd and Twm Poole.

> Jac y Pandy's estate included four counties, and it took a year or more for him to travel across his entire domain, so he didn't try the patience of his tenants very often. A man bewitched, or so it was believed, but I'm not sure he thought so, because he was cunning as a fox.[46]

In the magazine *Red Dragon* in 1884 'Merlin' writes knowledgably and warmly about a tramp he knew, 'a regular out-and-outer, who had received all the freedom of the roads, the towns and the gaols in the country'. He lists the man's complete possessions:

> ... a bit of mottled soap in brown paper, two rusty needles in red flannel, a reel of black cotton, three horn buttons, two yards of twine wound round a cork, a clasp knife with a broken blade, the half of an old comb, an inch of tallow candle, a diary ... and a map of the road, with the police stations where relief tickets were given marked with a cross.[47]

One of the last of the 'clerwyr barddonol' or wandering minstrels was 'Professor' William Owen or 'Gwilym Meudwy' ('Gwilym the hermit'). Born in Llandybïe, he took to tramping when his father and mother died, limping along with his pamphlets on his back. He moved between the spas of Llanwrtyd and Llandrindod in summer and Brynaman, Llanelli and Swansea in winter, but wandered all over south Wales. The poet David Rees Griffiths ('Amanwy') recalled his visits to the family home in Betws, Ammanford:

> We often heard him approaching the back kitchen door in the old house, a small round man, his wooden leg and his stick striking the path in turn, and his squeaky voice saying, 'Marged Griffiths, it's William here, calling for something to eat.' He received the usual welcome, and sat, relaxed, in the armchair by the fire, while

mam would make him a meal. Soon it was ready, and William set about eating it. I never saw such a glutton! I don't remember a line of his rhymes, but the impression his peerless guzzling left on me still lives in my memory.[48]

Throughout the nineteenth century tramps and vagabonds on the road were still likely to pass by people at the other end of the social ladder: comfortably-off visitors to Wales from England and elsewhere. Only a small fraction of these were pedestrians, and, as the train, and later the bicycle and the motor car gained popularity, 'tourists' walking long distances came to seem more and more eccentric.

Jenkin Jones

After the early years of the nineteenth century fewer visitors wrote or published extensive 'pedestrian tours'. One was written by Jenkin Jones, a tough navy captain who walked alone from Swansea to Caernarfon in May-June 1819. His journal offers an idiosyncratic mix of observations on scenery, people and food and drink. Jones doesn't reveal why he chooses to travel on foot, though he refers to his need to 'live within my pay'. His original plan, according to his surviving manuscript diary, involved an extraordinarily long walk, from Exeter to Inveraray. He'd already walked from Barnstaple to Ilfracombe before taking a boat to Mumbles Head ('all the passengers but myself were sick').

Jones stays his first night in Wales at the Bush Inn in Swansea's High Street. After dinner he strolls along the streets: 'I liked the effect of the hat on the women and saw many very pretty ones.' Moving north, he passes through Llandybïe and Llandeilo, and is sitting on an old bridge at Taliaris on the Lampeter road when

A singular looking figure mounted on a dirty half-starved Welch pony with a piece of cord round its nose by way of bridle, issued from the wood close by me. The man was about 5 feet 2 inches high, looked about 70, his beard full 6 months growth, his skin the collor of excrement, an old patched drab-colored coat, no shirt, a ragged handkerchief round his neck, a pair of greasy leather breeches, patch'd with sheep's skin with the wool on, and large jack boots, with a cole-heaver's hat on.[49]

Jones is surprised when the man – he introduces himself only as Mr J.N. of Llethr Mawr – says he owns a large estate here. Later Jones learns that the man is the richest man in the county, but a notorious miser: he carries brown sugar to satisfy his hunger when travelling, and has never been known to offer anything to anyone.

After a diversion to Cilcennin to pay homage to his ancestors who are buried there, Jones walks on to Aberystwyth. Here he stays at the Little Black Lion ('had a thing they called veal-cutlet, but it tasted like a chip stewed in rancid oil'), and admires the sunset and the pretty girls. In the library he finds a map and 'Evan's Tour' to plot his route into north Wales. Beyond Machynlleth he calls in the Blue Lion inn at Minffordd, and meets its landlord, Edward Jones, whom Coleridge and Peacock had met. Edward refuses to act as guide to Jenkin Jones up Cadair Idris, pleading old age: 'he would rather walk 20 miles on the road than ascend the mountain.' But for the price of a pint of ale he agrees to sketch a plan of the best route.

Jones continues on foot, via Maentwrog, Ffestinog and Beddgelert, to Caernarfon. At the Goat Inn he meets a grocer from Chester and persuades him to come with him to the summit of Yr Wyddfa. After an evening meal at the Snowdon Ranger inn the two of them share a small bed for a few hours, like Ishmael and Queequeg in Herman Melville's *Moby-Dick*:

He undressed entirely, I kept my drawers & stockings on, and in we tumbled, the sheets were very clean, we had a pie-dish for a wash-hand-bason, a broken flower-pot, with a cork in the hole at the bottom, by way of chamber utensil. My little friend was soon asleep, but my squeamishness kept me awake, till his sleep was so sound, and his snoring so loud as to occupy the whole of my time in nudging him, which only had the effect of changing his note, & was in general accompanied by the same token that King Harry, as the song goes, gave the miller's son. At first I grew vicious, and farely pinched the poor little man, but this only drew additional vollies from him – I entertained myself by farting an accompaniment ...[50]

They set off with a guide at 2.15am, and, with the help of large draughts of brandy, arrive at the summit by sunrise, despite the cold, a strong wind and the Chester grocer's ailments.

By 10.00am they're back in Caernarfon, enjoying 'a famous breakfast'. Next day is Sunday, and the town is quiet. Jones walks east from Caernarfon in the company of his Chester friend, who suffers from the cold and fortifies himself regularly with rum and water. At Penmaenmawr they're discussing the dangers of the road 'when about ten yards before us, about five hundred weight of loose stones came rattling down, and the wall just there having been knocked down by a previous fall, some of the stones killed a sheep that was grazing on a little grassy part beneath.' At Conwy Jones says farewell to his companion and continues his walk along the coast and into Cheshire and Yorkshire.

Chapter 5: Scientists, mountaineers and writers

In the same year as Jenkin Jones made his journey on foot across Wales, a young man who would achieve much more fame than him started on a similar walking tour. Michael Faraday, the son of a blacksmith from Newington, south of London, was 27 years old. He'd received little formal education, except at Sunday school, but Humphrey Davy recognised his talent for science, trained him as an apprentice, and helped him become skilled in analytical chemistry. Josiah John Guest, the owner of the Dowlais ironworks in Merthyr Tydfil, had exchanged letters with Faraday about the processing of iron, and now invited him to visit Dowlais.

Faraday's journal of the trip is unusual for combining a keen scientific and technological curiosity with an open and sympathetic interest in the people and places he passed through.

Accompanied by a friend, Edward Magrath, Faraday set off by coach from London on 10 July 1819, reaching Cardiff two days later. A post-chaise took him to Merthyr, and he was given a tour of the ironworks at Dowlais, an experience that shook him:

> The operations were all simple enough, but from their extensive nature, the noise which accompanied them, the heat, the vibration, the hum of men, the hiss of engines, the clatter of shears, the fall of masses, I was so puzzled I could not comprehend them, except very imperfectly.[1]

Faraday and Magrath now took an extended pedestrian tour of Wales. From Merthyr they walked to Glynneath, staying in the Lamb and Flag inn, where Faraday dined on local trout and found the cwrw (beer) 'by no means ... so dangerous a beverage as I expected it would be'. Then they walked down the Vale of Neath. Arriving at Swansea, they were met by 'an immense cloud of sulphurous smoke' from the copperworks. They crossed the Tawe by ferry:

> Being market day our boat contained a motley group; there were

some barelegged market women; some neatly dressed tidy farmers' wives and one or two private persons. Folks saw we were strangers one required of another whether we were welchmen who had lost their way; others whispered that we must be runaway schoolboys; guided probably in their judgement by our scrambling appearance and the similarity of our dress.[2]

Mention of dress reminded Faraday to note down the clothes he and Magrath wore, and what they carried with them, 'light enough for pedestrian excursions, not exhibitory of dirt and easily cleaned':

A blue coat, black silk waistcoat, fawn coloured trousers, half hose. I wore quarter boots and Magrath Wellington boots. We each had on a cravat and a round hat. Neither of us wore flannel, or drawers. Each had a common 5/- umbrella and in his parcel, 2 shirts, 4 cravats, a pocket handkerchief, 2 night caps, 3 pairs of half stockings, a pair of shoes, a nightshirt, a razor, tooth and nail brushes etc., which were packed up in a piece of oilskin into a bundle of a few pounds weight.[3]

Faraday and Magrath visited J.H. Vivian's Hafod copper works. Faraday was familiar with the properties of copper from his laboratory work. He also tried, but failed, to visit the Cambrian Pottery.

The two walked back up to Glynneath. His description of a waterfall he visited, Henrhyd near Coelbren, combines observational exactness with a lyric sensitivity that recalls the manner of Coleridge:

The air carried down by the stream, the more forcibly in consequence of the minute division of the water, being resisted by the surface of the lake beneath, passed off in all directions from the fall, sweeping many of the descending drops with it. Between us and the fall the drops fell brilliant and steady till within a few inches of the bottom, when receiving a new impulse they flew along horizontally, light and airy as snow. A mist of minute particles arose from the conflicting waters, and being driven against the rocks by the wind, cloathed them with moisture, and created myriads of miniature cascades, which falling on the fragments beneath polished them to a state of extreme slipperiness.[4]

Next Faraday and Magrath walked to Brecon via Ystradfellte, and then, after a false start, where 'we had lost 4 hours and covered about 9 useless miles of a very bad kind for pedestrians', to Builth, then Rhayader via a post-chaise, and Hafod and Devil's Bridge. Faraday found the next stage north hard going, summing up the difficulties as '1 no roads, 2 no houses, 3 no people, 4 rivers but no bridges, 5 plenty of mountains'.

The few people they met had 'dim Sasnach' and nodded in agreement with whatever direction Faraday pointed to as 'the way to Machynlleth'.

On the road north of Machynlleth Faraday and Magrath met people walking in groups of two or three, wearing shoes and stockings and kerchiefs 'properly adjusted', and carrying books. They were clearly on their way to chapel. And soon the two men came across 'a small simple building with plain latch doors'. From it came the slow, plaintive melody of children chanting a Welsh psalm. 'Never did music give me such pleasure before.'

Intent on traversing Cadair Idris, Faraday and Magrath arrived at Minffordd in a thunderstorm and took shelter in the Blue Lion. The landlord, Edward Jones, said there was no guide available to lead them across the mountain, but drew them a map and gave instructions on how to find their way – exactly as he'd done for Jenkin Jones a month earlier. They climbed to Llyn Cau, scaled the steep slope to Craig Cwm Amarch, and turned towards the peak. Their boots were soaked and they were exhausted. 'Magrath tied his bundle around his neck to have it in case of a fall and mine was actually rolling down the sleep side but was luckily stopped in time or it would have been gone into the lake.'

More strenuous walking took Faraday and Magrath 28 miles from

Dolgellau to Beddgelert. As they tried to shelter from the rain along the way a woman invited them into her cottage. Faraday gives a detailed picture of its appearance and contents, and praises its orderliness and comfort. He also describes the local women and their way of walking:

> Every girl and woman in going from their houses to the town takes her shoes and if she has stockings, them also with her. She walks however without them on but on nearing the town washes her feet in a brook, puts herself in order and then makes a respectable appearance.[5]

They reached Caernarfon, and then crossed by boat to Anglesey, noting the preparations for 'a new hanging bridge over the Straits projected by Mr. Telford'. They 'fagged on without any rest or refreshments' to Amlwch. From Bangor the friends continued to Capel Curig, Llangollen and Shrewsbury.

Today Faraday's account of his 1819 Welsh tour is most valuable for his detailed descriptions of the pioneering industrial sites that especially interested him. But his observant eye was trained on everything he saw on his journey: scenery, geology and people. It was not a cold eye. He felt a ready sympathy for the ordinary people he met on his walks, and found it easy, thanks to his own origins, to appreciate their strengths. At Corwen on 30 July he noticed an innkeeper's son:

> He could not be more than 10 or 11 years of age and yet he certainly had the advantage over a young gentleman apparently an Oxonian who endeavoured to joke him on his country.[6]

Anne Lister

Like Faraday other travellers had special reasons for embarking on tours of Wales. Few shared the same motivation as the Yorkshire diarist and inveterate traveller Anne Lister. She came, three years after Faraday, in order to explore sexuality. She'd always been clear and open about her lesbianism – 'I love and only love the fairer sex and thus beloved by them in turn, my heart revolts from any love but theirs'[7] – and in July 1822 she came to north Wales, in the company of her aunt, also called Anne, to seek out others in her position. In Chester she said farewell to her married lover, Mariana Lawton. Their relationship had been long-lasting and complex.

Anne made straight for Llangollen, hoping to fulfil her twelve-year old ambition to visit Plas Newydd. This was the home of the 'Ladies of Llangollen', Sarah Ponsonby and Eleanor Butler. For over forty years these upper-class Irishwomen had been famous for their eccentric Gothic-converted house and gardens, for their hospitality to writers and other visitors, and, most of all, for the intimacy of their long relationship (they'd run away from Ireland together). It was this relationship that fascinated Anne Lister. On successive days she and her aunt walked up through the town to Plas Newydd. They failed to meet the Ladies – Eleanor Butler was ill – but the visit affected Anne deeply: 'my expectations were more than realized & it excited in me, from a variety of circumstances, a sort of particular interest tinged with melancholy – I could have mused for hours & dreampt dreams of happiness.'

The Ladies of Llangollen, by Susan Murray Tait (Lady Sitwell), 1819
(*National Library of Wales*)

With a local boy as guide Anne and her aunt walked above the town to Castell Dinas Brân ('I never slipped once even with my bright iron-heeled boots on'), afterwards visiting the boy's family home and listening to his father reading Welsh ('I think I could get the language in a few months'). Then they set out on a conventional tour. Anne climbed to the summit of Yr Wyddfa, followed more laboriously by her aunt, and at Bethesda she took a particular interest in the Penrhyn quarry.

After the tour Anne returned to Llangollen to try again to meet the Ladies. She was granted an evening audience with Sarah Ponsonby. After some nervous preparations she walked on her own to Plas Newydd, to find

> a large woman [so as to waddle in walking but] tho' not taller than myself – in a blue shortish waisted cloth habit, the jacket unbuttoned shewing a plain plaited frilled habit shirt... altogether a very odd figure – yet she had no sooner entered into conversation than I forgot all this & my attention was wholly taken by her manners & conversation – The former, perfectly easy, peculiarly attentive & well bred & bespeaking a person accustomed to a great deal of good society – mild & gentle, certainly not masculine, & yet there was a je-ne-sais-quoi striking.[8]

Anne probed Sarah by making several coded enquiries about the real nature of her relationship with Eleanor. Did they like [sexually explicit] Greek and Roman authors? No, 'thank God', Miss Ponsonby replied, 'from Latin & Greek I'm free'. Had she read Byron's [immoral] *Don Juan*? 'She was ashamed to say she had read the first canto.' Had they ever quarrelled? Only the occasional 'difference of opinion'. Every question met with an evasion, as was the usual reaction by the Ladies to prying enquiries. It seems that the closest they got to admitting a physical relationship was to call a succession of their dogs 'Sappho'. However, Sarah ended the conversation by giving Anne a rose, which she intended to dry and keep. 'I know not how it is, I felt low after coming away – a thousand moody reflections occurred.'

When Mariana asked her later whether she thought the Ladies' association 'has always been platonic', Anne answered 'I cannot help thinking that surely it was not platonic. Heaven forgive me, but I look within myself and doubt. I feel the infirmity of our nature & hesitate to pronounce such attachments uncemented by something more tender still than friendship.'[9]

Anne left Llangollen and returned home via Denbigh, St Asaph and Holywell. All through the Welsh trip she'd been turning over in her mind the troubled relationship with Mariana. Back in Chester she wrote, 'I sat musing on M thinking I wasted my life in vain expectation'. In the end Mariana could never bring herself to leave her husband, and in 1834 Anne met and married (at least in her own eyes) another, younger woman, Ann Walker.

Charles Darwin

Nine years later another remarkable visitor stayed in Llangollen, and visited Castell Dinas Brân. Charles Darwin was twenty-two years old, had just graduated from the University of Cambridge, and was accompanying Adam Sedgwick on a geological tour of north Wales. Sedgwick was Professor of Geology in the University, and a cleric who clung to the old biblical chronology of the earth's development. His aim was to search for evidence in north Wales of Old Red Sandstone strata, but his value to Darwin lay in his expertise as a field geologist. Darwin, suddenly 'mad about Geology', had just bought a clinometer and spent some days in July testing his surveying skills in the quarries at Llanymynech on the Welsh border, making notes and colouring maps.

The two started out in August 1831 from Shrewsbury, where Darwin had been born and educated. His family had been in the habit of taking holidays across the Welsh border, often staying near Tywyn on the Merioneth coast. As a young man Darwin was strong and energetic, and enjoyed roaming the hills. 'During the summer vacation of 1826', he recalled later, 'I took a long walking tour with two friends with knapsacks through north Wales. We walked 30 miles most days, including one day the ascent of Snowdon.'[10] In July 1828 he wrote to a friend, 'I only wish you would make a trip here, & I would cicerone you up & down the mountains, untill you had not a particle of wind left in your lungs.'[11]

Sedgwick and Darwin travelled by gig to Llangollen, then Conwy and Bangor, stopping on the way to walk to geological sites.

Walking to Cwm Idwal, they searched all day for fossils, without, Darwin later recognised, understanding the remarkable geological formations that surrounded them. In 1842 he returned to the area and published an article on the valley's glaciation. He later wrote, in sadness, 'This excursion interested me greatly, and it was the last time I was ever strong enough to climb mountains or to take long walks such as are necessary for geological work.' After Cwm Idwal the two men climbed Moel Siabod to study its rocks.

Darwin may or may not have accompanied Sedgwick to Anglesey, but at some point in the trip the two men parted. Starting from Capel Curig, Darwin recalled 45 years later, he 'went in a straight line by compass and map across the mountains to Barmouth, never following any track unless it coincided with my course. I thus came on some strange wild places, and enjoyed much this manner of travelling.' It's hard to take Darwin's words literally, since a direct route, over some of the most difficult and rugged terrain in Wales, would have taken more than two days, and his own notes suggest that, after an overnight stay in Ffestiniog he crossed the Harlech Dome at Bwlch Drws Ardudwy and followed Cwm Nantcol towards the coast road. At Barmouth he met Robert Lowe, later Viscount Sherbrooke, who recalled,

Here I met for the first time the illustrious Darwin. He was making a geological tour of Wales, and carried with him, in addition to his other burdens, a hammer of 14 lbs weight ... I walked twenty-two miles with him [to Mallwyd] when he went away, a thing which I never did for anyone else before or since.[12]

Darwin's 1831 Welsh trip came at a crucial time in his intellectual evolution. It gave him a grounding in geological method and thinking that was central to his later work. In a letter to his Cambridge friend, John Stevens Henslow, the Professor of Botany, he wrote:

> Tell Prof: Sedgwick he does not know how much I am indebted to him for the Welch expedition.— it has given me an interest in geology, which I would not give up for any consideration.— I do not think I ever spent a more delightful three weeks, than in pounding the NW mountains.[13]

When Darwin returned home to Shrewsbury on 29 August he found a letter waiting for him: an invitation from Henslow to be a naturalist on Captain Robert FitzRoy's ship HMS *Beagle* during its voyage around the world. The *Beagle* sailed in December 1831. When it returned in October 1836 Darwin was already famous as a geologist. He'd read Charles Lyell's gradualist theories of geology, and the seeds of the theory of natural selection had been planted in his mind.

Guidebooks and mountain guides

As the number of visitors to Wales increased, there was a market for practical guidebooks, to help them find their way around the most appealing areas. In her travels in north Wales Anne Lister refers to earlier tour accounts, but also to newer guidebooks such as George Nicholson's *The Cambrian traveller's guide*. A particular need was help with the linguistic challenges of travelling in a country where many people had limited or no English, especially outside towns. In 1831 Thomas Roberts, a Quaker, goldsmith and political and religious radical living in London, published the first edition of *The Welsh interpreter*, a Welsh vocabulary and phrasebook for the use of tourists 'who may wish to make themselves understood by the peasantry during their rambles through Wales.' In his introduction Roberts writes

Pedestrians, who may chance to wander from the beaten track, will occasionally find it convenient to ask for information of a peasant, and even to take shelter in his humble cottage ... It would be but a poor consolation to a weary traveller, who sought the nearest way to the next village, to receive for answer to his earnest enquiries, the eternal repetition of 'Dim Saesneg', and thus be compelled to continue shivering in the cold, and exhausted for want of a dinner.[14]

Numerous phrases in the book concerning mountains testify to the popularity of mountain walking as a pastime for visitors, and to some of the difficulties they met with: 'How long shall we be going up?', 'It is dangerous to take neat brandy when ascending a mountain', 'Can you carry my greatcoat, cloak?', 'Must I have nails in my shoes to ascend that mountain?', 'You are giddy because you look down', 'Where is the nearest surgeon to be found?'

A popular general guidebook was *Black's picturesque guide to North Wales*. First published in 1858, this work had reached its 23rd edition by 1907. Its editorial emphasis was on the practical. The high-flown descriptive prose of earlier 'tours' was sternly rejected:

... there will be a uniform aim at perspicuity and conciseness, and a studious avoidance of overwrought description and needless or burdensome details; in other words, the endeavour will be to convey the greatest possible amount of information in the smallest possible space, and in a form best adapted to the use of the traveller.[15]

Modest walks are recommended ('a very agreeable walk of nearly two miles'), but *Black's* assumes that visitors make longer journeys by other means. Railways loom large in the text and on the map provided. The itineraries are arranged according to railway routes, and journey times are based on train speeds. Much space is given to railway architecture, like Robert Stephenson's Britannia Bridge across the Menai Strait, and other monuments of Victorian engineering. A pony is advised for visitors wishing to ascend Yr Wyddfa.

By the time these two guidebooks were first published mountain walking had a lengthy history in Wales. Mountaineering and rock climbing had also become established sports. Visitors developed a taste for climbing Yr Wyddfa by more difficult routes, and in harsher weathers. Local guides, familiar with the mountain in all its guises, may have encouraged them, and were certainly better prepared for mountaineering. This rarely prevented the gentlemen amateur climbers from treating their professional guides with condescension.

One of the bravest Yr Wyddfa guides was William Williams, known locally as 'Will Boots'. He was described as 'active as the goat of his native mountains' and 'a most daring cragsman'. He was a keen botanist and specialised in taking bolder visitors to see rare plants on the higher slopes of Yr Wyddfa, using fixed ropes to abseil down rock faces to collect specimens (he died in 1861 after a fall on the mountain). Williams fostered a distinctive self-image: he 'dressed

himself in a suit of goat-skin, consisting of cap, coat and trousers which made him appear like a savage from the land of perpetual snow.' In 1838 he led a Worcester botanist, Edwin Lees, to Clogwyn y Geifr, above Cwm Idwal. Lees recalled a moment of panic:

At this point my nerves actually quailed at the prospect, and I could move no farther. But my little guide soon gave me a recipe for my nervousness, occasioned by my looking down into the cloudy gulph beneath. 'Look up', said he, 'creep close to

William Williams, 'Will Boots', anonymous watercolour painting, undated
(Storiel, Bangor)

the rock, and there is no danger'. I still hesitated, till measuring the distance with my eye, and at last forming my resolve, I closed my eyes on the fearful view, felt my way with cautious steps, crossed the dreaded ledge in safety, and gathered my plant![16]

Williams later came to understand that, through their hunting, and his own collecting on their behalf, botanists were quickly stripping the mountain of its rarest plants. He devised a plan to build a reserve for them near Llanberis.

Another Snowdon guide was Robin Hughes of Capel Curig. At the age of 61 he led the experienced Alpine mountaineer John Tyndall and his friend T.H. Huxley up Yr Wyddfa in thick snow in December 1860. The two were ill-prepared. They lacked gaiters and had forgotten to bring ice-axes: in Bethesda they paid a blacksmith to improvise using rake handles fitted with rings and iron spikes. Tyndall found the ascent through the knee-deep snow painful, but they reached the summit, Hughes being powered, Tyndall implied, mainly by whisky.

Some visitors ventured on to the mountains without guides or maps, wearing unsuitable clothing, and with a poor appreciation of weather, terrain or distance. The results could be fatal. On Sunday 20 August 1882 George Norton and Thomas Dismore, two solicitors from Liverpool, decided to 'do Snowdon', without a guide. They'd reached the summit and started to descend, straying towards Clogwyn Coch and then trying to reach Pen-y-Pass. Near Crib Goch they reached a 'steep declivity'. Norton turned back, sensing danger in the wind and mist, but Dismore, a 33-year-old 'ardent mountaineer', was confident he could negotiate the slope safely and pressed on. Norton heard behind him 'a noise as of a scuffle of some sort', and turned to watch as his friend disappeared over the edge of a precipice, without a sound, falling over 300 feet. Later Norton found the body, 'completely shattered' and the skull smashed. At the inquest the jury returned a verdict of accidental death, adding that 'it was certainly not right or proper for strangers to attempt to cross over Snowdon, particularly on misty days, without the assistance of guides.'[17]

Mountaineers

Apart from the paid guides, few local people viewed rock-climbing and winter mountaineering as pleasures. Farmworkers and slate quarrymen had already spent too many hours in the week battling against the harsh climate of the mountains to seek more dangers there in their few leisure hours.

More serious climbers began to arrive in Eryri as the fashion for mountaineering took hold among the upper middle classes in England from the late 1850s (the Alpine Club was founded in London in 1857). They tended to treat the Welsh peaks as a training ground for the challenges facing them in Switzerland. They'd often stay in Pen-y-Gwryd, a farmhouse converted into an inn. From 1847, under the ownership of the mountain guide Harry Owen and his wife Ann, Pen-y-Gwryd gained a reputation for hospitality to mountain climbers. One of its most frequent guests was Charles Edward Mathews, a Birmingham solicitor, who climbed Yr Wyddfa and Cadair Idris a hundred times each and pioneered many Alpine climbs. He was one of the founders of the Climbers' Club, established in Pen-y-Gwryd in

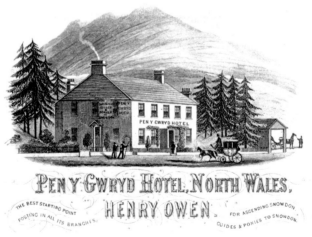

Pen-y-Gwryd, business card, undated
(Trustees of the British Museum)

1898 to encourage rock-climbing in Wales and England (of the 265 members in 1910 only four had Welsh addresses[18]). Earlier, in 1870, Mathews had set up a predecessor, the Society of Welsh Rabbits, an informal group that aimed to promote winter climbs in Eryri. Charles Kingsley, in his 1890 novel *Two years ago*, paints a vivid picture of the warm kitchen in Pen-y-Gwryd at night, and its occupants: Harry Owen, who had climbed to the summit of Yr Wyddfa earlier in the day and would lead a German back there at midnight, Ann Owen and her mother providing food, locals singing 'Codiad yr Ehedydd' (singing being 'the one gift still left to that strange Cymry race'), several English visitors drinking, and assorted small children and dogs playing.[19]

The generation that followed the 'golden age' of Alpinism was less interested in climbing mountains in winter, amid snow and ice, and more taken with finding routes up difficult rock faces. Two of their leaders were England-born Welshmen, Owen Glynne Jones and William Jones Williams. They came from working-class backgrounds, which set them apart socially from the English, public school-educated climbers. O.G. Jones was the son of a carpenter and builder from Barmouth, while Williams's father was a warehouseman, originally from the Llanrwst area. Jones, an athletic and naturally gifted climber, pioneered climbs in the Lake District, and often visited the Alps, but he was also active in Eryri. In May 1888 he climbed alone the east ridge of Cyfrwy on Cadair Idris, pioneered routes on Tryfan, and he was preparing a guide to rock climbing in Wales when he was killed in a climbing accident in Switzerland at the age of 32. His cousin Winifred Davies was also an accomplished rock climber. W.J. Williams, small in stature but 'agile and tough', climbed with his wife Mary, also a mountaineer, in the Alps every year from 1894 till 1914 and took part in the first ascents of many Welsh rocks.

Most of the new breed of climbers were men, but Welsh women too developed a taste for mountain adventure. Emmeline Lewis Lloyd of Nantgwyllt in Cwm Elan climbed in the Alps in the 1860s and was a member of the first party to ascend Aiguille du Moine. As a girl Mary ('Minnie') de la Beche Nicholl went on long walks with her father,

Lewis Llewelyn Dillwyn, in the Swansea area, before becoming a lepidopterist, and, in her late thirties, a keen mountaineer in the Alps, north America, north Africa and Asia Minor.

Frances Ridley Havergal, who ended her life in Newton, Swansea, was well known in her day as a religious poet and hymnwriter, but she'd lived in Germany as a girl, and made four climbing trips to the Alps between 1869 and 1874. She found walking on Yr Wyddfa and Moel Siabod a tame experience. She and her sister were warned that Moel Siabod could be difficult, and that guides could be engaged: 'we set all this at defiance'. On 16 July 1872 she stayed at Pen-y-Gwryd and wrote to a friend:

> I am finishing this at the top of Snowdon; the ascents are all so easy; no need of ponies or guides, when we can walk twelve to fifteen miles. We shall run from down this the Llanberis side, and camp for a week, half way down, with one of my sister's charming old women.[20]

Havergal found it impossible to divorce her experience of mountains from her intense religious faith. She thanked God for 'letting us see his handiworks' by providing a sunny day for climbing Yr Wyddfa.

The Alpine mountaineers were seldom interested in religious revelation, or the collecting of botanical or geological specimens that motivated earlier climbers. Nor were they always inspired by the same nature Romanticism as Wordsworth, Coleridge and their successors. For them climbing was an end in itself, akin to other extreme sporting pursuits that challenged the limits of the (mainly male) human body. Taking physical risks was an important element of the process. The experienced eye, and even more important, the touch of hand and foot on rock became of critical importance in success or failure. For these privileged people, mastering new environments – 'conquering' new peaks or rock climbs – paralleled the drive to empire that was in full swing in this period. With some exceptions, like the pioneering climber J. Archer Thomson, their interest in the particularities of the land of Wales and its people was limited; in this, they differed little from ordinary tourists. When they needed names for the places where they pursued their sport, for example in their published guides to climbs, they made up English terms, like Heather Terrace and Milestone Buttress, instead of using Welsh names: Yr Wyddfa lost ground to Snowdon, and Eryri to Snowdonia. Before the First World War climbing in north Wales was still dominated by the English upper classes, and it was only from the 1930s that talented climbers from other backgrounds, like Colin Kirkus and John Menlove Edwards, dislodged their position.[21]

George Borrow

Some tourists and travellers continued to come to Wales to walk rather than to climb. Few were more singular than the man who set out from Chester in July 1854 for a walking tour of north Wales. His name was George Borrow. Eight years later he published a narrative of his travels, *Wild Wales: its people, language and scenery*. The book sold poorly at first, but later became a classic account of travel in Wales and has never been out of print since.

Borrow was fifty years of age when he came to Wales. Born at East Dereham, Norfolk in 1803, he was the son of an army recruiting officer, and as a child moved from place to place throughout Britain and Ireland. His education was sporadic. He started training as a lawyer but was much more interested in languages and literature and as a young man he earned a precarious living as a writer. In 1833 he worked as an agent for the British and Foreign Bible Society. This work took him on long travels, many on foot, in Europe and Asia. In 1840 he came home, married and settled in Lowestoft, where he began writing a series of books based on his wanderings.

In 1851 Borrow published *Lavengro*, a work of what would now be termed autofiction. Its theme was the Romany people. His interest in gypsies began early, perhaps stimulated by the parallel with his own peripatetic experience. He sought them out wherever he could during his continental travels, and spent time with them, learning their traditions and language. Roma appealed to Borrow for their outsider status as well as their romance, and all his life he retained a respect for minorities and classes often held in contempt by respectable society.

Borrow arrived in Wales predisposed to sympathise with its people. He also came well equipped to speak with them. He was a talented linguist and had learned Irish, Latin, Greek, Hebrew, German, Danish, French, Italian, Spanish and Portuguese. As a young trainee solicitor, he claimed, he'd been taught spoken Welsh by 'Llwyd', a Welsh groom in Norfolk, and by the end of his training he'd read widely in Welsh prose and poetry, including Dafydd ap Gwilym. In 1830 he composed an English translation of Ellis Wynne's *Gweledigaethau y Bardd Cwsg* (Visions of the sleeping bard), but failed to get it published.

In two respects, then, Borrow differed from almost all English travellers in Wales during his period. There was a further difference: he was a committed, even fanatical pedestrian. In *Wild Wales* he records only one journey not made on foot. A railroad he described as 'one of those detestable contrivances.' Borrow was a tall, well-built man, and all his life had been an energetic long-distance walker. His preference was to walk alone, on paths rather than roads, with the minimum of baggage: a small leather satchel containing a white linen shirt, stockings, a razor and a prayer book. He also

George Borrow, oil painting by Henry Wyndham Phillips, 1843-68
(*National Portrait Gallery*)

carried notebooks, and an umbrella, which, he said, protected against rain, could be used as a defence against bulls, dogs and footpads, and acted as a badge of respectability: 'Oh, a tent, a shield, a lance, and a voucher for character is an umbrella.' He never seems to have carried a map, preferring to ask locals for directions.[22]

Walking gave Borrow an immense advantage over horsed or wheeled travellers: it offered a guarantee that he'd meet on the road dozens of ordinary local people. He was keener to have conversations with them, especially in Welsh, than he was to mix with the Anglicised gentry within their walled estates. On his tour he talked to a huge variety of people. On the first leg of his trip, between Chester and Llangollen, where he joined his wife Mary and step-daughter Henrietta, he'd already had conversations with a bookseller, a waggoner, a fighter, a church clerk and a woman beggar. Trampers, he thought, were 'the only people from whom you can learn anything'.

Borrow chose the words of the title and subtitle of his book with care. By the time it appeared, so many tours and guides had been published that many parts of Wales were very familiar to readers. Wales, it seemed, had been domesticated. Borrow was determined to visit less frequented, upland areas of the country, and to explore the country through conversations with its ordinary people. He aimed to re-wild Wales, bringing to light aspects of the past and present of its people that would surprise outsiders with a superficial or second-hand acquaintance with the country. The subtitle, 'its people, language and scenery' reflects the priority of Borrow's concerns, and dictates how he set the stage for his book: Welsh people are in the spotlight, the Welsh language and its literature are a constant theme, and the landscape of Wales, the highlight of most Welsh tour literature for the last century, is relegated to the background.

Borrow spends the first weeks of his Welsh stay with his family at Dee Cottage, Llangollen. For remoter walks out of Llangollen he hires a guide, John Jones, a shepherd and ex-weaver, whom he deplores for his Methodism but admires for his walking speed and botanical knowledge.

Next, Borrow leaves his family and starts out on his tour alone: 'I had determined to make the journey on foot, in order that I might have perfect liberty of action, and enjoy the best opportunities of seeing the country.' His first stop is Cerrigydrudion, twenty miles away. At the Lion Inn he falls into conversation with others. 'Rather hot weather for walking, sir!', says one. Borrow replies, '... as I can't observe the country well without walking through it I put up with the heat.' He's the most sociable traveller and an inveterate recorder of conversation – conversation that often takes its cue from surprise at his Welsh language prowess.

Borrow continues to Bangor, and from Llanberis climbs Yr Wyddfa, with Henrietta and a local guide. Many tourists are on the mountain, and the cabin on the summit is selling refreshments to them, but Henrietta is first obliged to listen to Borrow reciting from memory Goronwy Owen's poem on the mountain. 'Three or four English ... stood nigh, with grinning scorn.' The family now leave Borrow as he walks on to Anglesey, to visit Owen's birthplace at Llanfair Mathafarn Eithaf. The village turns out to be 'desolate place', but the local miller and his wife invite him to have a meal with them. He's deeply moved by this act of hospitality.

The miller and his wife have no English, so the conversation is in Welsh. Throughout this trip Borrow takes every opportunity to practice his Welsh, and is almost childishly delighted when complimented on his grasp of the language. On one occasion he dares to explain at length the etymology of a Welsh place-name to a native speaker, who professes to be grateful: irony verging on embarrassment is common throughout *Wild Wales*. Many people have difficulty in understanding his mainly book-derived Welsh: in the north he's assumed to be from south Wales, and in mid-Wales and south Wales he's taken for 'a man from the north country'.

On Anglesey Borrow twice allows us to laugh at his expense. On the way to Llangefni he has met a person, described, very doubtfully, as Anglesey's leading contemporary poet, who says he keeps an inn in the town. He seeks out what he assumes is the inn, a magnificent building, and orders a pint and a chop, only to discover, after much misunderstanding, that he's in the wrong place and should have gone to another, much meaner 'mug house' of the same name. In Holyhead a group of Irish reapers mistake Borrow for 'Father Toban', a character as dubious as the great poet, and insist he blesses them before they commit themselves to the Irish ferry. Toban, 'a powerful priest in these parts' and 'the greatest scholar in the world', makes several other fictional appearances in *Wild Wales*. These excursions into fantasy show how far *Wild Wales* strays from being a simple travel book.

From Holyhead Borrow takes the train, for his only time in Wales, to Bangor. To his dismay the inn there is crammed with working-class visitors the railway has brought from Manchester and Liverpool, 'the scum of manufacturing England' (for Borrow, peasants are acceptable, the proletariat beyond the pale). Passing through Beddgelert, Aberglaslyn and Tan-y-Bwlch, he enters the vale of Ffestiniog. On the road he has a frustrating conversation with a man who refuses to speak Welsh with him, and, instead of answering Borrow's questions about the obscure fifteenth century poet Rhys Goch Eryri, insists on telling him about the English royal family. 'I told him he was a bad Welshman, and he retorted by saying that I was a bad Englishman.'

At Bala Borrow meets an American, and allows him to think that he too is from the United States – a kind of deception that he uses several times in *Wild Wales*, one of whose chief themes is identity and identification.

Borrow rejoins his family in Llangollen, and from there walks to Wrexham, to buy a book on the history of Methodism, via Dinas Brân and the Eglwyseg Rocks. At Plas Uchaf a farmer advises him that a respectable person should not walk back along the common road on a Saturday night: 'you will perhaps meet drunken colliers who may knock you down.' On the moors at the top of the valley Borrow gets lost, 'steeplechases' it through the knee-length heather and bogs, and, with the help of some surly colliers, finds his way to Wrexham and buys his book.

At Machynlleth Borrow stays the night at the Wynnstay Arms. He talks to a lawyer, here to defend a man accused of illegally spearing fish in a river whose fishing belonged to Sir Watkin Williams Wynne. Borrow decides to go to the town hall to attend the trial, presided over by 'Lord V.', the defendant's landlord. The witnesses conspire to lie, and the man is convicted and fined. 'What an ill-treated individual' is Borrow's own verdict.

Despite his social conservatism Borrow is hostile to landlordism. At Sycharth, home of Owain Glyndŵr, he learns that the landowner is Sir Watkin, 'the Marquis of Carabas of Denbighshire'. In a pub in Llansilin he's interrupted by a loud and violent group of Sir Watkin's 'gamekeepers and river-watchers'. When John Jones remarks near Chirk Castle that it's a pity that 'the halls of great people no longer flow with rivers of beer, nor have mountains of bread and beef for all comers', Borrow replies

> No pity at all, things are better as they are. Those mountains of bread and beef, and those rivers of ale merely encouraged vassalage, fawning and idleness; better to pay for one's dinner proudly and independently, at one's inn, than to go and cringe for it at a great man's table.[23]

One of his criticisms of his fellow Englishmen is their 'crazy admiration for what they call gentility, which made them sycophantic to their superiors in station'.

By contrast, Borrow almost always has time for ordinary people. He feels a special attraction to marginal groups, like the Irish who wandered about Wales at the time in the shadow of the Great Famine, and gypsies and tinkers. (Only once, on the Black Mountain, does he meet Romany travellers: they explain that Irish immigrants have made their life in Wales harder.) But while the rural poor often evoke sympathy, he tends to view industrial workers with suspicion and sometimes horror. He spends little time in the south Wales valleys. Swansea, at its height as a copper smelting centre, he finds 'a large, bustling, dirty, gloomy place'.

There's one group of Welsh people Borrow holds in the highest regard: poets and other writers. He loves to track down the homes and haunts of writers, often to the bemusement of local people. Since his youth he'd studied the works of many of them, and his trip to Wales is in part an act of literary pilgrimage. Having tracked down the birthplace of Goronwy Owen on Anglesey, he searches out the burial place of Huw Morus in Llansilin and of Dafydd ap Gwilym in Strata Florida.

Wild Wales acts as an introduction for Borrow's English readers to the traditional poets of Wales, several years before Matthew Arnold, who never mastered Welsh, pontificated in his lectures about them. But all of Borrow's literary heroes belonged to the past. He seems to be unaware of living exponents of the Welsh poetic tradition, and has a blind spot for nonconformist writers like William Williams Pantycelyn. What interests him far more is the Welsh language. All aspects of it interest him: its accents and vocabulary, its geographical and class distribution, its linguistic sociology.

Borrow records where the Welsh language is already in retreat, as rapid economic and social change begin to privilege English as the language of the future. Welsh place names are being changed to English ones by incomers. English settlers are attracted by industrialisation, at Wrexham and in the south Wales valleys, and by tourism, as at Betws-y-coed. English people long settled in Wales have failed to learn the language, to Borrow's disapproval. Some Welsh speakers are beginning to turn against their own tongue. A woman in Llangollen tells Borrow that 'Welsh people at the present day were so full of fine airs that they were above speaking the old language.'

Though he breaks with many of the traditions of the Welsh tour, Borrow follows his predecessors in paying much more attention to the north of Wales than to the south. He covers his journey from Llanddewi Brefi to Chepstow, via Swansea, Merthyr Tydfil and Caerphilly, in just fourteen out of the 109 chapters of *Wild Wales*. The scenery is often spoilt for him by industry. In the Rhymney valley he's appalled by 'a horrid black object, a huge coal work, the chimneys of which were belching forth smoke of the densest description.' The river is 'filthy and turbid owing of course to its having received the foul drainings of the neighbouring coal works.'

At Chepstow he spends a final mid-November night 'drinking wine and singing Welsh songs'. He has walked 250 miles. In the morning he buys a first-class ticket for a 'comfortable carriage' in a train to London.

Eight years separated Borrow's tour of Wales and the publication of *Wild Wales*, leaving plenty of time for him to fashion his notes into an ingenious, novel-like mix of fact and fiction. It's far from being a plain travel narrative, as an anonymous reviewer of the book would have wished:

> We are dubious whether it is simply a record of his walks through Wales, or whether he has mingled a quantity of very mild and not very amusing fiction with actual experiences. In any case the book is extremely defective, and contains an unpardonable proportion of triviality and self-glorification ... In one volume, instead of three, the work might have been an attractive guide-book for pedestrians.[24]

The 'George Borrow' of the book is a carefully constructed character. If a common hero of the eighteenth-century novel is the 'man of sentiment', Borrow sets up his alter ego as the 'man of prejudice', constantly grumpy and irritable about religion, trains, tourists and much else, and also as comically conceited and proud of his linguistic ability. He plays on the fluidity of the self. On many occasions 'Borrow' allows himself to be mistaken for others – a Breton, or Father Toban, an American or a Baptist minister – and his anecdotes often hint at self-mockery. The true subject of *Wild Wales* is not Wales but George Borrow himself. As the poet Edward Thomas noted in his study of Borrow, 'in all his best books he is the chief subject and the chief object.'[25]

Poets

George Borrow tried his hand at poetry, though would never have claimed to have to be a poet of distinction. But walker-poets continued to come to Wales throughout the nineteenth century, many drawn by the dramatic landscapes of the north. For Alfred Tennyson, Eryri provided a strong contrast to his native Lincolnshire. He first visited Wales in July 1839, already attracted by the Arthurian myths that would later preoccupy him as a poet.

He walked from Aberystwyth to Barmouth, and later stayed in Llanberis, the setting for a poem entitled 'Edwin Morris; or, The lake', with its reference to Dolbadarn castle. A second poem written there, 'The golden year', recalls a climb up Yr Wyddfa and a walk near the Dinorwig slate quarry:

> He spoke; and, high above, I heard them blast
> The steep slate-quarry, and the great echo flap
> And buffet round the hills from bluff to bluff.[26]

Industry was beginning to elbow its way into the poetic imagining of Eryri. By the time of Tennyson's visit hundreds of workers were employed by Thomas Assheton Smith at Dinorwig, and a horse-drawn tramroad delivered thousands of tons of slate every year to Y Felinheli (Port Dinorwic) on the coast.

Tennyson returned to Aberystwyth in 1844, walked to Barmouth and Caernarfon, and climbed Yr Wyddfa on three occasions. In 1856 he brought his family for a holiday. Alfred insisted in climbing Cadair Idris, and was caught in a storm. His wife Emily waited anxiously below. She noted in her diary,

> Pouring rain came on. We waited a long time for him. I heard the roar of waters, streams and cataracts, and I never saw anything more awful than that great veil of rain drawn straight over Cader Idris, pale light at the lower edge. It looked as if death were behind it and made me shudder when I thought he was there.[27]

By now Tennyson was deeply absorbed in Arthurian myth. From 1838 Lady Charlotte Guest had been publishing her versions of the Mabinogi stories, and Tennyson was in search of inspiration from the places mentioned in them. During the trip he and Emily employed schoolteachers to teach them Welsh, and together they studied books on early Welsh poetry and history. They revisited Caerleon, a site of Arthur's court in *The idylls of the king*.

The family returned to Wales in 1868, and Tennyson revisited Llanberis with his son Hallam in 1871. The two climbed Yr Wyddfa – Tennyson was 71 years old by now – and wandered among the mountains.

Wales and his slow passage through it had left their mark on Tennyson. What he saw and what he read about early Welsh literature and history made their way into his early poems and into the Arthurian world of *The idylls of the king*.

For another, younger English poet, Wales became a more central experience, and an intense part of his poetic development.

Gerard Manley Hopkins was 30 years old when he arrived at St Beuno's College, near Tremeirchion in the Vale of Clwyd, on 28 August 1874, to begin a three-year course as preparation for becoming a Catholic priest. He'd converted to Catholicism in 1866 while a student at Oxford University, and had already completed courses on religion and philosophy. At times he'd doubted whether writing poetry, which he'd done as a younger man, was compatible with his severe sense of religious duty. But coming to Wales released in him a flow of poems that combined his strong faith with a rapt exultation in the rural landscape around him. They were poems of a new kind, full of unusual rhythms, newly-coined words and abrupt swerves of thought. They'd have puzzled his Victorian contemporaries if they'd read them – but they remained unpublished until 1918.

It was several weeks before courses were due to begin at St Beuno's, and Hopkins spent many of them, often in the company of his Jesuit friends, walking in and around the Vale of Clwyd. The college students led a spartan life, and walking was their only way to travelling around the country surrounding them. On 6 September Hopkins climbed the Clwydian Hills behind the College. He recorded in his diary:

With Wm. Kerr, who took me up a hill behind ours (ours is Mynefyr), a furze-grown and heathy hill, from which I could look round the whole country, up the valley towards Ruthin and down to the sea. The cleave in which Bodfari and Caerwys lie was close below. It was a leaden sky, braided or roped with cloud, and the earth in dead colours, grave but distinct. The heights by Snowdon were hidden by the clouds but not from distance or dimness... Looking all round but most in looking far up the valley I felt an instress and charm of Wales. Indeed in coming here I began to feel a desire to do something for the conversion of Wales. I began to learn Welsh too but not with very pure intentions perhaps.[28]

Here Hopkins unifies his intense, detailed observations of weather and landscape in a single word he'd invented years before, 'instress'. Instress is the means by which the 'inscape', Hopkins's term for the unique character of a thing in nature, has an effect on the poet's perception, memory and imagination.

Moel Maenefa

(photo Chris West)

169

Four days later Hopkins took a longer walk, to the Elwy valley, and on 24 September he was back on the hills above the College, on Moel Maenefa, and observed a sunset, which he sketched in his diary, using a palette of verbal colours:

Afterwards a lovely sunset of rosy juices and creams and combs; the combs I mean scattered floating bats or rafts or racks above, the creams/ the strew and bed of the sunset, passing north and south or rather north only into grey marestail and brush along the horizon to the hills.[29]

On 8 October Hopkins walked with a fellow-trainee, Clement Barraud, to Holywell. They bathed in St Winefride's Well and 'returned very joyously'. The trip also fed Hopkins's poetic imagination. His diary entry describes the water of the well as 'clear as glass, greenish like beryl or aquamarine, trembling at the surface with the force of the springs, and shaping out the five foils of the well'. This and subsequent walks to Holywell led to the writing in 1879 of his unfinished verse play 'St Winefred's Well'.

In his free time Hopkins took full opportunity to wander through the Vale, making all-day trips with friends to Cwm, St Asaph, Ffynnon Fair and Denbigh. He used a mental map of his walks in his 'Dominical', a practice sermon he gave to his fellow initiates at St Beuno's in March 1877, in which he conjured up a picture of the Sea of Galilee by mapping its outline on to places in the Vale of Clwyd that they were all familiar with.[30]

More significantly, the walks also became a reservoir of images and sensations that Hopkins drew on as he broke his moratorium on writing verse and began to write his most revolutionary poems.

Hopkins began to learn Welsh, in part with the help of a local Catholic, Susannah Jones. As he told his mother, he'd always felt half-Welsh, and he wanted to be able to speak to local people in their own language. His main reason, though, was poetic: a desire to understand *cerdd dafod*, traditional verse craft, and the different forms of *cynghanedd*, whose alliteration and word patterning were so close to his own evolving poetics. By 1876 he'd mastered the language well enough to write a Welsh *cywydd*, and many of the English poems he wrote at St Beuno's show the influence of *cynghanedd*.

The series began with a long poem, 'The wreck of the Deutschland', the first to show Hopkins's new 'sprung rhythm' and innovative use of language. Hopkins contrasts the drama and horror of the wreck with his own place of safety, 'away in the loveable west, / on a pastoral forehead of Wales'.[31]

The eleven 'Welsh' sonnets that followed were derived much more directly from Hopkins's reactions to the glory of the natural world he found on his walks. They include 'Pied beauty', God's grandeur' and 'The windhover', generally regarded as among his greatest achievements. Some of the poems are connected with specific places, and others reflect the walker's view of them.

Of 'Hurrahing in harvest', the last of the sonnets, Hopkins wrote to his friend Robert Bridges, 'the Hurrahing Sonnet was the outcome of half an hour of extreme enthusiasm as I walked home alone one day from fishing in the Elwy.' Walking, on earth and in the heavens, is woven into the start of the poem:

> Summer ends now; now, barbarous in beauty, the stooks rise
> Around; up above, what wind-walks! what lovely behaviour
> Of silk-sack clouds! has wilder, wilful-waiver
> Meal-drift moulded ever and melted across the skies?
>
> I walk, I lift up, I lift up heart, eyes,
> Down all that glory in the heavens to glean our Saviour
> And, eyes, heart, what looks, what lips yet gave you a
> Rapturous love's greeting of realer, of rounder replies?[32]

Hopkins finds delight in harmonising God and nature, perception and faith. The cloud images could almost have come direct from the weather observations in his journal: Denbigh castle, for example, in an entry in February 1875, looked 'dead mealy grey against the light'.

In 'Moonrise', a quiet nocturne, the poet wakes 'in the

Midsummer not-to-call night, in the white and walk of the morning',
to see the crescent moon rising above Moel Maenefa. A very different
kind of walking appears in 'God's grandeur': the repetitive tramping
of industrial workers yoked to economic necessity and alienated from
the natural world and the religious impulse:

> Generations have trod, have trod, have trod;
> And all is seared with trade; bleared, smeared with toil;
> And wears man's smudge and shares man's smell: the soil
> Is bare now, nor can foot feel, being shod.[33]

In 1877, having failed his theology exams, Hopkins left Wales, 'much
against my inclination', for the north of England and, later, Ireland.
He returned once, on holiday, in September 1886, staying with a friend
at Caernarfon and Tremadog and climbing Yr Wyddfa ('we walked so
much').[34] Hopkins always considered his years in the Vale of Clwyd
as the happiest and most settled of his life and north Wales as 'the
true Arcadia of wild beauty'. 'Wild Wales', he wrote, 'breathes poetry';
it is 'always to me a mother of Muses.'

Chapter 6: Map-makers, protesters and poets

Map-makers

When we read about the tours of Hopkins, Borrow, Faraday, Kilvert and other regular walkers we can't help noticing that when they needed directions they'd almost always ask local people for help. They'd almost never consult a map. Although road maps existed, they tended to be on too small a scale, and therefore lacking in detail, to be of practical use to off-road pedestrians. They were also often too expensive and bulky. The Ordnance Survey (OS) began work in Wales in 1803, with the aim of mapping the country as accurately as possible to a scale of one inch to one mile. Its first map, Pembrokeshire, was not officially published until 1820, and the last in the 'First Series' appeared in 1841. The original aim of the OS was to assist military planning, and throughout the first century of its existence its main audience was the government and industry. It took many decades before its directors understood that walkers too might benefit from having pocket versions of their maps. In 1901 a pocket map of Pembrokeshire was issued, which 'should also prove serviceable to cyclists and pedestrians.' Other one-inch-to-a mile maps followed.

Strenuous walking was an inevitable part of the work of the surveyors employed by the OS, who were paid by the square mile. At the start they were usually Royal Engineers. Whether they were calculating triangulations or sketching the contours of the countryside, they needed to leave roads behind and travel on foot, carrying theodolites and other heavy equipment with them. Often their work obliged them to climb to the tops of mountains. In north Wales a regular destination was the summit of Yr Wyddfa, from which they could plot triangulations to other points in Wales, England and Ireland. Often survey teams had to spend days in accommodation below the mountain, or in tents upon it, in the hope of hitting on a day of good visibility.

In 1811 an 'object' was planted on the summit of Yr Wyddfa, and in 1826 or 1827 a more permanent cairn, incorporating a staff, was

Trig point, Pen-y-gadair, Cadair Idris, looking west

(*Andrew Green*)

raised. Triangulation points began to appear on other peaks. In 1848 a complaint was made to the Cambrian Archaeological Association that the summit of Carnedd Dafydd 'has been altered by the engineers of the ordnance survey, and any carnedd which may have existed in former times, is now replaced by a pyramid of stones used for the purpose of triangulation.'[1]

In 1842 J.G. Kohl, a visitor from Germany, observed a party of Royal Engineers on the peak of Yr Wyddfa, and was told that in two months the men had not seen Ireland more than four times:

The mountain tapered at last into a complete cone, terminating in a summit, on which there was just room enough to spread out a tent for the protection of some mathematical instruments. The soldiers in charge of this tent, erected with a view to a new survey of the country, had constructed a small path of stones around their canvas mansion, and thus it became easy to enjoy the prospect on every side. The officer of engineers in command of the post had pitched several tents, a little lower down, for the accommodation of himself and his men.[2]

The earliest OS maps of Eryri, drawn by Robert Dawson and his son Robert Kearsley Dawson from 1816, were widely admired, especially for their vivid relief drawings of the mountains. But behind their elegance lay weeks of tough walking and meticulous observing. An obituary of R.K. Dawson, who died in 1861, gives a glimpse of his

> ... toilsome marching which can be appreciated only by those who have had experience of it. Unlike the hardy hunter of the red deer, in search of manly sport, and healthy recreation and exercise, the station hunter has no comfortable home to receive him at night. He must take up his quarters in the nearest shelter, and resume his walk at earliest dawn.[3]

OS maps were as welcome in Wales as elsewhere. One newspaper reported that, 'it is safe to say that an intelligent student examining one of these productions may obtain a much more vivid and accurate idea, than an ordinary individual going unintelligently over the ground itself!'[4] Some complained, though, about the slow pace of mapping, and others about the erroneous forms of place-names that were chosen to appear on maps. The OS retained advisers on Welsh place-names, but rarely employed Welsh-speaking staff.

The advent of definitive mapping put an effective end to one walking custom. This was the practice of 'beating the bounds' in order to reconfirm parish and county boundaries. It was known as 'cerdded plwyf' or 'cerdded terfynau', and in Glamorgan as 'cerdded corporasiwn'. Hugh Evans recalled how it operated in mid-nineteenth century Denbighshire:

> The custom in Cwm Eithin when I was a lad was to walk the boundaries, that is, the boundary between one parish and another, and between one county and another. This was done every few years. I'm not sure who was responsible for the task. It's likely it was the overseer, and that it was an old custom. At that time the ordnance maps hadn't been completed, most likely, and it was necessary to be sure how much land belonged to each parish so that it could be tithed. I remember a group going around – two or three old people and two or three youngsters; and so the boundaries were fixed from age to age.[5]

The 1870s saw the brief, late flowering in Wales of a peculiar kind of solo walking. It might be called 'endurance walking', 'professional walking' or 'commercial walking'. Its practitioners were men and women who performed astonishing feats of walking for money. Spectators would bet money on whether they'd succeed in completing a specific route or task within a set period of time.

The early nineteenth century was the heyday of pedestrianism. A Sussex walker, John Townsend, came to Wales in 1825. His speciality was walking well over sixty miles in one day, a feat he achieved twice, between Abergavenny and Monmouth in July, and, between Brecon and Hay-on-Wye in August. 'It is for no wager', he claimed, 'but merely to shew the people of Abergavenny and Monmouth what he can do.' But walking long distances for bets continued for many years. On 13 June 1871 Francis Kilvert recorded in his diary that his mountain guide, Robert Pugh, had once been challenged by 'a reading party of 4 or 5 Cambridge men' to climb Cadair Idris three times in a day, for £10. He succeeded, and 'could have gone up the fifth time.'[6]

William Gale was born in London and trained as a bookbinder. He was already well known for his pedestrianism before he married and moved to Cardiff. Between 28 June and 25 July 1877, at the Canton Running Grounds, Cardiff, he walked a thousand quarter miles, one quarter mile each consecutive ten minutes. This feat of endurance (and sleeplessness) captured the imagination of the public, and of the press:

> He has had all sorts of weather – hot, sultry, oppressive; undecided, shifty, meaningless weather; treacherous, erratic, saucy weather; flood and deluge weather; hours of bite-your-nose-off weather; a rough, hard, uneven path for some time, then a duck's running ground, so to speak, soft and sloppy; up, down; down, up; puddles and pools; sawdust and muck, ashes and clay, grass and snails – all sorts of weather, all sorts of ground ... Three times, just a week apart, has Gale shown symptoms of breaking

down. On the first occasion he was delirious, on the second physically weak, on the third he suffered bodily and mentally – in each case he picked himself up in A1 style.[7]

Journalists often remarked on Gale's figure, describing him as a 'plucky little man'. He was in his forties, stood little more than five feet three inches in height, and weighed less than nine stone. In August 1877 he succeeded in an even more challenging feat in London, walking 1,500 miles in 1,000 hours, a mile and a half to be completed at the start of each consecutive hour.

During his Cardiff walk Gale received a visitor, an actress and recently-widowed London theatre manager called Ada Anderson. After receiving six weeks of training from him she began her own endurance walking career in Newport in September 1877. It was said that she covered 1,000 half-miles in 1,000 half-hours, taking only twenty minutes' rest at one time. In October Anderson joined Gale in another walk in Plymouth. By the summer of 1878, with several more walks completed, she became known as 'Champion Lady Walker of the World'. In October she set off for the United States, where new audiences awaited her. Paying spectators, rather than gamblers, now provided income. She was successful, and William Gale followed her across the Atlantic, later becoming a boxing manager and taxidermist in Cincinnati.

Almost the last walker in the tradition was William Buckler. He was born in Newport in 1848, went to sea at the age of twelve, and remained a seaman for thirty years. He started out as a road walker rather than a course walker, and came to wide attention in 1885 when he set out to walk 300 miles on a route between Newport and Cardiff within 72 hours. One newspaper's special correspondent noted:

There is a hollowness about the cheeks and eyes, which might have been produced either by the work and dangers he has been subjected to as a sailor or by hard training. He certainly seemed as 'hard as nails,' and though brusque in manner, I found him by no means a badly-disposed fellow or an unpleasant companion.

'Dirty work, this,' said I. 'Devilish,' said he, 'an' don't care how soon it's over.'[8]

In October the same year, after walking for fifty miles a day for six days through the streets of Aberdare, William Buckler was summoned to the police court in the town for obstruction, 'by causing crowds to collect on the occasion of his recent pedestrian feat'. He was let off with a warning.[9]

In September 1896 at the Vetch Field, Swansea Buckler broke Gale's 'quarter hours in ten minutes' record in front of 7,000 people. Afterwards he was taken in procession to the Empire Theatre (later renamed the Palace Theatre) and appeared on the stage, to general delight. William Buckler died in 1908 in a lodging house in Hull, where he was employed as a dock labourer.[10]

In the Edwardian period this 'heel and toe' walking slowly evolving into a regular working-class sport as competitive racing. At six o'clock on the morning of 9 June 1903, for example, thirteen 'coloured' contestants gathered at the Angel Hotel, Cardiff to race to the sixth milestone on the Newport Road and back. They were accompanied by spectators on bicycles and in traps. Chester Maurice won the gold medal. 'Considering that all the competitors were seafaring men', wrote the reporter, 'the walking was of good quality.' The same newspaper story

A NEWPORT MAN'S WALK AGAINST TIME.

EXPERIMENTAL TRAMP BY OUR SPECIAL COMMISSIONER.

William Buckler, from Western Mail, 2 February 1885
(National Library of Wales)

announced that twelve entries had been received for a forthcoming walking race of Cardiff wooden-legged men. Prizes included a silver cup and a peg-leg. 1903 saw a sudden craze in such walking, as all kinds of work-based groups took to the roads: licensed victuallers, accountants, gas stokers, coal merchants, dockers, and 'lady assistants' at the Park Hotel, Cardiff.[11]

Nineteenth century pedestrianism had a dark counterpart in the harsh prison regime of the time. In around 1818 William Cubitt, an East Anglian engineer, devised a treadmill as a form of hard labour for prisoners. It took the form of a large iron wheel with wooden steps arranged around the outside. Several inmates at a time would step in unison to turn the wheel for a set period. The wheel might be used to grind corn, pump water, saw timber, or simply rotate freely for no other purpose than to cause fatigue and pain. By 1824 treadmills were in use in over fifty prisons in England and Wales. An example survives in Beaumaris Gaol, built in 1829. Housed in a lean-to shelter, it consists of twenty-four steps attached to a large cylinder. Prisoners 'walked' in teams of two, each spending ten minutes on the wheel before yielding to the other. Each was divided from his neighbour by a wooden partition. In a ten-hour day the two men together would climb 23,000 feet. Their labour wasn't entirely pointless. The mill was used to pump water from a well beneath to a cistern at the top of the building, which provided cells with sanitation (a rare amenity in gaols of the time). The monotony, injury and exhaustion suffered by prisoners on this machine will have far exceeded the experiences of those 'working out' on treadmills in modern gyms, the new industrialised factories of muscle.[12]

Processions

By the second half of the nineteenth century 'respectability' was a dominant value in society. Individual conduct, from dress and speech to how people interacted, became subject to widely-accepted norms. Collective behaviour was similarly regulated. Tensions between different social groups were played out more peaceably than in the past, and the growth of civil society – voluntary associations, friendly societies, chapels, schools, libraries, sporting bodies and many others – tended to smooth out the divisions and antagonisms that followed rapid industrialisation, urbanisation and migration.

Collective walking, too, became 'respectable'. From the 1840s, uncontrolled, often violent marches and demonstrations began to give way to that quintessentially Victorian form of outdoor communal expression, the procession. 'Such walking', wrote Rebecca Solnit, 'is a bodily demonstration of political or cultural conviction and one of the most universally available forms of public expression.' It could be described as marching, she adds, though participants don't, like soldiers, merge their individuality in obedience to authority.

Processions were events licensed by the authorities and moved in an orderly way through the streets of a town, usually watched by crowds. But they varied a great deal according to who organised them and why.[13]

In 1839 the streets of Newport had been filled with angry workers wielding weapons. The Rising was suppressed, but at the expense of many deaths and bitter social divisions. In October 1842 the élite of the town designed a very different street event. Ostensibly it was intended to celebrate the opening of the new Newport Dock, which they hoped would transform the town's ability to act as a major exporting port. But the organisers also wished to show that Newport and its hinterland had rejected violent workers' rebellion in favour of a new social contract based on economic growth and prosperity. They also wanted to co-opt other parts of society into sharing their vision of social cohesion.

Local newspapers carried detailed descriptions of the Dock opening and the procession that accompanied it. It was a Monday, and the organising committee succeeded in having the day declared a public holiday, with local shops closed. Visitors came from afar, including travellers on steamers from Bristol. The procession formed at eight o'clock in the morning at St Julian's Inn on the road to Caerleon. First came Police Superintendent Hopkins and the mace-bearer, in a carriage, over which was a banner bearing the town's arms.

Then a brass band from Bristol, the Mayor and members of the Corporation, also in a carriage, and the Dock Committee. Then, on foot, local groups and societies: Freemasons, shipwrights, the Hibernian Society, charity boys, Oddfellows, Teetotallers, and, at the rear, 'inhabitants of the town, in immense numbers, and decorous in conduct'. The Dock Committee had gone to great lengths to include all parts of the community in the procession, including the local Irish population, whose loyalty to the establishment was sometimes questioned. They were careful, however, to organise groups in strict order of social hierarchy.

Thousands of cheering people thronged the streets to watch, as the procession moved down High Street and Commercial Street towards the Dock. There a grandstand had been erected for spectators, the Dock Committee boarded a boat, and soldiers played music and fired cannons. The reporter estimated that up to 25,000 people were present, waving flags. Boats ceremoniously processed into the Dock. As the grandees, led by Sir Charles Morgan, retired for a grand meal, the crowd was entertained by boating races, and fireworks in the evening.

CEREMONY OF OPENING NEWPORT DOCK, MONMOUTHSHIRE.

Ceremony of opening of Newport Dock, 1842, from Illustrated London News, *22 October 1842*

(National Library of Wales)

At the dinner the Chairman obliquely referred to the Rising when he reminded the diners of how, in his view, 'during all the late trying events, the Army has displayed a good temper, firmness, and propriety, which entitles them to our warmest thanks. We have seen the public peace preserved without any act of oppression being committed.' Colonel James Love, who had been prominent in quelling the Newport uprising, thanked him and said, of the procession, 'I never witnessed a large assembly which conducted itself with so much decorum.'

In short, the Dock procession was an elaborate and expensive event that served to expunge the bloody memory of the Rising.

Only a few months earlier Chartists had marched through the town in support of a petition to Parliament for political reform, with banners bearing portraits of the transported 'martyrs' of the 1839 uprising.[14] Although there was no trouble, and the demonstrators were outnumbered by troops, the planners had been nervous about the behaviour of crowds attracted to the Dock event. During the dinner of the Dock opening Mr George Lawrence sang a song, which included the words, 'The peaceful flag of commerce waves triumphant now before thee ... while Oblivion, looking back, will wipe all bloody spots away.'

Large 'top-down' demonstrations of order and loyalty were arranged only occasionally. Much more frequent were smaller processions organised by many of the individual friendly societies and mutual-aid groups, like the Oddfellows, Ivorites, Foresters and Ancient Druids. Though their origins lay within the middle classes, their membership tended to cross class divides, and included unskilled as well as skilled workers. Each group was keen to make a visual and aural impact on their societies by organised walking through the streets. Members, mostly male, wore distinctive, sometimes exotic or theatrical dress. The Foresters dressed in green as Robin Hood and his merry men, and the Druids spent their money, according to one critic, on 'robes, velvet caps, and long flowing white beards.' Starting often from club rooms in local pubs, they walked with banners and were accompanied by brass bands, or, in the case of the Ancient Druids, harps, before finishing with a meal in the club room.

The presence of friendly societies on the streets sometimes excited suspicion, for example, that they provided a disguise for trade union agitation, or appropriated ritual elements of organised religion, or enjoyed themselves too much. But society members felt keenly the importance of being seen publicly, and having spectators to watch them. Their symbolic occupation of public space was a way of asserting their legitimacy as respectable elements of civil society. They were proud that their marching was self-regulated; there was rarely a need for a police presence. And although they had their own internal hierarchies, reflected in how their processions were arranged, they were far more democratic than the wider society they were part of.

Religious organisations, especially nonconformist chapels, also organised street events, sometimes by denomination, sometimes jointly. Their processions were timed to coincide with religious festivals, like Easter, Whitsun and Christmas. From the early nineteenth century well into the second half of the twentieth century Whitsun was the occasion for town processions organised by chapels, featuring banners, hymn-singing, tea parties, sports and games in open spaces, and excursions. In 1936 the novelist Gwyn Jones recreated a Whit Monday procession in his fictional 'Jenkinstown':

The Procession was timed to start from the open space opposite the Hearts of Oak at exactly one-thirty of the clock. The Wesleyans, who this year headed the Sunday Schools, would set off as near that time as proved possible, and be immediately followed by the Baptists. They then turned to the left down the main street ... and a short way down the incline were supported by the Congs, from the tin Congregational Chapel. At the New Bridge would advance the forces of Salem and Moriah, headed by a silver band ... At this point they would be reinforced by the strictly marshalled Salvation Army, rich in captains of the guard, and only recently admitted to the higher company they were now to enjoy.[15]

Often the aim of Whitsun festivities was to attract public attention away from fairs – Whit Monday fairs were common – and other secular counter-attractions, and, later in the nineteenth century, to add weight to the campaign for disestablishment of the Church of England by showing what numbers they could muster. For both churches and chapels Sunday School processions were important as 'nurseries of faith', demonstrating that the next generation of worshippers was being prepared. Respectability was as important to chapels as for other groups, although the Salvation Army was unafraid to court controversy and sometimes confrontation when taking its aggressively proselytising message to the streets.

Most of these groups 'laying claim to the streets' wanted to make a public assertion of their rightful role in Victorian society, but their prime intention was not to challenge that society. Other groups emerged, however, who aimed precisely to press for major social change. For them walking the streets was an important weapon in their struggle. One of first was the temperance movement, which campaigned to reduce, and sometimes prohibit, the consumption of alcohol.

Street procession in Neath, by an anonymous photographer, 1905
(*National Library of Wales*)

From the 1830s temperance societies organised themselves, especially in industrial areas, to counter what they saw as the damaging effects of alcohol on individuals and society. Some of their members aimed for moderation in drinking, while others aimed for complete abstinence or prohibition. Societies had enough resources to build Temperance Halls to hold their meetings in and act as alternative cultural centres to public houses. They received much of their support from churches and chapels, and they benefited from the enthusiasm generated by periodic religious revivals.

Temperance processions were vivid and loud, and could transform a town into a 'theatre of social action', in Lewis Mumford's phrase. Music, including brass bands and the singing of hymns, was common, and elaborate theatrical tableaux were devised, to entertain spectators and ensure the anti-drink message was not lost:

> On Thursday [6 September 1866] an interesting anniversary demonstration was made by the Cardiff Sons of Temperance. A procession mustered at the docks, many features of which were strikingly and ingeniously illustrative of the objects of the association. After the band came a vehicle, which had been fitted up as a wretched-looking apartment, representing the home of the drunkard. In the wagon was a stalwart-looking man, ragged, with a pipe in his mouth, holding in his hand a bottle, with which he indulged himself in smashing a quantity of crockery which had been placed on an old ricketty table... Then followed the reverse side of the picture, viz., a car adorned with evergreens and flowers, and a well-dressed mechanic, his wife and family, all taking tea together in a room comfortably furnished on the platform of the car.[16]

Teetotal campaigners targeted bars and public houses and tried to persuade employers to support them. Sometimes, as in Neath in 1859, their processions provoked counter-demonstrations by those who failed to share their views. The cause became a political movement, which culminated in 1881 in the passage of the Sunday Closing

(Wales) Act, the first statute in modern times to affect Wales alone. A Grand Temperance Demonstration at Swansea in 1882, organised to celebrate the Act, attracted, it was claimed, over 20,000 people. Street processions remained an important way of winning new supporters, and of demonstrating strength in numbers.

Coal and slate miners

If the temperance movement had the potential to make enemies by trying to overturn long-established assumptions about the place of drink in Victorian society, other movements emerging towards the end of the century provided a more direct challenge to structures of power. The trade union and labour movement, which grew rapidly in Wales from the 1880s, understood well the value of occupying the streets. Marching through them in large numbers became an important means of demonstrating unions' own social and economic power, and of protesting against injustices, in direct opposition to the interests of the owners of industry and their supporters. The south Wales coalfield, now one of the largest in the world, was the main focus of street protests by workers.

As the demand for coal increased, the numbers employed in the coal industry exploded. In 1851 only 951 people lived in the Rhondda valleys; by 1891 their population had risen to 88,351, and by 1911 to 152,781. Workers were attracted from rural areas of Wales, and later the west of England, by higher wages. Coal mining, however, was one of the most dangerous and physically demanding of all jobs. It could also mean a great deal of walking. The day's work began early, with the walk to the pit. Bert Coombes, who migrated from rural Herefordshire in 1910 to work as a miner in the Vale of Neath, recalled his first day of work, aged 17, in a mine at Resolfen:

> John was waiting for me near the colliery screens at ten o'clock. I was silent, and on edge for what the night would teach me. We climbed uphill between a double set of narrow rails, and the

woods shut us in on either side. It took us half an hour of steady climbing before we halted on top of a grey pile that was the rubbish-tip and we could look back on the lights in the village below.[17]

After that there was the walk to the coalface. This could add more miles, in dark, wet and dangerous conditions:

As soon as we entered under the mountain I was aware of the damp atmosphere. Black, oily water was flowing continually along the roadway and out to the tip. It was up to the height of a man's knees, and to avoid it we had to balance carefully and walk along the narrow rails. I slipped several times, and then tried crouching up on the side and swinging myself along by the timber that was placed upright on either side.[18]

When Coombes later moved to another pit, the walk to work meant climbing for three miles up a mountain, along lanes, across streams and through rough grassland and bogs; even in summer coats and leggings were needed, otherwise just five minutes of driving rain would drench a man to the skin.

Earlier, in the mid-nineteenth century, children were employed in mines. They too were expected to walk underground, in the most difficult of conditions. Watcyn Wyn, who later became a teacher and poet, first started working in a coal mine in the Amman valley in the early 1850s at the age of eight. His job was to move the carts of coal for transport to the surface:

Underground again, to cart for the 'Bwli bach', and I can say the work was hard enough. I got eight pence a day as pay, and I had to work hard to earn it … How we boys chattered about carting. How hard it was to get a light, easy cart – a tidy little cart! How pleased we were to find headroom, to avoid hitting our backs on the roof, and losing our skin and getting a scar … How many fingers were wounded, how many knees injured, how many backs broken, how many tears, how much sweat and blood were lost with the carts.[19]

Ben Davies, later a nonconformist minister, recalled working underground in the 1870s. He worked a twelve hour shift every day, except on Saturday afternoon and Sunday, and his pay was a shilling a day. 'It was a strange prison to a boy of the hills', he recalled. Once at his post, standing in the darkness, he'd often see nobody for hours:

> Within a month of being twelve years old, I had to face the colliery, like my brothers. I remember descending to the bottom of the old Cwmllynfell pit, led by William, my brother. Having arrived at the bottom of the mine, we would walk down for about a mile to the bowels of the earth.[20]

For many years relations between coal owners and workers were often managed without major conflict, but in 1898 came a decisive rift. The miners demanded an end to the 'sliding scale' system, which linked the level of wages to the selling-price of coal, and asked instead for a 10% wage increase and a basic minimum wage. The owners responded by rejecting the claims and locking the miners out, in a bitter dispute that lasted for six months.

During the lock-out and strike the miners used many methods of winning public opinion to their side and of maintaining solidarity. These included use of the press, protest meetings and rallies, often held on mountains above valleys towns, and marches. A common aim of the marches was to put pressure on 'blacklegs' who defied the strike by continuing to work.

In June at Merthyr Vale miners marched against blacklegs who refused to join them:

> A tremendous procession of strikers marched on Merthyr Vale on Tuesday night for the purpose of demonstrating against

persons who are alleged to be engaged in cutting coal at Messrs. Nixon's colliery. The procession was made up of two sections – one being composed of the men of Dowlais, Merthyr, Abercanaid, and Troedyrhiw, and the other of the men of Treharris and Merthyr Vale... The crowd first turned into Cory-street, where they made one stoppage, and afterwards visited various houses in other streets where the men complained of lived, the long staves of the marshals being held up as a signal for every place at which to halt. The mob insisted upon every person 'spotted' coming out of the house and giving a promise to cease working, and every time the promise was given, as was done in every case, loud cheers of victory were raised.[21]

Later the same month a large crowd of miners arranged to assemble at Troed-y-rhiw. On the walk there they were prevented from marching past mines with working colliers by soldiers, who had been drafted into the area as a 'precaution'. Five hundred marchers from Treharris, led by a local headteacher and a brass band, therefore kept to the public highway, but expressed their resentment of the military presence. The march culminated in a meeting, attended by between 5,000 and 6,000 men and 'a sprinkling of women and boys', at which motions were passed calling for a single trade union, and labour representation in Parliament.[22]

One of the 'martyrs' of the long dispute was the veteran trade union agent David Morgan ('Dai o'r Nant'), who was imprisoned for alleged intimidation of working miners at a strike at Abernant in 1896. A policemen joined the march of strikers to the pit and

... asked Morgan what was the meaning of the procession. Morgan said the men were simply taking a walk. The constable said it was rather an odd thing to take a walk at that time of day. Just as the men were leaving the pit the men went on to Ynysceinon House, which commands a view of the pit, and as the men were leaving the demonstrators set up a great booing. The result was that some of the men were frightened, and instead of going the ordinary way to their houses they went another way through a wood, with the result that it became unnecessary for David Morgan and his friends to go any further, for the frightening they had given the men had the desired effect, and after that no men went to work.[23]

By the end of August 1898, the miners, demoralised and physically weakened, were comprehensively defeated. They returned to work under conditions imposed by the owners. But the experience convinced them that they needed a strong trade union, and by October they'd established the South Wales Miners' Federation, which affiliated to the Miners' Federation of Great Britain in January 1899. By the end of that year, over 104,000 miners belonged to the 'Fed'. In 1903 it succeeded in having the hated 'sliding scale' abolished.

During the lock-out the miners had been supported by James Keir Hardie, already well-known as a miners' leader and founder of the Independent Labour Party. In June 1898 he spent two months in the coalfield, visiting several valleys and addressing fifteen meetings, in what he later called 'the best holiday I ever had'. A special correspondent for the newspaper *Tarian y Gweithiwr* gave a vivid and sympathetic eye-witness description of the procession, starting from Dowlais, that preceded Keir Hardie's speech at Troed-y-rhiw on 25 June:

About six o'clock I heard the sound of a brass band approaching, and by the time it reached High Street I recognised it as the Abercanaid band – and how they couldn't half play! Following it was a crowd of every kind of worker from Dowlais, Penydarren, etc., but I think most of them were miners, and they walked in an orderly way, with the Dowlais Fife Band behind. I joined them, and I was told that the men of Merthyr Vale, Treharris, etc, were coming up to meet them in the field near Cross Yew Street, Troedyrhiw, where it was intended to hold the meeting in the open air. By the time it came to the bottom of the town the march had grown large, and the spectators were doing their best to keep the boys and children out of the columns, a difficult task considering what enthusiasm took hold of them as they heard the band playing so brightly.[24]

After the strike, support grew quickly for Keir Hardie's Independent Labour Party, as a political expression of workers' aspirations. In 1900 he was well enough respected to be elected in Merthyr Tydfil as the first MP of the Labour Representation Committee, renamed the Labour Party in 1906.[25]

Coalminers were not the only workers to become involved in bitter battles with employers in this period, or to use marching as a weapon. In 1885 slate miners were locked out of the Dinorwig quarry near Llanberis after a dispute. On 15 December strikers gathered on the quarry road, some armed with sticks, to dissuade strike-breakers. The Llanrug brass band marched into the quarry at the same time. The strikers joined the band, and were followed by women and children. When they arrived at the quarry office they found themselves face to face with the two quarry managers, Vivian and Davies. They gave the two men ten minutes to leave, 'or take the consequences.' Vivian and Davies fled, amid screams and hoots of derision from the crowd. The strikers cleared away the remaining working miners, leaving the quarry deserted, and walked home. This comic victory, however, could not avert eventual defeat for the strike.[26]

The same result followed 'Y Streic Fawr', the Penrhyn lock-out of 1900, a dispute that dragged on for three years. Some of the strikers' tactics, like threats and violence towards individuals, pre-dated the age of 'respectable trade unionism', but boycotts were a common weapon, and so was marching, as strikers tried to deter their fellow-slate workers, 'cynffonau' (flatterers, or tails) from breaking the strike. During 1901 they held many demonstrations and marches through the streets of Bethesda. These often culminated in mass meetings. Keir Hardie was one of the speakers on 3 August after a large procession had walked peacefully past a force of foot soldiers and dragoons. The aim of marches was to solidify support among and for the strikers, and to show the strength and depth of their

Unemployed miners marching along Richard St., Cilfynydd, during the
Cambrian Colliery dispute of 1910-11, by an anonymous photographer
(Pontypridd Museum)

determination. Women joined the ranks of the men, a sign that the whole community aimed to unite behind the strike. Marchers would pause outside the houses of known blacklegs and hoot and hiss their disapproval. In August 1901 the authorities became nervous of these events and sent troops to keep order in Bethesda.

In the early years of the twentieth century, as workers became more organised and assertive and as disputes with employers became more frequent and more combative, the 'respectable procession' model of demonstration and protest lost ground. Less controlled, sometimes violent confrontation took its place, as at Tonypandy in 1910 and Llanelli in 1911.

Women's suffrage

Victorian and Edwardian Wales was a masculine culture, and 'processional culture' was usually a reserve of men. But there was an important exception, a campaign that aimed to overthrow part of that male dominance. In the Welsh women's suffrage movement, which gathered pace from 1906, petitions, printed propaganda and meetings were crucial methods in its campaign to win the vote for women, but organising marches and processions was also a common tactic. This was true both of the 'constitutional' campaigners like the National Union of Women's Suffrage Societies (NUWSS) and those prepared to break the law, like the Women's Social and Political Union (WSPU), set up by Emmeline and Christabel Pankhurst.

Members of the WSPU, 'the shriekers, the raiders and the martyrs'[27] of the suffrage movement, realised from their start, in 1903, that protesting, marching on Parliament, heckling, breaking up meetings, smashing windows, arson, being imprisoned and other forms of agitation gave them a public prominence much greater than their numbers suggested. They also held frequent meetings and outdoor demonstrations. 365 women travelled by train from south Wales to London in June 1908 to join a WSPU-inspired procession to Hyde Park, attended by up to half a million people and described by one newspaper as 'a demonstration unparalleled in the history of British politics.'[28] They sang Welsh hymns, and carried banners and Welsh dragons on poles.

In Bethesda in September 1909 the Women's Freedom League (WFL), a group that had broken away from the WSPU, organised a large procession and public meeting, which, unusually, did not provoke opposition:

Hundreds of men and women crowded the streets, waiting in the rain, with an eager tensity that made one tingle. Up went our banner, and, followed by a cheering multitude, we wended our way to the hillside field, where, on a natural platform, we took our stand. There as we stood the public streamed and streamed until over 2,000 stood around us in a silence that could be felt.[29]

The WFL were ingenious in their campaigning methods. In Tenby in 1909 they hired a bathing machine to preach their message. In the following year, members paraded the streets in Swansea, one of their Welsh strongholds, to advertise their meetings:

Swansea rubbed its eyes in the morning to see a dozen well-dressed women, in brilliant sunshine, walking in the road with umbrellas up and wearing the regalia of the League. The *raison d'être* of the umbrellas became apparent as each passed when huge bills announcing the forthcoming Albert Hall meeting in Swansea were seen pinned to the outside.[30]

Taking part in the suffrage campaign enabled many women to discover in themselves capacities they were unaware they possessed. Elsie McKenzie, the WSPU's organiser in Cardiff, wrote to a friend in 1909, 'I do not know what is happening to me. I seem to be changed into somebody else. I never thought I could write articles, confound politics on a public platform, etc.'[31] The militancy of the WSPU and the WFL, often in the face of official and public hostility, elevated suffrage to being one of the leading public issues of the day. Without it the NUWSS, the constitutional wing of the movement, would not have flourished as it did.

The NUWSS concentrated on trying to influence Parliament through private members' bills and election campaigns, and on building local support through meetings and other activities. After 1910 its branches proliferated in Wales, with enough members to form a Welsh stream of walkers in the 'Great Pilgrimage' of summer 1913. A group of women started from Cricieth in July, rested around the Reformers' Tree in Bangor, gathered more marchers along the north Wales coast, and joined an English stream of 'pilgrims' at Chester for the onward march to London. Margaret Elias gave a lyrical report of the trip:

I wish I could bring before you some of the vivid scenes that lie splashed across my memory – the long procession winding slowly down the hill to Colwyn Bay with bristling pennants and banners blazing in the sun, and every window a flutter with handkerchiefs – the vast changing sea of faces on the sands at Rhyl, the silent listening group under the castle walls at Conway, and every morning the beauty of sea and hills, and the insistent call of the long white road between them.[32]

Women's suffrage pilgrimage in Cathays Park, Cardiff, 1913, by an anonymous photographer

(*Amgueddfa Cymru – National Museum Wales*)

The procession paused frequently to hold meetings. One, at Rhyl, attracted 4,000 people, 'but the crowd was greatly annoyed by the disturbances of hooligans hired by a local Anti-Suffragist.' At Llandulais the women held an impromptu meeting for 200 quarrymen who came to join them.

South Wales tributary pilgrimages converged on Cardiff before moving on to Newport and London, where 70,000 people gathered in Hyde Park. The word 'pilgrimage', with its echoes of sacred searching, was well chosen. For opinion formers it distinguished the peaceable protesters of the NUWSS from the lawless suffragettes. A Barry newspaper editor wrote:

> The women who have tramped the roads have not beguiled the time with stories of love and adventure as Chaucer's famous pilgrims did. They have carried banners, distributed literature, and made speeches, all with the object of demanding the vote,

enforcing their orderly methods of expressing that demand, and enlisting support.[33]

When the Great War began in August 1914 most of the suffrage groups placed patriotism before emancipation, and ceased their activities, but the WFL, pacificist in outlook, continued its campaigning. In December 1914 members of its active Swansea branch 'paraded the streets with a brilliantly decorated box organ' to advertise a talk by Nina Boyle on 'men, women and the war'.[34]

Women fighting for the suffrage faced fierce and powerful opposition. They didn't achieve even a limited franchise until 1918, and parity of voting with men took another decade. But ultimately the anti-suffrage campaign was futile. And by 1914 the suffragettes and suffragists alike had established as an accepted fact that women could combine in processions, march through the streets together, and demonstrate and organise publicly in support of a common cause. Welsh women would never again be dissuaded from collective action by such objections as 'Oh! Ye restless agitators for women's rights, do not try to subvert the order which your wise creator has long ago settled for the best.'[35]

Public parks and public footpaths

Demonstrators, protesters and campaigners claimed possession of streets and other open spaces for short periods of time only. But as more and more people lived in often dense urban areas, they found it ever harder to gain access to public spaces they could use daily for walking and recreation. They lacked the ready access that the upper- and upper-middle classes had long enjoyed to spaces for walking: the private parades, promenades and terraces that surrounded their homes. In England the Commons Preservation Society was set up in 1865 by leading Liberals, as well as the radical William Morris, with the aim of preventing the loss of commons and other public lands, and ensuring that ordinary people could take advantage of them.

It may have been the Commons Preservation Society that was in the mind of William Thomas, when he made a powerful speech in Swansea on 9 July 1874. He argued passionately for the importance of parks as spaces where working people and their families could rest and exercise after a week of relentless industrial labour. Known as 'Thomas of Lan', he was one of a new breed of elected councillors in Swansea, eager to use political power to improve the conditions of ordinary people, in a town that had seen large increases in population without a parallel growth of public amenities. He was particularly anxious about working-class parts of Swansea, where parks were absent. He later recalled of Morriston, 'the children there had no more playground than there was under the school; they had nowhere to go except the street to play and the gutter (which was a sewer).'

The speech was a turning point in Thomas's life. 'From that hour to the present', a writer recalled in 1896, 'the subject has been the nearest of all things to Mr Thomas's heart; and the public parks and playgrounds in various parts of Swansea stand as an everlasting monument to the full and complete success of his life's best humanitarian purpose.' Luckily, the Public Health Act of 1875 allowed local authorities to buy or lease space to be used for 'public walks or pleasure grounds', and Thomas began to approach local landowners for help. One of them, John Dillwyn Llewelyn of Penllergare, responded by donating a 42-acre farm above Morriston, and money to convert it into a public space. It was opened to the public as Llewelyn Park in 1878, when Thomas was mayor of Swansea. At the opening ceremony Llewelyn's son emphasised the democratic nature of the new space: 'the park was the people's own, and in using it they need ask the kind permission of no one'.[36]

Several other parks and playgrounds were opened in densely populated parts of the town in the following years, though never as many as Thomas wanted: in 1906 he lamented that 'they had still only 100 acres in the town – 100 acres for 100,000 people, a mere flea bite.'[37]

Swansea wasn't alone. Many other Welsh towns acquired public parks from the 1860s.[38] By the First World War most towns enjoyed some form of space open to the public for walking and relaxation.

William Thomas of Lan, statue in Victoria Park, Swansea 1906
(photo Andrew Green)

Other parks and walking routes were designed with tourists in mind. They tended to spare pedestrians long distances and over-steep gradients, but rewarded them with fine views over sea, estuary or mountain. Examples were the Panorama Walk at Barmouth and the Precipice Walk near Dolgellau, both laid out in late Victorian times.[39] The most developed by far was Constitution Hill in Aberystwyth. In 1895 the Aberystwyth Improvement Company constructed numerous walks and gardens on the slopes of the much-quarried hill, lighting them on summer nights with Japanese lanterns. Non-pedestrians could ascend via a cliff railway, operated by water balance technology. At the summit they'd find pavilions, kiosks, refreshment rooms, a bandstand, a camera obscura, a hall and free reading room, and 'a charming greensward for roamage'. Firework displays, concerts and other amusements entertained visitors. But 'Luna Park' didn't last long. The railway survived, but the other attractions fell victim to several summers of disappointing weather. Aberystwyth failed to develop into what a railway poster advertised as 'The Biarritz of Wales'.[40]

More mundane walking routes were beginning to receive

attention during the same period, as ancient footpaths and the public right to use them came under increasing pressure from landowners and developers. The National Footpath Preservation Society was established in 1884, with the aim of preserving 'ancient foot and bridle paths, and all other public rights of way', and occasionally intervened in cases in Wales where footpaths were under threat. Local footpath associations were formed to maintain and defend established paths. In 1864 an association was formed 'for the protection of public footpaths in Wrexham and the neighbourhood'. A Cardiff society was busy from 1888, protesting against the blocking of footpaths, and from 1890 the energetic Aberystwyth Footpaths Association was active in arranging signposts for paths and a map of them, erecting seats, reopening closed paths, and investigating legal rights.

In 1888 the fiery Liberal MP for Merioneth, Thomas Edward Ellis, a proponent of land reform and no friend of large landlords, introduced his private member's bill, the Mountains, Rivers and Pathways (Wales) Bill, to the House of Commons. It contained truly radical proposals, which would have enlarged public access to the countryside of Wales to an extent not yet achieved even today. Ellis wished to give the public the right, 'for the purposes of recreation, or whinberry gathering, or scientific research', to move freely, not only over mountains, moor and wasteland, but also on the banks and beds of rivers, streams and lakes. If footpaths had been used for five successive years during the last half-century, he suggested, they should become rights of way.

A writer in the north Wales press welcomed the Bill's ambition 'to release the greedy landlord's grip', so that 'men and women in Wales may breathe the Welsh mountain air without optical darts in nervous quest of the obsequious keeper and steward'. Ellis probably knew that his Bill would meet with fierce opposition, and would not have been surprised when it failed to advance beyond a Second Reading.[41]

The period before the Great War, it could be argued, was the golden age of walking in Wales, before the motor car took permanent and near-exclusive possession of the road and reduced the pedestrian to the margins of physical and mental space, and before the War's slaughter cast a long shadow on the lives of those who experienced it. It was the last time that walkers were free enough to wander the highways with safety, and to ramble across open country without fear of persecution by landlords.

O.M. Edwards

A Welshman for whom walking was essential to his way of thinking and writing about his country was the scholar, educationalist and writer Owen M. Edwards. His walking book *Cartrefi Cymru* (Homes of Wales), published in 1896, quickly became a classic, selling almost 20,000 copies before his death in 1920.

By 1896 Edwards was well known to Welsh speakers as an editor and popular writer. Six years earlier he'd founded the influential magazine *Cymru*, and himself contributed much of its content. Together with its sister magazine for children, *Cymru'r Plant*, it helped shape a new generation of those who cared for the future of Wales and especially the Welsh language and its use in education. All but one of the chapters in *Cartrefi Cymru* were reprinted from articles Edwards had written for the pages of *Cymru*. He used the collection, which he dedicated to the parents and children of Wales, to construct a coherent, positive picture of his country that would give him, and them, inspiration and hope.

Each chapter takes the form of a personal journey to the home, and usually the grave, of a man or woman Edwards regards as of emblematic significance to Wales. Of the eleven figures he chooses, two are poets, two prose-writers, three preachers and two hymn-writers, while one is a saint and another a religious martyr (there are no aristocrats, soldiers or politicians). Almost always Edwards travels slowly, by foot, spending as much time on the journey as on his destination. He himself uses the word 'pilgrimage':

Perhaps I have stirred the desire in you, through the pages of this book, to go on pilgrimage to some of the homes of Wales, or to wander over the dear mountains of our country? Does the land of our fathers seem a little more like holy ground to some of you now that you have read my words? ... There are homes scattered everywhere, and in them children, full of life and hope, like the heroes who lived in them before; is it not a good thing to show children the direction taken by those who walked out from those homes before them?[42]

The first of Edwards's walks takes him to the grave and home of the eighteenth-century hymn-writer Ann Griffiths. He frames the journey carefully. In the inn at Llanfihangel-yng-Ngwynfa in Montgomeryshire, he rests after the day's exertions. While he waits for the weather to clear he tells us the events of the day.

Dolwar Fechan, engraving from O.M. Edwards, Cartrefi Cymru, 1896
(*National Library of Wales*)

His walk had started from Llanfyllin, amid scents from shrubs and trees. He passes a small chapel nestling by the river, asks a stonemason the way, spots carts on their way to the new reservoir dam at Llanwddyn, and meets a man waiting for his son to return from England. Ann Griffiths is little remembered in these parts, says the man, and her hymns are seldom sung. In the churchyard at Llanfihangel a man cutting grass points out Ann's grave. A group of village children gathers around him. He asks them what is the current price of good, healthy children like them. They flee in mock horror, and he's left alone to contemplate the grave.

Next Edwards walks towards Ann's home, Dolwar Fechan. On one side of the road are rocks, on the other steep green fields. A clear stream murmurs, shadowed by birch and hazel trees, and a redshank peers into one of its pools.

> I paid attention to everything, because I knew that Ann Griffiths had walked this path thousands of times. I knew that it was gazing at some stream or mountain that set off her singing, and then her mind flew far away towards things that last for ever.[43]

Further along, amid the heat of the day, Dolwar Fechan comes into view in the distance. At the brow of a hill, Edwards catches a view of the far, green mountains, 'like the dream of a young man'. An old woman comes out of the house to welcome him, and offers him food after his eight-mile walk. He refuses but accepts a glass of milk and meets the lodger, a teacher who admits how difficult it is for the children to learn Welsh since he's an Englishman who does not know the language. He's never heard of Ann Griffiths.

This opening chapter is typical of *Cartrefi Cymru*, where the walk narrative mixes comfortably with biography, nature writing, literary anthology and cultural sermon. Its style is informal but polished, the first-person narrative inviting the reader to match the writer's leisurely stride. Edwards travels incognito, and none of the people he meets would know him as the Oxford don he was. He's clearly aware of George Borrow's similarly hybrid style and withheld identity in *Wild Wales*.

The scene by the riverbank and the view of distant mountains reflect Edwards's intense, almost sacred feeling for the upland landscapes of Wales, inseparable from his belief in the special character of their inhabitants, *gwerin Cymru*, the common people of Wales. These rural cottagers keep alive the ancient tradition of simplicity of life and of hospitality to the stranger, symbolised by the near-sacred gift of fresh milk.

Central to Edwards's ideal of Welsh life, itself moulded by the experience of his own childhood near Llanuwchllyn, were a rootedness in the rural landscape of north Wales, a serious and moral nonconformity, liberalism and anti-landlordism in politics, a cultural nationalism informed by a common awareness of Welsh history and literature, and, above all, a lived commitment to the Welsh language. The comparative poverty of the material lives of Edwards's people, he felt, was compensated for by spiritual, cultural and educational riches, as he shows in his story about the preacher Robert Thomas ('Ap Fychan'), who overcame childhood destitution with the help of a cultured father and generous minister. Edwards's purpose in *Cartrefi Cymru* is to strengthen and revive this complex of ideals for his own time, and in the future.

But there's a problem. The Wales Edwards is walking through often fails to live up to the model he felt should exist. He's dismayed by the lack of knowledge among local people about Ann Griffiths, and encounters similar ignorance of the achievements of some of his other heroes. How will the Welsh language be transmitted through education when teachers lack the language? *Cartrefi Cymru* is full of anxiety about language: a monoglot English policemen is unable to speak to local people; a girl knows current English songs, but none in Welsh; a carriage-driver in Haverfordwest is ignorant of Welsh culture and dismissive of Welsh-speakers. Language is not the only loss. When he visits Llandovery, Edwards is shocked by the dilapidation of the town, and its depopulation.

All the same, Edwards never tires of urging Welsh people to preserve their culture and language, and put them to use. In 1907 he was appointed as the first Chief Inspector of Schools for Wales, and began to have a practical impact on how Welsh was taught.

It's easy to criticise Edwards's view of Wales as exclusionary and backward-looking. His modernism is selective, and he shuns industrial Wales, as ugly, Anglicised and a threat to the traditional Welsh-speaking culture he loves.

Today the more didactic and patriotic aspects of *Cartrefi Cymru* hold less interest than what Edwards's small pilgrimages tells us about his own experience and perceptions. At the time of writing the pieces he was an unhappy man, overworked and prone to depression. Despite the disappointments he encounters, he uses his walking journeys as a way of finding personal tranquillity, through his precise appreciation of the natural world and his weaving together of landscape, literature, history and social observation to create a coherent, diachronous vision of his country. For years he'd lived an exile's life, as an academic in Oxford. Re-exploring the rural Wales of his youth returned him to a world he knew was his own.

For Edwards walking was crucial to this process of rediscovery, a slow, meditative way of approaching his heroes and their homes that gradually uncovered the landscape, the people and the history that gave meaning to them. Here he is in Ardudwy, searching for the home of the seventeenth-century writer Edmwnd Prys, and reviving his childhood love of mountains:

> I have never been so happy in walking any path as when I walked the Roman road in Ardudwy. The breeze was refreshing and mild, the murmur of the streams sweet-sounding, the flowers overflowed with life, and the intense silence of the mountains revived me. The water was so crystal, the colours so fiery, and the weather so sunny that I could hardly believe I was in Wales.[44]

Robert Graves

Visitors to Wales couldn't hope to match Edwards's insider understanding of 'deep Wales' or to be alert to the cultural resonance of specific places. Few would even have heard of any of his chosen heroes and heroines. In Carmarthenshire he's dismissive of the

English gentleman tourists he meets, who prefer to visit the cave of the semi-mythical Twm Siôn Cati than join him in searching for the home of William Williams Pantycelyn.

For two later writers from England, Robert Graves and Edward Thomas, the roads and hills of Wales proved an irresistible magnet – and an idyllic interlude before they were enveloped in the Great War, in which one was badly wounded and the other killed.

In 1898, when Robert Graves was three years old, his mother, Amy found a plot of land just outside Harlech when out blackberrying, and on it built a house, Plas Erinfa, overlooking the Irish sea.[45] From that year until 1914 Robert would always look forward to travelling with his family from their home in London to spend the summer there. Graves's father, Alfred Perceval Graves, was an Irish educationalist, poet and folklorist who had a strong interest in Welsh culture (he was inducted to the Gorsedd in 1902 as 'Canwr Cilarne').

At Harlech the young Robert enjoyed almost complete freedom to roam. He'd often disappear after breakfast and not come home

Erinfa, Harlech
(*photo Crown Copyright: Royal Commission for the Ancient and Historical Monuments of Wales*)

until after supper time. He was drawn to the 'desolate, rocky hill-country' immediately behind the house. Thirty years later he recalled the places in Ardudwy that he and his sisters explored, in his memoir *Good-bye to all that*:

> As we grew older, we spent more and more of our time up here, and less and less on the beach and the links. There were occasional farms and crofts in these hills, but one could easily walk fifteen or twenty miles without crossing a road, or passing close to a farm. Originally we went up with some practical excuse. For the blueberries on the hills near Maes-y-garnedd; or the cranberries at Gwlawllyn; or bits of Roman hypocaust tiling (with the potter's thumb-marks still on them) in the ruined Roman villas by Castell Tomen-y-mur; or globe flower on the banks of the river Artro; or a sight of the wild goats which lived behind Rhinog Fawr, the biggest of the hills in the next range; or raspberries from the thickets near Cwmbychan Lake; or white heather from a nameless hill, away to the north of the Roman Steps.[46]

This passage is striking for its topographic precision, its naming of hills, lakes and farms – Graves had clearly absorbed over the years the Welshness of his new, joyful landscape – but immediately afterwards he renounces the particularities of place. Now he reimagines Ardudwy as a different landscape, stripped of its place-names and people, and standing outside time and culture. It becomes for him a special place of the imagination and memory, a childhood myth:

> This country (and I know no country like it) seemed to be independent of formal nature. One hardly noticed the passage of the seasons there; the wind always blew across the stunted grass, the black streams always ran cold and clear, over black stones … Winters were always mild, so that last year's bracken and last year's heather survived in a faded way through to next spring. We saw hardly any birds, bar an occasional buzzard, and curlews

wheeling in the distance; and wherever we went the rocky skeleton of the hill seemed only an inch or two beneath the turf.[47]

For Graves this abstracted version of the Harlech landscape had no room for Wales or the Welsh language or for the people who spoke it: 'we felt little temptation to learn Welsh still less to pretend ourselves Welsh, but knew that country as a quite ungeographical region'.[48]

Young Robert explored nearer to home. He overcame his fear of heights by scaling the walls and towers of Harlech castle, as Coleridge had done before him. But it was the hills that inspired Graves's earliest poems, including 'The mountain side at evening' and 'Rocky Acres'. Rocky Acres was his name for the hillside immediately behind Erinfa. The poem, whose complex alliteration possibly reflects the cynghanedd of Welsh poetry, of which Graves had some knowledge, presents not the real hills of Ardudwy but his empty, non-human, mythologised version of this beloved 'lost land':

Time has never journeyed to this lost land,
Crakeberry and heather bloom out of date,
The rocks jut, the streams flow singing on either hand,
Careless if the season be early or late,
The skies wander overhead, now blue, now slate;
Winter would be known by his cutting snow
If June did not borrow his armour also.[49]

The Harlech hill country, harsh and lonely, never lost its hold on Graves. In 1914, straight from school, he enlisted with the Royal Welch Fusiliers and saw action at the battles of Loos and the Somme, where he was badly injured and, for a time, given up for dead. Whenever he could take leave, he went back to Harlech. He was back there in April 1916, and again in August, to recuperate from his injuries. This time he was joined by his friend Siegfried Sassoon, fellow-Fusilier and another Somme-survivor. The two walked the hills, and wrote poetry together, trying out their drafts on each other and on Graves's family.

When the War ended in November 1918 Graves was on the north Wales coast, but, far from rejoicing at the victory, 'the news sent me out walking alone along the dyke above the marches at Rhuddlan (an ancient battlefield, the Flodden of Wales), cursing and sobbing and thinking of the dead'.[50] In 1919 he spent months in Harlech in a borrowed house, with his wife, Nancy Nicholson. On all these visits, and between them, the mountains retained for him the status of a lost paradise. His poem 'A letter from Wales', published in 1925, imagines that he and Sassoon both died in the War, and contains poignant echoes of his wartime wanderings with Sassoon on the hills:

> Anyhow ... We were eating blackberries
> By a wide field of tumbled boulderstones
> Hedged with oaks and nut-trees. Gradually
> A glamour spread about us, the low sun
> Making the field unreal as a stage,
> Gilding our faces with heroic light ...[51]

But there was a different, darker way of looking at the same landscape. At Harlech in 1919 Graves recognised that his mind been badly damaged. From time to time the violence of the war invaded his dreams and his waking life alike: 'shells used to come bursting on my bed at midnight ... strangers in daytime would assume the faces of friends who had been killed'. Ardudwy could also appear transformed by trauma:

> When strong enough to climb the hill behind Harlech and revisit my favourite country, I could not help seeing it as a prospective battlefield. I would find myself working out tactical problems, planning how best to hold the Upper Artro valley against an attack from the sea, of where to place a Lewis-gun if I were trying to rush Dolwreiddiog Farm from the brow of the hill, and what would be the best cover for my rifle-grenade section.[52]

Edward Thomas

Edward Thomas never had time for retrospection on the War: he was killed by a shell in the first hour of the Battle of Arras on 9 April 1917, aged 39. But he shared with Robert Graves, from an early age, a deep love of Wales. Like Graves, he explored it mainly on foot, and unlike Graves he often wrote about it.[53]

London was Edward Thomas's birthplace and early home. But his father was Welsh and his mother part-Welsh, he always thought of himself as Welsh, and from an early age he visited south Wales, to stay with relatives in Pontarddulais and Ammanford. He returned often and made close friends there, including the poet John Jenkins ('Gwili') in Ammanford and John Williams in Swansea. With their help he took long walks in the countryside. At Oxford University his tutor was Owen M. Edwards, who encouraged his love of Welsh literature (though he never mastered the Welsh language).[54]

By the time he left university Thomas was already married with a first child. To support his family he wrote for publication and money: book reviews – by 1914 he'd written over 1,900, about a million words – and a rapid stream of books and articles. In September 1904 the publisher A. and C. Black commissioned him to write the text for a book called *Beautiful Wales*, to go alongside pictures of Welsh scenes painted in watercolour by Robert Fowler. He knew parts of Wales well from previous stays, but now he decided to take a long solitary walk through the country, beginning from Ammanford. He made a start, reporting to a friend,

> My walk in the mountains of Carmarthenshire and Cardigan was splendid. It rained all the time as I walked through the wildest and yet most hospitable country I can imagine. The people and the land were adorable.[55]

But after three days and sixty miles his feet became badly blistered. He had to abort the walk, and never reached north Wales. This proved unfortunate, since almost all of Fowler's illustrations were of locations in the north. After the walk Thomas spent time on desk research, and wrote fifty pages of notes, but abandoned them, despairing of a historical basis for his book. But he completed the text and sent it to the publisher in March 1905. He was disappointed by what he'd produced: 'nearly all of it without humanity except what it may owe to a lanky shadow of myself – I stretch over big landscapes just as my shadow does at dawn.'

Many readers of *Beautiful Wales*, when it was published, may also have been disappointed. It's no guidebook, or historical summary, or personal journey through Wales. Very few places or people are named: one review of another of his topographical works complains that he 'localises virtually nothing' and 'individualises as seldom'. Instead, he presents an impressionistic series of stitched-together essays, short of detail about places or people, and wholly unconnected to the pictures. In the opening paragraph of 'January' the sullen valley and the moody walker watch each other suspiciously, and only the act of 'walking fast' sustains the traveller's morale:

> The road ran for ten miles between mountains on which woods of oak and fir moaned, though there was little wind. A raven croaked with a fat voice. I could hear a score of streams. But the valley would not speak with me. The sole joy in it was that of walking fast and of seeing the summits of the hills continually writing a wild legend on the cloudy sky. The road curved and let in the poor sunlight from the south-west; and there were interminable oak woods ahead, – one moan and one dull cloud.[56]

Walking performed several functions for Thomas. He enjoyed travelling alone, and welcomed the solitary hours that a long trek guaranteed him:

> I had walked for ten miles and had not seen a man. But it would be more just to ignore such measurements, since the number of milestones was unimportant; so also were the hours. For the country had given me the freedom of time.[57]

The road almost becomes a fellow-walker, a constant partner:

> We may go or stay, but the road will go up over the mountains to Llandovery, and then up again over to Tregaron. It is a silent companion always ready for us, whether it is night or day, wet or fine, whether we are calm or desperate, wet or sick.[58]

Walking, and later cycling, also offered Thomas escape: escape from Helen, his wife, and their children – family relationships were often strained and he found home life stifling – and escape from the depression, guilt and despair that plagued him throughout his adult life. Above all, for Thomas walking – the physical movement as well as the chance to observe – was closely connected with the process of writing. He developed, Lucy Newlyn has suggested, a 'pedestrian' prose style: sentences and paragraphs that combine the regular rhythm of forward movement with frequent digressions from the path.[59] Like Wordsworth he'd compose on foot, and always carried a notebook in which to jot his field notes. His account of the English walker-writer Richard Jefferies could equally describe his own practice:

> He describes a place, or more often a series of places, along the paths and roads of a day's walk at a particular season, with digressions, as memory or the need of comparison prompts him, to other seasons and places. There is no aim to exact unity and consistency of subject and treatment. He is always a walker, moving about and taking notes.[60]

Edward Thomas is usually regarded as a rural writer, but he was also one of the first walker-writers to take seriously the urban places of Wales. *Beautiful Wales* includes several far from conventionally 'beautiful' passages on industrial landscapes, familiar to him from his stays in Pontarddulais, Swansea and Ammanford. Thomas's reaction to the detritus of industry combines revulsion and admiration in equal part.

Thomas's close observation of urban landscapes ignored by most travel writers continued in June 1914, when the *English Review* published his descriptive essay 'Swansea village'. Deliberately ignoring the picturesque and bourgeois western parts of the town, he concentrated his walker's eye on 'the real Swansea', the waterside of the lower Tawe valley. It was a place crammed with factories, waste tips, and squalid and abandoned houses, where dereliction was left uncleared. But it was also 'one of the sublimest of all absolutely human landscapes'. From Townhill Thomas watched 'the furnaces in the pit of the town blazing scarlet'. Swansea was a 'a city of wondrous night', a phrase that locates Thomas directly in the tradition of the early Romantic poets.

Some town councillors were not pleased with 'Swansea village'. Members of the Library Committee met to discuss the article. Its Chairman complained that, at a time when the councillors had been spending large sums of money to 'boom Swansea' and attract visitors, Thomas was busy belittling the town. After the press picked up the story Thomas felt obliged to write to a local newspaper defending his essay.[61]

By this time Edward Thomas had begun his turn from prose to poetry, encouraged by the American poet Robert Frost. They first met in October 1913, and on long walks with Frost in the Gloucestershire countryside in the spring and summer of 1914 (Frost called it 'talks-walking') Thomas started to find his poetic voice, a voice more concentrated, direct and colloquial than that of his prose. Between December 1914 and his death he wrote nearly 150 poems. They look back to the rural landscapes of Wales and England that Thomas loved, but the Great War raging on the Continent casts a dark shadow over many of them. Roads, lanes and paths – observing them, walking them, choosing between them – are a constant theme, and often a metaphor for the uncertain journey Thomas was making towards the face of war. 'I have come a long way today' begins 'The bridge', a poem where friendships are left to the past. 'The path' runs parallel to a road, but is abandoned by the children who made it, and now leads nowhere. In 'Roads', written six months after he'd enlisted and begun military training, Thomas makes explicit the connection between roads, the war and his own imminent part in the fighting:

> Now all roads lead to France
> And heavy is the tread
> Of the living; but the dead
> Returning lightly dance ...[62]

In the short poem 'The cherry trees' (May 1916), the old road has been emptied of living walkers:

> The cherry trees bend over and are shedding
> On the old road where all that passed are dead,
> Their petals, strewing the grass as for a wedding
> This early May morn when there is none to wed.[63]

In one of his last completed poems, 'Lights out', written in November 1916, two months before he went to France, Thomas says farewell to love, despair, ambition, pleasure and trouble; sleep and walking combine as a sign for what he now sees as his likely death at Arras:

> I have come to the borders of sleep,
> The unfathomable deep
> Forest, where all must lose
> Their way, however straight
> Or winding, soon or late;
> They can not choose.[64]

The very last words Thomas wrote, found on a slip of paper with his diary on his body after his death, were 'Roads shining like river up hill after rain'.[65]

For a whole generation of young Welshmen, walking in the years 1914 to 1918 meant marching towards the battlefield. Another London Welsh poet, David Jones, looked back in 1937 to his own experiences of marching as an army private towards the horrific battle of Mametz

Wood, where he was wounded. In Part 1 of his late modernist prose-poem *In parenthesis*, he recalls the men of the 55th Battalion of the Royal Welch Fusiliers marching from Winchester to Southampton on 1 December 1915. Before dawn, 'Private Ball' and his comrades, weighed down by their heavy equipment and the bawled orders of their officers, plod miserably through the freezing rain. A delay ('the bastard's lost his way') stops the column, but gives no relief, only icy cold skin. Resuming the march brings pain: 'in brand-new overseas boots weeping blisters stick to the hard wool of grey government socks.' No cheering welcome awaited them in Southampton 'for it was late in the second year'.[66]

Many of those who marched away that day never came back. For those who did, Wales after the war would be a very different place.

Chapter 7: Miners, hikers and patriots

Cars, buses and schoolchildren

After the First World War a new, dark age dawned for walking. For most people trains had already all but eliminated long-distance walking – 1920 saw a peak in the number of passengers on Britain's extensive rail network – but it was the steady spread of motorised road transport in the nineteen twenties and thirties that began to make foot travel for all but short journeys a near-obsolete activity.

Only the richest people could afford to own cars before the Great War. But once factories turned to mass production, the cost of them reduced steadily, so that by the end of the 1930s many middle-class people could buy one: an Austin Seven or a Ford 8 cost £125 in 1938. Photographs and films of streets in the centres of Welsh towns in the nineteen twenties show a few cars, but ten years later there are many more. Over two million vehicles were travelling Britain's roads by the time of the Second World War.

Though car ownership in Wales was less prevalent than in England, its growth saw the same trend. By 1938 there were 76,000 privately-owned cars in Wales.

Even more important than the rise of the car was the spread of 'charabancs' and 'motor omnibuses', and of motorised vans and lorries. A network of bus routes grew up all across Wales that allowed quick and easy travel for almost everyone, and reduced the isolation of even remote rural communities. Goods transport

Aberystwyth Central Garage van at Llan-non, by an anonymous photographer
(*Ceredigion Libraries*)

was likewise revolutionised by motor vehicles: horses and carts began to disappear from roads.

Eironwy Llewellyn was brought up on her grandmother's farm in the Vale of Neath in the 1930s. She recalled the existing order of transport by cart, trap and foot being overturned by the coming of the car, and how bewitching the new technologies seemed to her family:

> Outstanding in my happy memories of those years are 'BNY750' and 'CNY616'. 'BNY750' (always referred to as this) was a shimmering, black Ford 8, complete with carrier on the back, two doors, gleaming chrome handles and bumpers, green, real leather upholstery. She revolutionised Mamgu's life, for now she could go to chapel in style, deliver milk and eggs, collect sand for the cegin floor from sand-dunes 15 miles away, even carry the occasional calf or pig, hens and ducks, all in double-quick time and come rain or shine.[1]

Advertising amplified the appeal of the new technology. A poster of 1932 bears the words 'Everywhere you go you can be sure of Shell', framing a scene of Llansteffan, based on a painting by H.E. du Plessis. It shows, beneath a summer sun, the Norman castle, estuary and shoreline street, devoid of traffic. The village, picturesque and distant from railway lines, was a shrewd choice as a destination of desire for the new car owner.

As motor traffic increased, so did pressure to improve the condition of the roads they travelled on. From 1910 income from vehicle excise duty and licences had financed a Road Fund that introduced tar and bituminous surfaces for the first time to major roads. Two years later these were classified into A and B roads, and in the 1930s many A roads were substantially upgraded.

All these changes affected walkers and walking. In towns, as motor vehicles began to dominate streets, pedestrians were increasingly elbowed on to pavements. In the country, on main roads, they were pushed on to verges and into hedges. Motor accidents were common. Even by 1930 over 7,000 people, many of them children, were killed on British roads every year (in the same year the legal limit of 20 miles per hour was lifted).

In the 1930s, and since then, the assumption that roads belonged to car drivers proved impossible to shake. John S. Dean, the chair of the Pedestrians' Association, wrote in 1947 that the private driver

> ... is most strongly influenced by the sense of ownership of his car ... It is 'his' car to do with as he pleases, and, as he often believes, it is 'his' road too, and the other road-users are merely intruders who are there at their own peril.[2]

The Pedestrians' Association, founded in 1929 to press for measures to improve road safety for walkers, achieved some limited successes, like the introduction of pedestrian crossings in 1934 and the reintroduction of speed limits. But in effect pedestrians had been banned from roads for decades to come. Early photographs show people walking boldly in the middle of streets, moving aside only for the occasional vehicle; now, they were relegated to pavements and needed to be wary at junctions. Walking on main roads in the countryside became more and more dangerous. It also became unnecessary for many people, as cars and buses proliferated, unless you were poor or destitute.

Motor vehicles began to affect how workers reached their place of work, and how children arrived at their school. Previously, walking was the normal way of getting to school. Kate Roberts paints a vivid picture of children walking to secondary school in Caernarfon in her historical novel *Traed mewn cyffion* ('Feet in chains'). Published in 1936, it recalls Roberts's own childhood in the slate-mining village of Rhosgadfan in Dyffryn Nantlle at the end of the nineteenth century.

> Owen started in the County School. There was no transport in those days, so he had to walk the four miles between home and school. He had plenty of company, lads on their way to shops and offices. They started out at exactly the same time every day, and met everyone at the crossroads. If they passed a friend's house,

they whistled as they approached, and the next moment he would be out at the gate. Owen had never known a more sociable crowd in his life. There was a certain silent understanding between them. No one spoke about it, but it was there.[3]

In the 1910s E. Llwyd Williams walked through fields to his primary school in Llandysilio, Pembrokeshire:

> To go to school we had to walk through three fields before coming to the main road from Cardigan to Narberth. ... we walked on past Pwllaca, Parc-y-brwyn and the Bîg to get to Brynconyn school ... carts and horses were the only thing then, and I knew all the horses' names, and who was sitting or standing on the cart. I knew whether I'd have a ride or not before the cart came near us.[4]

Gradually, though, for children as for adults, walking declined, so that by the twenty-first century almost no one in Wales did their daily travelling by using their own bodies for locomotion – with serious consequences for the health of individuals and the well-being of the planet.

Coal miners: depression and protest

Coalminers in south Wales had usually lived and worked in the same villages or towns where their mines were located. But during the Depression, as local mines started to be closed, many were forced to travel to find alternative jobs in surviving pits. A survey in 1936 found that an average of a third of miners used buses or trains to get to their work, travelling up to ten miles. Some, especially where unemployment was highest, had a longer journey. They might then face a lengthy underground walk, perhaps of one or two miles. Moving house to be closer to a new place of work was difficult, especially when the new job might be as uncertain as the last.[5]

After the defeat of the miners following the lock-out of 1921, men had no choice but to search for new work at more distant pits. Bert Coombes travelled up and down the Vale of Neath every day to see if work was available, but he found that hundreds of others were doing the same. When he finally found a job, his day became much longer:

> I had to get up about half-past four in the morning and be on my way before half-past five. The darkness and the wind and rain were all hindrances. I had to ride about seven miles, leave my cycle at a house, then walk nearly a mile and a half up the mountain; after that I walked some distance inside the colliery and started the real work.[6]

The opening paragraph of Gwyn Jones's novel *Times like these* recreates the moment miners finish the night shift and walk away from the colliery:

> Soon after half past five it started again – the hard, slaggy tramp of nailed boots on a well-metalled road. They came out early at the Cwm to suit the trains. No other sound is like the walk of the night shift returning from work. You hear the firm, clipped ring of the young and vigorous, the deliberate crumping of the strong colliers, the less decisive scrape and scrabble of those whose shanks are spindly under them. Hear it long enough, and you fancy you recognise the walkers.[7]

Coombes remembered the arrival of the first buses, or 'charabancs'. The first one was paraded around the village, so that the inhabitants could get used to it and see that it was safe. Charabancs were used for leisure purposes, but also to take miners to work. By the end of the 1930s men would often travel up to twenty miles using buses and trains. These commuting miners, Coombes adds, were favoured by the mine managers, because they were less likely to have time to take part in trade union activities. By contrast, union officials usually lived close by, and walked to work.

So extreme was the situation for unemployed miners and their families that some had to resort to begging, sometimes walking across the mountain to the next valley, where they were anonymous. Rhys Davies, in his 1938 novel *Jubilee blues*, introduces one such unemployed miner, who arrives at a pub. Cassie invites him in for some food:

> 'Thank you, Missus,' he said in that hollow voice, looking at her from his far-away eyes, water-grey. And told her that he had walked over the mountains since six o'clock that morning from the Aberdare valley. She understood that he had come to beg in a valley where he wasn't known. He had a wife and five children, he said, and had been out of work for six years.[8]

In times of crisis, miners and their families took to the streets together to seek help. During the lock-out of 1926 colliery bands and singing groups would walk across southern England seeking money to support soup kitchens. At home, costumed members of 'jazz bands', whose main instrument was the simple 'gazouka', paraded in strict formation through the streets of Valleys towns to collect money. There were over thirty of them in the Cynon Valley alone.[9]

The best-known form of walking in the coalfield communities of inter-war Wales was the mass demonstration by workers protesting against unemployment and cuts in unemployment pay. On many occasions, groups of miners and their wives marched in protest on the local offices of the Board of Guardians, and were often challenged by police. But activists soon understood the need to make sure that the plight of unemployed miners was felt more widely than in Wales, and that the government was put under pressure to respond. The first march from south Wales to London took place in 1927, in the wake of the failure of the General Strike. It was organised by the National Unemployed Workers' Committee Movement (NUWCM), a body set up by the Communist Party to organise and politicise out-of-work miners.

The aim of the 1927 march was to protest against the refusal of the government to give relief to unemployed miners, and against the new Unemployment Bill. Those who marched were men from the two Rhondda valleys who had been denied unemployment benefits. Collections were made locally so that each had suitable boots and clothing, and each carried a miner's lamp. The marchers began at Maerdy on 8 March and made their way down the Rhondda valleys. A surviving newsreel film shows cloth-capped miners walking through Porth. 'Thousands of miners', runs the subtitle, 'accompany their comrades the first few miles of their long march to London'.[10] They walk two abreast with banners, watched by friends and families lining the road. In Bristol, Bath and Swindon they were encouraged by local people who came out to see them. By the time they reached London the miners numbered 260, according to a police report. The next morning, the report continued, a large meeting was addressed, in the pouring rain, by the south Wales miner's leader, A.J. Cook.

The march to London had no impact on the government. Dai Lloyd Davies, an official of the Maerdy Lodge of the South Wales Miners' Federation, had marched to London in 1927. In November 1928 he wrote in a letter, 'I am very sorry to say that things continue very black in this Rhondda area, and will confess that the last was the blackest Christmas I've ever spent.'[11] Davies had been unemployed for two-thirds of the time since 1921. Two men died on the march.

Other hunger marches followed between 1928 and 1936, also organised by what by now was called the National Unemployed Workers Movement. Women as well as men marched. But they met with an equal lack of success, in part because, as Communist-inspired events, they were not supported by the Labour Party or the South Wales Miners' Federation, and because they met with hostility from the press and police in London.

Claude Stanfield, an unemployed miner from Troed-y-rhiw, Merthyr, was one of the leaders of the final hunger march from Merthyr to London in 1936. He left a vivid account of the journey – of the warm reception and hospitality shown to the marchers in the places they stayed in, of the self-discipline of the men, of the protest meetings and their brass bands and singing the Internationale, and of the alien culture of rural conservative England:

We saw Somerdale [near Bristol] out on our left, the huge Frys factory. What a different environment to our mine workers. The contrasts [in Bath] were plainly visible. Royalty, nobles etc. about 100 years ago, enjoying themselves in all vulgar ways. This year unemployed marchers sleeping there. Merthyr were chosen to lead the marchers out of this former cesspit of debauch & dissipation. Our leader said, let us leave this place cleaner at least, than the gallants of old left it ... Welsh people in Slough to meet us. Thousands lined the streets the accents were that Welsh we thought we were in Rhondda.[12]

The miners and their families, despite official indifference, refused to submit to their fate. When in 1934 the government passed a new Unemployment Act, centralising the administration of benefits, curbing local discretion in decision-making and reducing spending, they rose in protest. A wave of meetings took place from December 1934. A movement 'swept through the coalfield with something of the atmosphere of a religious revival, though with none of the hysteria, and it was an essentially outdoor phenomenon rather than an indoor one'.[13] It culminated on Sunday 3 February 1935 in what became the largest demonstration in Welsh history. Almost all parts of coalfield society supported the protests. The treatment of unemployed workers, and especially the hated 'means test', were no longer a sectional interest but a concern of everyone.

About 300,000 people took part in the 3 February events. In the Rhondda valley all road traffic came to a standstill as sixty thousand people converged on Tonypandy. 50,000 people marched through rain and wind, in a procession two and a half miles long, to Mountain Ash in the Cynon valley. In Pontypool over 20,000 people listened to a speech by Ernest Bevin, Aneurin Bevan spoke at Blackwood, and there were other events at Merthyr, Neath, Briton Ferry and Barry. As they marched down the valleys, the protesters carried banners, sang songs and were accompanied by brass bands. According to Gwyn Thomas, 'the political marches were great musical occasions ... it was the highest ratio of musician to marcher ever seen.'[14]

The *Aberdare Leader* correspondent was in the Cynon valley and noticed how diverse was the composition of the people on the streets. In addition to miners and unemployed workers there were teachers, tradesmen, council employees, printers, shop assistants, Salvation Army officers, British Legionnaires, Co-op employees, many women's organisations, representatives of churches and Sunday schools.

The reporter added that 'men, women and children wore their 'best' clothes.' This respectability was an inherited tradition from an earlier time, of 'best' dressing on Sunday or on special occasions like Whit weekend processions. In reality the marchers had so little money that they had difficulty making ends meet once their rent was paid. Surely the government must listen to the protesters' demands, 'a cry from humanity to humanity':

> When one remembers that thousands of these people, including women and children, had walked to Mountain Ash from Hirwaun, Llwydcoed, Cwmdare, Trecynon, and had to walk back again – many of them tramping sixteen miles all told in the wind and rain – one is impressed by the determination of the people in making this great protest. The Government *must* listen.[15]

Two of the marchers in the Rhondda valley that day were writers. Both were committed to the workers' cause, but were able to pause and put into words the overpowering impression of an entire community on the move, united against injustice and oppression. One was Gwyn Thomas from Cymer in the Rhondda Valley, later a novelist, playwright and journalist, but then a visitor from the Oxford University Labour Club. Looking back in 1964 he wrote:

> The world's brow was hot and we were out to fan it with banners … During the demonstrations against the Means Test and other bits of crass social legislation that put Britain in the deep-freeze during the Baldwin period, we marched almost as a way of life. We were trying to shout a little wisdom and compassion into the world's ear and the world was as deaf as a post … In 1935 some

climax of disgust brought the entire valley population on to the streets. As one watched the huge streams of protesters pouring up and down the two gulches on their way to Tonypandy, one could have sworn that the very blood of the place was on the boil.[16]

The other writer was Lewis Jones, a miner and communist who at the time was the Welsh organiser for the National Unemployed Workers Movement. In his second novel, *We live*, his hero Len stands with his wife Mary and surveys the moving crowd:

> The street behind him looked like a flowing river of human beings on which floated innumerable scarlet banners and flags ... Although directly in front of the band, he heard running beneath its thrumming wails the deep monotone of countless boots tramping rhythmically on the hard road ... The mountain which separated Cwmardy from the other valleys looked like a gigantic ant-hill covered with a mass of black waving bodies. 'Good God', the man next to Mary whispered, 'the whole world is on the move.'[17]

On 5 February the Minister of Labour, Oliver Stanley, announced that the government would suspend the rule changes affecting the payment of unemployment benefit. This 'Standstill Order' proved to be the only substantial concession that the marching miners extracted from the government during the 1930s. Even so, the victory was only temporary. The means test continued. There were more demonstrations, and even riots, as at Blaina in March 1935. A final hunger march of 504 marchers, left south Wales for London in October 1936.

Mass marches had been a powerful way of mobilising communities in support of workers' demands and grievances – spectacularly so at the high point of the movement in 1935 – and it helped to win sympathy and opinion outside Wales. But marching had limitations. Protesters were usually on the defensive, trying to protect themselves against attacks from coal-owners and governments.

Marching was legal, but police and government alike tended to regard marchers as potentially dangerous and unconstitutional. Crucially, the marchers tended to lack political impact, especially on central government.

In 1936 in the House of Commons, Clement Attlee, the leader of the opposition, complained that 'the Prime Minister has decided that he

Mid-Rhondda marchers 1936, banner
(South Wales Miners' Library, Swansea University)

will not see the marchers, the Cabinet has refused to see them, and the Prime Minister has refused facilities for the discussion of their petitions.'[18] Workers had to wait for the coming of the Labour Government before full employment became official policy, the means test was abolished and the coal mines nationalised. In the meantime, their hatred for their rulers hardened and their determination that things must be different blossomed. The foundations of the 1945 election result were laid in the years after 1926.

Women and peace

Industrial workers were not the only groups on the march between the wars. Many women, appalled by the slaughter of the First World War, were deeply committed to the cause of peace, and especially to the idea of arbitration and conciliation as the only means of avoiding future conflict. Welsh women were already known for their bold advocacy of peace. In 1923 over 390,000 women signed a 'women's peace appeal', organised by the Women's Committee of the League of Nations Union, and presented it to the women of the United States. They called on the US to join the League of Nations and reinforced their message with a nationwide American peace tour.[19]

On 27 May 1926 a group of about 2,000 determined women 'pilgrims' from Cricieth, Pwllheli, Nefyn, the Nantlle valley and other directions gathered in Pen-y-groes in Gwynedd, under the banner 'Hedd nid cledd' (Peace not the sword), to deliver a political message to London. Led by Gwladys Thoday, Mary Silyn Roberts and Charlotte Price White, they aimed to join streams of women from other parts of Britain and converge on Hyde Park in London for a mass demonstration on 19 June. The pilgrims walked in procession through Caernarfon and Bangor, carrying banners, blue and orange streamers and 'name poles', bearing small boards with the names of places they passed through. Others joined the route from Anglesey and Bethesda. They held meetings at Llanfairfechan, Penmaenmawr and in the castle at Conwy to gather support for the cause. Everywhere they went they received hospitality and encouragement, from local people and a wide range of societies, including religious and political bodies. By the time they'd passed through Colwyn Bay, Rhyl and Prestatyn to reach Chester on 31 May many women had walked 150 miles over five days, holding fifteen meetings on the way.

Women's peace pilgrimage, by an anonymous photographer, 1926
(*Bangor University Archives and Special Collections*)

A second Welsh stream of pilgrims set out from Swansea and moved east to Cardiff. Some of the Welsh groups walked all the way to London. At Hyde Park the North Wales group formed the largest contingent of long-distance travellers, carried the largest number of banners, and sang the loudest songs. Gwladys Thoday and Mary Silyn Roberts both addressed the crowd, the latter in Welsh. 'For the number, size and enthusiasm of its meetings', it was reported, 'the palm must be awarded to north Wales.'

'Pilgrimage' as a description of the event echoed medieval religious practice, but with a difference. 'In olden times', according to a leaflet published by the movement, 'the object of a pilgrimage was to do homage to the dead bones of saints. The object of the modern pilgrimage is to do homage to living ideals.'[20] The pilgrims continued to promote peace with vigour in the following years, but the ideal of solving international conflict by arbitration gradually faded in the face of fascism and aggression in the 1930s, and there were no repeats of the women's pilgrimage of 1926.

Hikers

Cars, buses, better roads and more professional advertising brought many more visitors into Wales after the First World War. Guidebooks proliferated to help them and often suggested walking routes for the more energetic. Train companies published guides to the country their lines passed through. Great Western's *The Cader country: how to explore it* appeared in 1926, and *Rambles and walking tours around the Cambrian coast* and *Rambles and walking tours in the Wye valley*, both written by Hugh E. Page, in 1936 and 1938.

More adventurous walkers made for Eryri. Some may have carried 'Snowdon', the first one-inch to one mile 'tourist' map ever produced by the Ordnance Survey, published in 1920, with a striking colour picture of Yr Wyddfa on the cover by the Survey's chief illustrator, Ellis Martin. (The OS was slow to see the commercial potential of its maps: Bartholomew had begun producing half-inch to the mile tourist maps of Wales in 1903.)

Cover of Ordnance Survey map of Snowdon with design by Ellis Martin, 1920
(National Library of Wales)

Hiking was becoming less solitary and more organised. From the 1870s rambling clubs began to spring up in England. In Wales, the Cardiff Ramblers were active by 1923. In 1931 local clubs came together in an umbrella body, the National Council of Ramblers' Federations, four years later renamed the Ramblers Association. Young walkers too were organising, or being organised. The British Youth Hostels Association was formed in 1930. It soon became the Youth Hostels Association (YHA), covering England and Wales.[21]

Some of the impetus behind this organisation-building came from men with socialist and communitarian ideals, who were determined that workers could have the chance to escape from the dirt and squalor of the industrial cities they lived in and enjoy the countryside. The Clarion Cycling Club, attached to Robert Blatchford's weekly newspaper *The Clarion*, had been founded in 1894, originally as the Socialist Cycling Club. It had its local hiking equivalents. The Sheffield Clarion Ramblers was established in 1900 by G.H.B ('Bert') Ward, an original member of the Labour Representation Committee. It was the first of several in the north and midlands of England. Ward's motto. 'a rambler made is a man improved', was widely adopted by the movement.[22]

Other 'outdoor' organisations, like the Cooperative Holidays Association and the Holiday Fellowship, offered organised walking holidays. Both organisations were founded by T. Arthur Leonard, a Congregational minister in Colne, Lancashire, who was also influential in setting up the Ramblers Association and the Youth

Hostels Association. He promoted countryside activities not only to instil a love of nature but also 'healthy companionship' and freedom from 'the enslaving attractions of the superficial things in life'. In 1918 Leonard moved to Conwy, living in the Holiday Fellowship's headquarters and first centre at Bryn Corach.[23] The first youth hostel in Britain was opened in Pennant Hall near Llanrwst in 1930 and others soon followed.

Ramblers organisations sprang up throughout Wales. The Newport Hiking Club was formed in summer 1932, and immediately arranged four walks. The first, to Wentwood, was not a success: only six members finished the walk, late at night, having taken the wrong paths and got lost. The second was to Twmbarlwm. Over fifty years later Cecil Granville remembered the day (he was sixteen years old):

> I only remember standing on top of that mountain, where I had never been before in my life, and feeling the joy of human achievement, then sitting on the tump for a picnic lunch which was suddenly interrupted by the wonderfully frightening sight of an Air Ship flying into view, and circling overhead. It was the R100 or R101 on a test flight from its mooring at Cardington, Bedfordshire.[24]

The third outing used a Great Western Railway 'hiking ticket', costing 2s 6d, which allowed members to walk along the Wye from Chepstow to Monmouth, past the early youth hostel at Whitebrook, where walkers could stay for one shilling a night. The fourth walk was abandoned after a thunderstorm in Caerleon, and the Newport Hiking Club came to an end. In December, however, a new club began, the Newport Ramblers Club ('hiking' was judged out of fashion), and soon affiliated to the South Wales Federation of Rambling Clubs. The subscription was 2s 6d a year. The members were mainly women, schoolteachers and office workers. Money was short, and it was decided that the cost of an outing should not exceed 2s 6d, including refreshments and travel fares.

In England and Scotland the influx of leisure walkers into the uplands, especially on the Pennines between the two urban conurbations of Lancashire and Yorkshire, was not always welcomed by farmers and landowners. Demands for greater access became more insistent, and more political, in the early 1930s, and culminated in the Kinder Scout trespass of April 1932. Five trespassers were arrested, prosecuted and imprisoned. The shocked public reaction to the severe sentences contributed to the movement to gain free access to the countryside.

There were no 'mass trespasses' in Wales, where opposition to public access to uplands was rarer. After the end of the First World War hostility to rambling was less concentrated and fierce in Wales than in England or Scotland. Between 1918 and 1922 most of the great Welsh landowners sold their estates, to benefit from high land prices, to meet debts or death duties, or because they chose to invest in other forms of wealth. About a quarter of Wales's land changed hands, and large numbers of tenants became freeholders. The gentry quickly lost their influence, and their interest in defending their acres against common people. The result was that

> Over the greater part of [Wales] you may walk where you will. There are few barriers physical or legal. There are no deer forests as in Scotland, and hardly any grouse moors ... You may walk from Cardiff to Carnarvon almost without taking a highway or breaking through enclosures.[25]

It was not that Welsh people were indifferent to gaining access to the mountains and hills around them. Many, like the inhabitants of Manchester and Sheffield, lived in heavily urbanised areas like the coal valleys of south Wales, and they appreciated the cleanliness and freedom of the mountain-tops that were so close by. For Bert Coombes they were an escape from the tension and depression of the General Strike of 1926 and the long conflict between coal-owners and miners that followed:

> All through that summer the stoppage was continued. We walked

up the mountains because the grass was soft and because we could not endure the sight of those prosperous-looking cars flashing along.[26]

Lewis Jones opens his first novel *Cwmardy*, of which *We live* was a sequel, with a similar mountain-top scene. 'Big Jim' and his young son Len have climbed up on a midsummer evening and through the heather and bracken they look down into the valley, with its 'belt of smoke that hung half-way up the mountain like a blanket blotting out everything underneath'. Len follows a sheep track downhill until it ceased to be green and 'buried itself in the murk and hid as if ashamed of its eventual destination'. The mountains offered a means of brief escape from the grimness of daily existence.

During hard times like strikes and lock-outs miners walked the hillsides and coal tips for a more urgent reason, to search for fuel. 'Coal picking' on the tips was a way of gathering coal to heat homes when there was no other supply and money was very scarce.

In 1937, the novelist James Hanley observed, in his study of unemployment in the coalfield,

> Men and women, children, dragging after them all manner of vehicles, battered prams and bicycles, all manner of rude carts, two planks of wood and a wheel, all went forward, some quickly, some dragging wearily behind, the old and the women carrying children. Some of them were looking up at the wagons skirting the slag-heap now, others went along with their heads bent, as though the going were hard.[27]

Inter-war visitors

The view of most interwar visitors to Wales who wrote about their experiences tended to be narrow, for two reasons. They tended to avoid industrial areas, unless, like the Quakers visiting their settlements, they had specific intentions there. And they used cars rather than their own feet to go from place to place. H.V. Morton's *In search of Wales*, the best-known travel book of the period, was first published in 1932 and went through ten editions before 1938. Morton was a perceptive and sympathetic observer, but his default view of the country was the one from the car window. He lamented that modernity had invaded the land he imagined as a fortress of tradition and otherness. Modernity included the radio, bottled English beer – and motor transport.[28]

Another popular guide for visitors was *Wales for everyman*, first published in 1935. The 'laziest and most care-free' way of getting about the country, wrote its author, H.A. Piehler, 'is to hire a car and the services of a chauffeur', although the steep and tortuous roads provide 'the adventurous motorist with the maximum of thrills.' Little wonder that 'in these days of heavy motor traffic the plight of the pedestrian on a main road is unenviable', quite apart from walking's other disadvantages, like the uncertain climate and poor accommodation in remoter parts.[29]

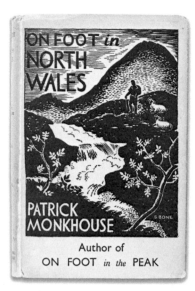

Cover of Patrick Monkhouse, On foot in north Wales, 1934
(*National Library of Wales*)

Relatively few visitors published accounts of their pedestrian travels in Wales between the wars. One was Patrick Monkhouse, who combined in his 1934 guidebook an impressive knowledge of mountain walking routes in Eryri with a frank admission that he knew little about other aspects of the land he passed through: '... let it be here clearly understood that I know little or nothing of the Welsh people, of Welsh history and culture, or of the Welsh language, beyond what is needed for making a guess at the meaning of the place-names.'[30]

Monkhouse made no secret of his preferences in walking gear:

I am all for shorts on the hills (even for women, if their figures will stand it, which is not often). On warm days they ventilate the legs. On wet days, they are the best of all. For flannel trousers, or knickerbockers, when wet, cling around the knee in a most exasperating way, and dry slowly ... For hard Welsh walking there is only one thing in it – good hobnail boots. You do not need a whole armoury of nails but they must be of the sort that stay in.[31]

Another author who made a deliberate choice to explore Wales on foot was John C. Moore. Born in Tewkesbury and privately educated, he developed an early taste for writing and the outdoor life. He'd already published a novel when in 1930, aged twenty-three, he packed his rucksack and set off by train for north Wales, intending to walk 400 miles.

Self-sufficient hikers like Moore were still uncommon. On his back he carried a tent, sleeping bag, groundsheet, clothes and cooking equipment, including a Primus stove, in a large 'Bergen' rucksack: enough to provoke 'obvious disapproval' from other train passengers. It is not his first time in Wales, and he even has some words of Welsh, but he seems dismayed by rain, wind and even sun. Road walking gives him no pleasure. He leaves Abergele on the coast road:

More and more cars and charabancs tried to run me down. The road was wide, so that two of the monsters could pass abreast on it ... on and on I went, pressing myself into the hedge whenever it was necessary in order to avoid making myself an involuntary sacrifice to the new Juggernaut.[32]

Moore is happier on country paths, and his youthful energy takes him across Yr Wyddfa, the Glyderau, Cadair Idris and the Black Mountain. He finds exultation on the mountains, but knows their dangers, describing vividly how paths can disappear, how mist can disorient the walker, and how easily ankles can be twisted. He has a keen eye for wildlife and is careful to note flowers and birds he sees (later he became known as a naturalist and conservationist).

Moore's main problem is that from the start he dislikes much of what he sees in Wales – many of the places, and most of the people. Flint, just over the border, is 'dull and uninteresting'; Rhyl, 'a chaos of pink sugar-rock', is 'like the wrath of God'; on a Sunday, Colwyn Bay resembles *uffern* (hell), and is 'not Wales at all, but a bit of Lancashire transplanted beside a Welsh sea'.

Welsh nonconformist culture Moore finds an affront. He reserves special contempt for chapels and Sunday closing. Welsh chapels, 'wickedly ugly', are often 'painful milestones' for the traveller, unlike the charming country churches to be found in England. He recalls coming across a hideous example on a previous visit with a friend to Merioneth:

> It was called Capel Bethesda, and it was without dispute the very ugliest building we had either of us seen in our young lives. Its ugliness was almost magnificent, so complete, so thorough, so perfect was it. Its colour was slate-grey, which is the colour of tombstones in those parts, and a sort of mosaic of yellowish bricks, inserted among the grey, decorated its exterior. We just sat in the car and stared at it.[33]

To make matters worse, on the opposite side of the street stands Capel Moriah, which surpasses Bethesda in ugliness. Moore is even more outraged by his failure to find alcohol or even food in Colwyn Bay on a Sunday. The chapels, with their allies the Welsh Liberals and teetotallers, hold a fierce grip on society:

> In the country-side and the villages they are the sole arbiters of morals and behaviour; they possess still a power of boycott, and they still exercise it ... The chapels are like a great black fungus, rotting away the very basis of sanity and freedom. Their influence has created the lying, thieving, deceitful hypocrite which Mr. Caradoc Evans holds to be typical of his countrymen.[34]

Moore has clearly been feeding his prejudices by reading *My people*,

Capel Sion and other stories by Caradoc Evans, with their vitriolic attacks on the perceived dishonesties of rural nonconformity.

Moore's intolerance of Welsh institutions translates into suspicion and dislike of the individual Welsh people he meets on his travels. In a pub in Llanbedrycennin he ignores the farm labourers 'gabbling in Welsh' to chat about West Bromwich Albion to the landlord from Birmingham. When a farmer near Beddgelert tells him about his seriously ill brother-in-law, Moore assumes he's eagerly awaiting his death so that he can inherit his land. As Moore nears the English border he senses the people getting friendlier. Having crossed it, he looks back on Wales, with a shudder of relief: 'The crimson sunset faded over Wales. The mountains were black as night already. Soon the darkness would fall over the dark land behind me ...'

What accounts for Moore's animosity? He may have been demoralised by the failure of his original hiking plan, or worn down by the injuries he sustained. His youthful arrogance and class privilege cannot have endeared him to those he met. And he may have calculated that the persona he adopts of a fault-finding and anti-puritanical chauvinist would find an echo in the prejudices of many of his readers. His inclusion of legends, reported conversations and personal commentaries show that he was familiar with George Borrow's *Wild Wales*. But he lacks Borrow's spirit of curiosity, and his respect for Welsh people and cultural traditions.

Moore's delight in the Glyderau, 'the most eerie and unearthly place I have ever been in', was shared by serious mountain walkers and climbers who flocked to Eryri after the First World War. Though many of these were products of the public schools and universities of England, and tended to regard themselves as the pioneering, heroic aristocracy of climbing, Welshmen maintained their long tradition of excellence on the rock faces. The outstanding figure was the Liverpool-born psychiatrist John Menlove Edwards, who pioneered new routes and wrote outstanding guides to Y Lliwedd, Tryfan and Cwm Idwal. He and others laid the foundations for the feats of Joe Brown and other working-class Manchester climbers on Clogwyn Du'r Arddu and other rock-faces after the Second World War.[35]

Women climbers became more prominent in the interwar years. The Pinnacle Club was founded in 1921 in the Pen-y-Gwryd Inn by Emily (Pat) Kelly, to 'foster the independent development of rock climbing amongst women', and included among its leading figures Dorothy Pilling, a noted Alpine climber. Several English climbing clubs came regularly to north Wales, and some, like the Climbers' Club and the Rucksack Club, adopted huts as their headquarters, in part because inns tended to be monopolised by motorists at weekends.[36]

Rural homelands

Visitors to Wales, even if they moved slowly and observantly, and encountered many people on their travels, caught only a brief sight of a land that for them was different, sometimes perplexing. By contrast, those who had known the country as their home since childhood had a very different relationship with it: a connection that was intimate and dear, but often complex and contradictory. This is most obvious in the case of poets and other creative writers, when they fused together their walking and their writing.

Robert Williams Parry was a slate quarryman's son who became a poet, a teacher and a lecturer. He was born and brought up in Dyffryn Nantlle, where slate mining dominated the lives of the local people, and from the early 1920s he lived in Bethesda, another slate-mining village. 'Eifionydd', written in 1924, sets the harsh, grey industrial landscapes of these areas against the green ease of the rural landscape just to the south. The poem seeks an escape from the ugliness of work, the competition of capitalism and the bitterness of 'progress', into an older, more harmonious world. This country refuge is precisely located in two Eifionydd locations: the hamlet of Rhoslan, and the 'Lôn Goed', the old wooded lane that linked Afon-wen on the coast near Cricieth with Hendre Cennen, five miles to the north-east.

The Lôn Goed had been laid out across open country in the early nineteenth century as a way of transporting lime from the coast to be spread on the uplands. It had long outlived its economic use and had become a secluded path, for the enjoyment of walkers in search of tranquillity. Overhanging trees on either side gave shade from the summer sun and shelter from winter winds. Earlier poets had sung in Welsh of the magic of the Lôn Goed, but for Williams Parry it held a special significance, as a haven, even a paradise, where, by walking, he could regain composure and connect himself with an older, better nature:

A llonydd gorffenedig
Yw llonydd y Lôn Goed,
O fwa'i tho plethedig
I'w glaslawr dan fy nhroed.
I lan na thref nid arwain ddim,
Ond hynny nid yw ofid im.

O! mwyn yw cyrraedd canol
Y tawel gwmwd hwn,
O'm dyffryn diwydiannol
A dull y byd a wn;
A rhodio'i heddwch wrthyf f'hun
Neu gydag enaid hoff, cytûn.

It's a finished calm,
the calm of the Lôn Goed,
from the arc of its woven roof
to the grass-green floor under foot.
That it goes to nowhere, parish or town,
bothers me not at all.

I feel delight when I reach
the heart of this quiet domain
from my industrial valley
and the way of the world I know;
and to walk its peace alone
or with a dear, like-minded soul.[37]

'Eifionydd' became a favourite poem for many, as a metaphor for passage through life, and the Lôn Goed became closely associated with its author. Thirty years later Williams Parry was photographed walking there, as he had as a young boy and a student at Bangor. He'd meet his old friends, including John Roberts, who later recalled:

R. Williams Parry on the Lôn Goed,
photo by Geoff Charles, 1950
(National Library of Wales)

Williams Parry and William Jones Tremadog and I would meet on the Lôn Goed in Eifionydd after I went to live in Porthmadog. It would happen on sunny days in the summer... I don't remember us talking about anything important in these sessions. Just being in the Lôn, under its woven branches, was the real pleasure.[38]

Williams Parry's poetic instincts were largely Romantic, and his contrast of urban and rural belonged to an old tradition. His cousin, the scholar and poet T.H. Parry-Williams, had lived and studied in Freiburg and Paris before the First World War, and absorbed the influences of modernism. Modernism's new ideas, and especially the feeling of alienation, the conviction of not belonging in one's world, are reflected in his poems and a long series of varied and subtly written essays. In one of his short early pieces, 'Dieithrwch' (Strangeness), written in 1927, he examines, like a cubist painter picturing an object from several angles at once, the simple act of returning on foot to one's childhood home.

Parry-Williams, the son of a teacher, grew up in Tŷ'r Ysgol, the schoolhouse in the small village of Rhyd-ddu, in the shadow of Yr

Wyddfa. It was a happy time, when he'd roam the lanes near the village, imagining that if he walked far enough along he'd meet 'Tylwyth Teg and ghosts and supernatural spirits'.[39]

From the age of eleven he left his beloved home to become a pupil, lonely and unhappy, in a secondary school in Porthmadog, twelve miles away. He'd walk most of the way there, lodge in the town and come home at the end of term. 'Dieithrwch', written over twenty years after leaving the school, begins with the final section of this journey home:

In those days, when I used to go home from school for the holidays, I would often have to walk the last four miles, and so, one by one, all the haunts of my childhood would come into view. Sometimes I felt something like disappointment to begin with, because my old friends – mountain, wall, rock, field and even the doorstep – seemed strange. Some clear distance existed between us for a while, even though I tried to remove it, but gradually it lifted, and in its place came a comforting feeling of the splendour and enchantment of familiar things. I learned to be glad to feel the strange newness of the old familiar things, and to take pleasure in it, because I knew it would surely be followed by seeing anew the sacredness of an old acquaintance. Still, at first there was a sad element in the experience – a failure to feel at home with the only things I had a hope of being comfortable with in their company.[40]

These swirling, twisting thoughts of Parry-Williams continue in the same vein. Sometimes his own family, when he returns, seem to him like strangers, stirring feelings of shame. Yet it is this absence and alienation that produce the closest feelings of belonging when they do meet. All the same, the strangeness still oppresses him. His walk back to Rhyd-ddu passes stopping points, each with its associations.

Even Yr Wyddfa, when it comes into view, looks new to him, rather than familiar. He stops to read carefully the final milestone before the village, as if he were a lost traveller seeking direction. The sounds his feet make as he climbs the steps to Tŷ'r Ysgol seem unusual and make him shudder. This entire aura of strangeness he experiences on approaching his old home, he realises, has its counterpart in homesickness, another alienation effect, felt shortly after leaving it. The two feelings lie at each end of the pendulum's swing. It is the stages of the walk that gives them their affective power. The essay ends, 'And the old white stone and the milestone know, as it were, when I pass them by, whether I'm on my way up or my way down'.

Journeys around their familiar haunts carry a heavy load of associations and emotions for both Williams Parry and Parry-Williams. The country they walk is steeped in memories of childhood, close ties of kin relationships, and wider cultural and linguistic affinities. They can't walk innocently, as would a visiting traveller. Each stage of a journey has the capacity to excite reflection and reaction, thoughts that, for Parry-Williams in particular, are complex and conflicted, both abstractly philosophical and intensely personal.

A contemporary of the two poets, Ambrose Bebb, offers a more social perspective on walking in Wales in the period between the wars. Bebb was a political activist, a founder member of the Welsh Nationalist Party in 1925, and a prolific writer on history and travel. In a BBC radio talk in 1936 entitled 'Y cerddwr a'r ffordd' (The walker and the road) he defends walking as the only way to appreciate fully what the traveller sees. Walking, he insists, *is* life. Motorists, by contrast, are 'feeble idlers', in danger of losing their limbs through disuse. The Welsh word for walk, 'cerdded', he notes, has a rich variety of associations. In his native Cardiganshire, for example, 'gered', in the vernacular, used to mean to walk far from home in search of seasonal work. For him, 'cerdded' simply means 'to see':

To see flowers and twigs, nests and eggs, cascades and waterfalls, gorse and whinberries, blackberries and raspberries, sun and moon, haystacks and wheatsheaves, heat-haze of banks and cobwebs and marshes, peat cutters and sheep shearers, corn stackers and reapers, wet cotton-grass, sphagnum moss, hidden valleys, high peaks, the whole astonishing life of the open air and its natural and human inhabitants – all of this invisible to those trotting along on a bike or galloping frivolously in a car.[41]

A few places remain to the walker, according to Bebb, that are reliably free from motor vehicles. One is Cwm Nant yr Eira in north Montgomeryshire. He describes a walk he once made there, on a dry September day, from Llangadfan to Llanbrynmair, having heard of its welcoming inhabitants and their distinctive accents. He walks part of the way with a friend, who can identify for him the remote farms scattered through the valley on either side of the small river and dusty lane.

I often left the road, taking short cuts across fields. I called at some of the farms. They gave me a princely welcome and set me back on the path, which wound its way in circles towards a peat bank pool and river bed, tempting me to leave it and find the right way through the coarse moor-grasses. After a while I drew near to the top of the valley and approached the gap that opens the way down to the Old Chapel and the whole district of Llanbrynmair. By now the evening, fiery red, had begun to lift up layers of mist, and, enveloped in that damp whiteness, I ended my walk.[42]

Cwm Nant yr Eira, for Bebb, is an unspoilt Eden, a place of retreat from the contemporary mechanical world, where the Welsh language persists and where ancient traditions of hospitality are still strong (his welcome by the farmers echoes the reception O.M. Edwards received on his own rural walks forty years before). Like Williams Parry and Parry-Williams, he chooses to walk in a deeply rural, Welsh-speaking setting that preserves the signs and values of a traditional culture. He's aware, though, of how fragile that culture is. His detested motor cars and bikes are symbols of a powerful modernity that threatens to sweep away what he holds dear about the old Wales.

Antiquarians

Reflections came naturally to Welsh walkers travelling alone. Those belonging to groups were more single-minded. One group for whom adventurous walking was a habit was the antiquarians and archaeologists. The Cambrian Archaeological Association had been founded in 1847, and its members were long used to striding over hills and moors to reach their antiquities. In her anecdotal memoir *Out with the Cambrians*, published in 1934, Evelyn Lewes recalled some of their events, including the 'Dolgelley Archaeological Week',

> ... a cross-country walk which not only entailed steady walking during several hours but the constant climbing of substantial stone walls, which, by the way, are a great feature of the district known as Dyffryn Ardudwy. I believe that those who did not feel equal to that arduous tramp, under what was quite a scorching midday sun, remained in the pleasant grounds of the ancient house of Corsygedol... Among those eager pedestrians and persevering wall-climbers were names well known, not only in the Principality, but much further afield.[43]

One of the 'well known names' was Mortimer Wheeler, who helped bring professional rigour to archaeology and sidelined the 'antiquarians'. By far the most 'eager pedestrian' among the antiquarians was George Eyre Evans, a Unitarian minister who dedicated his long life to the history and archaeology of Cardiganshire and Carmarthenshire. He was a prolific writer, he founded the Carmarthen Museum, and for eighteen years he acted as Inspector for the Royal Commission on the Ancient and Historical Monuments of Wales. He was also a considerable eccentric. He could often be seen walking the lanes with his thumb-stick, pointed white beard and Norfolk jacket, or the shorts and hat of his Boy Scout uniform. According to Evelyn Lewes,

> Philip Sidney [Evans's early *nom de plume*] was an exceedingly

energetic person, and disdaining the help of carriages, trains, or bicycles, walked from parish to parish in order to look at church registers and church plate, whilst collecting information from clergy, clerks, and churchwardens with the same boundless enthusiasm displayed by George Borrow in 1854. But as a hiker Borrow could not have competed with Philip Sidney, who covered in his rambles no less than 30,000 miles.'[44]

Walking enabled him to meet all manner of people he could use as sources of information:

Parsons and police, ministers and stonebreakers, lecturers and librarians, professors and ploughmen, all have readily given of their substance, their time, and their knowledge wherever the tramping enquirer has come to them.[45]

According to one obituary, 'in his closing years [he] was a picturesque figure surviving from an era of peace and leisure into the gloom that had gathered around our speed-loving mechanical life which he so thoroughly detested.'[46]

To Mortimer Wheeler, who knew him well and had little time for his amateurism, Evans seemed a character of unbeatable energy, the 'self-appointed leader' in all matters relating to local antiquities, with an 'unquenchable zest' for acquiring antiquities. Wheeler tells the story of how Evans escorted a coffin, draped in a flag and containing the body of his newly-deceased Aunt Delia, from Devon to Woking. Wishing to fill a gap in his knowledge of southern England, he stopped the hearse frequently along the way, to walk around Stonehenge and assorted historic churches.[47]

George Eyre Evans died in 1939. With him died the heroic age of polymathic walkers, begun by Edward Llwyd and continued by George Borrow and Iolo Morganwg. For all these figures observational walking was an essential means of gaining a rounded and detail picture of both past and present. Walking in the post-war era would be very different.[48]

Chapter 8: Long walking and slow walking

Long-distance paths

After the Labour Government came to power at the general election of July 1945 walkers at last began to gain statutory access to many parts of rural Britain previously barred to them. A firm legal status was given to public footpaths, and a series of national parks and national trails came into existence.

The new government set up a committee, under Sir Arthur Hobhouse, to prepare a law on national parks. The plan had two aims: to preserve nature and to establish public access. Hobhouse's committee, when it reported in 1947, put forward a list of twelve areas to become national parks, including Eryri (Snowdonia) and the Pembrokeshire Coast.

Hobhouse also recommended 'long distance paths and bridleways in and between National Parks and Conservation Areas'. The idea of long-distance paths had been in the air for years. In 1935 Tom Stephenson, a prominent ramblers' campaigner, published a passionate article entitled 'Wanted: a long green lane', in which he pressed for a 'Pennine Way' from the Peak to the Cheviots. The Hobhouse Committee suggested designating twelve long trails, including the Pennine Way and other routes in England, as well as Offa's Dyke, on the England-Wales border, and a Pembrokeshire coast path.[1]

The government accepted most of Hobhouse's ideas, though not his proposal for a legal right of access to all open country. The National Parks and Access to the Countryside Act was passed in 1949. Lewis Silkin, the Minister for Town and Country Planning, described it as 'the most exciting Act of the post-war Parliament'. Earlier, in the House of Commons, he expressed the egalitarian principles underlying it:

It [the Bill] is a people's charter – a people's charter for the open air, for the hikers and the ramblers, for everyone who loves to get out into the open air and enjoy the countryside. Without it they are fettered, deprived of their powers of access and facilities needed to make holidays enjoyable. With it the countryside is theirs to preserve, to cherish, to enjoy and to make their own.[2]

The new Act allowed for the setting up of National Parks, Areas of Outstanding Natural Beauty and National Nature Reserves. It also required local authorities for the first time to create and maintain definitive maps of rights of way across England and Wales. Councils moved at different speeds and with varying levels of enthusiasm to confirm the rights of way in their areas, but paths now received at least some degree of legal protection for the first time.

Eryri was one of the first four national parks to be set up in 1951. The Pembrokeshire Coast, the only entirely coastal park, followed in 1952, and Bannau Brycheiniog (Brecon Beacons) in 1957. The long-distance national trails took longer to establish. The first in Britain was the Pennine Way, opened in 1965, while the first to be planned in Wales was the Pembrokeshire Coast Path. (A proposal, first made in the mid-1940s, to create an Eryri path, along the route of the disused Welsh Highland Railway line, was dropped.) Surveying the route would be no easy matter, but in September 1950 a suitable person, Ronald M. Lockley, was found to carry out the task on behalf of the National Parks Commission.

It was a happy choice. Lockley was already well known as a pioneering naturalist and island-lover.[3] In 1927 he went to live on Skokholm island, off the coast of south Pembrokeshire. There he became the first person in Britain to set up a bird observatory.

Ronald Lockley at Island Farm, photograph, c1943
(Family of R.M. Lockley)

During his time there he produced several books, including a study of the Manx shearwater, and, with Julian Huxley, one of the earliest nature film documentaries, *The private life of the gannets* (1934). The Second World War forced him to leave Skokholm, but in 1940 the Royal Navy employed him on a secret mission to survey the coastline of west Wales to identify locations where enemy craft might land. He took this opportunity to study the grey seals he found there, but the task would also have given him a detailed picture of how walkers might be guided round the coast.

Lockley conducted his survey of a possible Pembrokeshire coast path in April and May 1951. He was paid only his expenses, but worked quickly and single-handedly. In the introduction to his report he laid out the principles he used for deciding on the path's route. It was to keep as close as possible to the sea, avoiding metalled roads and bypassing defence establishments. The route was to include 'the finest viewpoints for scenic beauty', while avoiding good agricultural land. Paths and bridleways already existed in many stretches, but were often disused and choked with vegetation. In his schedules Lockley included mention of cafés and inns along the route (some stretches lacked either). The schedules themselves are full of helpful notes, as well as warnings for future planners:

> Old footpath entirely choked by dense shoulder-high sloe and furze. Needs complete re-opening.
> Proposed revived passenger ferry.
> Parts of public footpath slipped into sea, new path formed on private land.
> Footpath blocked by rusted wire.
> Wild waste of heather, gorse and stones. Gradually ascends above Pwll Deri, with magnificent views inland and towards St Davids Head. This is a grand wild spot, the north-west facing cliffs of Pwll Deri being full of sea-birds.[4]

In February 1953 the report was submitted to the National Parks Commission. It was a remarkable achievement. The coastline was 167 miles long, deeply indented in parts, and it lacked existing public footpaths for much of the route. Lockley's naturalist's voice can be heard in his insistence on the natural world: 'the path affords opportunities for extensive journeys along the wild cliffs and sandy dunes of this area, enriched by bird and animal life and historical associations.' Sixty-six miles of new rights of way would need to be created; the costs involved, together with other costs, were estimated at something over £10,000.[5]

The plans for the coast path were accepted by the Minister in July 1953, and all that remained was to put them into action. This is where the difficulties began. Some local councils dragged their feet. Much of the proposed route lay across private land, without existing statutory public access. District councils had to negotiate routes for the Path with each landowner in turn. Over 150 agreements were needed, and resources to produce them were limited. Then, there were a few landowners who, according to the naturalist John Barrett

> ... used every legal and administrative device to postpone the day on which strangers might walk the rough edge of the cliffs round their land – in most cases a rough edge so overgrown with gorse and blackthorn that the owner had no possible alternative use for it.[6]

There were also serious physical challenges, as Lockley foresaw. Existing stretches of path were overgrown, and new stretches needed to be created from scratch. One of the tractor drivers carving out the new path in the 1960s later recalled,

> Following this test run, the tractor was taken to Strumble Head lighthouse and the supervisor, Paul Blick, advised me to take all the time I needed and we quietly but steadily carved out the Coast Path all the way to Harbour Village, Goodwick. My instructions were simple; keep the Path as close to the cliff edge as possible![7]

Paul Blick was the first Warden of the Path. It was his task to negotiate with landowners, overcome the physical obstacles, and provide the path with hundreds of stiles, bridges and steps.

> Nobody used initiative and diplomacy as he did; nobody received so many brickbats and ignorant rudery. Had Paul Blick always kept to the usual channels our path would not have been walkable for another decade.[8]

At last, in May 1970, the journalist and broadcaster Wynford Vaughan Thomas declared the Pembrokeshire Path open near its southern terminus, Amroth.

A year later a second Welsh long-distance path was opened. At 177 miles, the Offa's Dyke Path is almost the same length as the Pembrokeshire Coast Path, but is mainly linear, as it weaves its way across the border between England and Wales, and up and down across the west-east river valleys of the border. For much of its route, which begins at Sedbury near Chepstow and ends at Prestatyn, it follows the course of the Dyke, said to have been built in the eighth century by Offa, ruler of the powerful Anglo-Saxon kingdom of Mercia.

The Hobhouse Committee, no doubt aware of the pioneering survey work of Sir Cyril Fox in tracing the Dyke's route during the 1920s and early 1930s, had suggested an Offa's Dyke Path in 1947. Surveying the route began with early enthusiasm. By 1953 a proposal was ready for consultation, with local authorities and other bodies. A report was sent to the Minister, and the route was officially designated in October 1955.

But progress after that was painfully slow. Overall momentum was lacking. The route passed through the territory of as many as 36 local councils, each responsible for the detailed planning of the Path. There was reluctance and opposition from some landowners. By 1965 only a quarter of the new rights of way that were needed had been negotiated, and only twelve stiles had been erected.

However, the Offa's Dyke Path gained a powerful people's champion. In 1967 Frank Noble, a Knighton schoolteacher and archaeologist with a strong belief that people should be able to understand a landscape by walking within it, set up the Offa's Dyke Action Committee. Disappointed by the failure of the National Parks Commission to complete the Path, he and his friends pressed for urgent progress to be made.

The Committee set up an Offa's Dyke Information Centre and issued information and publicity in order to gather public support. Volunteers did their best to clear the route of the path from encroaching vegetation. Noble later wrote,

> Our fear then [in 1968], as we hacked our way along overgrown tracks, was that wild nature would win and that with a few more years of neglect the enthusiasts who were interested enough to find out where the National Footpath was supposed to run, would find it physically impossible to follow.[9]

Some stretches, Noble added, were suitable only as 'training for jungle warfare'. In 1969 he and others transformed the Action Committee into the Offa's Dyke Association, a membership body dedicated to promoting the Path and its conservation. Inspired by Noble, who possessed political skill and a talent for organisation, the Association persuaded the authorities to act swiftly and to appoint a full-time National Trail Officer. Its own members, with the help of the Workers' Educational Association, worked to clear the ground and sign the Path. In July 1971, at a ceremony at Knighton, attended by dignitaries and a large crowd, the Path was officially opened by Lord Hunt, the leader of the 1953 Everest expedition. Today the Association flourishes as a 'friends' group', operates a visitor centre in Knighton, at the rough mid-point of the Path, and works to conserve the Dyke.[10]

The Pembrokeshire Coast Path and the Offa's Dyke Path were both recognised as 'National Trails', with guaranteed standards of maintenance and signposting. In 1968 a third long route was devised independently by a keen rambler, Tony Drake, who presented his plan at the opening ceremony of the Offa's Dyke Path in 1971. The year before it had occurred to him 'to wonder why no one had proposed a long distance route over the principal mountains of Wales'. The Cambrian Way runs from Cardiff to Conwy. It's a strenuous, 298-mile high-level trail and takes in many of the highest mountain peaks. From start to finish a walker will have climbed over 70,000 feet. Drake's route, described in the guidebook he first published in 1984, included much open moorland. It encountered opposition from landowners, national parks, conservationists and even some ramblers. This prevented it from being recognised by official organisations for decades. But Drake and other campaigners persisted, with the help of a Cambrian Way Committee, and later the Cambrian Way Trust, thanks to a generous legacy from Drake, who died in 2012. In 2019 the route, now much changed, was finally recognised and partially signposted, and it's now included on Ordnance Survey Explorer maps. At Tŷ'n Cornel hostel in Cwm Doethie Fawr, one of the remotest spots along the Way, Tony Drake is commemorated by a bench, plaque and panel. The panel reads, 'through his dogged determination in the face of many obstacles, his vision became reality'.[11]

These long-distance walks have brought within reach of most people an experience previously denied them. In practice most journeys made along them are short, but more energetic walkers gain the chance to extend their range and stride out, aided by signposts, gates, and other path facilities, guidebooks, and cafés and overnight accommodation on the way. Walking a long-distance path helps you to become surprisingly fit and strong. It lets you experience close-up the natural world and human culture as they change from place to place and through time, to deepen friendships if travelling with others, or discover more about yourself if alone, or to learn about new places, cultures or languages. Some walkers treat the route as a physical and mental challenge, setting themselves targets. Others again walk to raise funds for charities. The rhythm of walking for a long period, at a remove from ordinary life, can be a means of overcoming loss or trauma, reducing stress, and improving mental well-being. There are cognitive as well as emotional benefits to a long walk. It allows the mind to detach itself from mundane anxieties and open up space for more constructive forms of thought: ruminating, musing, theorising, recollecting, planning, imagining, daydreaming, or even emptying the mind of thought altogether.

New long-distance paths were devised to join the initial three routes, including the Wye Valley Walk in 1975, St Illtud's Walk in 1994, the Cistercian Way in 1998, Glyndŵr's Way, which gained 'national trail' status in 2002, and the Snowdonia Slate Trail in 2017. Several paths followed the Pembrokeshire pattern in taking seaboard routes. The Anglesey Coast Path and the Llŷn Coast Path were both opened in 2006. The Ceredigion Coast Path followed in 2008. To mark its opening the poet Dic Jones, who farmed at Blaenannerch near Aberporth, wrote lines, 'Llwybr y glannau', that capture the essence of its grey, rugged cliffs. The words of the poem are inscribed on a stone overlooking Ynys Lochtyn, near Llangrannog:

Hyd lannau Ceredigion
Mae'r tir a'r môr yn leision,
A golwg ar bellterau'r Bae
O gribau'r creigiau geirwon.

All along Ceredigion's shore
Land and sea are grey as slate,
And far round the Bay appear
The rocks, rough-edged, serrate.[12]

The Wales Coast Path

In 2012 Wales became the first country in the world of any size to create a public footpath around its entire coastline. The Wales Coast Path became possible because by now Wales had its own devolved government, established in 1999, along with an elected parliament, the National Assembly for Wales (now the Senedd). The authority, policy determination and resources that a national government had at its command were able to overcame the barriers that had hindered the planners of earlier long-distance routes.

The idea of a continuous footpath along the coast was conceived, according to oral tradition, in the kitchen of the First Minister, Rhodri Morgan, during a conversation with Jane Davidson. Both were keen walkers and could see the attraction of adopting the Path as a government commitment. When he opened the Anglesey Coast Path in June 2006, Rhodri Morgan announced the new Wales Coast Path, emphasising its twin objectives: to boost the Welsh economy, especially through tourism, and to promote health benefits for everyone.

The Government asked the Countryside Council for Wales to prepare plans, and from 2007 Davidson, by now Minister for Environment and Sustainability, guided the Path's progress and directed the funding now available. Responsibility for action was in the hands of the Countryside Commission, in partnership with other government agencies, Ramblers Cymru, local authorities and the national parks. The planners faced the usual difficulties with some reluctant landowners. Even with the threat of compulsory purchase in their pockets, they couldn't overcome all problems, and some stretches of coast, for example near Gwbert and Cwmtydu and on Anglesey, had to be by-passed. Other areas, like Pendine, Castlemartin and Aber-porth, were occupied by the military and remain inaccessible.

Much new building was needed to complete the Path: 248 new stiles, 1,282 gates, 159 bridges, 818 culverts, steps and boardwalks and 1,432 fingerposts, each bearing the Path's logo, a dragon-tail conch. The planners were helped by the presence of the three existing coast paths, and the fact that large areas of coastline had been bought by the National Trust. The Trust was founded in 1895, and in the same year Fanny Talbot, a friend of John Ruskin, was the first person to donate property to it, Dinas Oleu in Barmouth. The Trust began its programme of preserving environmentally important coastal areas in 1965 with 'Enterprise Neptune' – Whiteford Burrows in Gower was the first purchase in the UK – and it now owns over 150 miles of coastline in Wales.

Six years after it was first announced, the Path was complete. It was officially opened on 5 May 2012. It's 870 miles long and runs from Chepstow to Queensferry and on to Chester, taking in the perimeter of Anglesey. Unlike other long-distance paths, it includes urban and 'edgeland' stretches, around Newport, Cardiff and Swansea, and in Flintshire, as well as conventionally picturesque areas. Some sections of the Path are accessible to cyclists, horse-riders and people with restricted mobility. Natural Resources Wales, the successor of the Countryside Commission for Wales, is responsible for maintaining the Path, in collaboration with local councils and national parks.

In its first year the Path saw 2.8m visitors. A report on the economic impact of the spending of Path visitors estimated that adult visitors to the Path spent £547m in 2014. After only a year, 18% of tourism-related businesses reported increased customers. Researchers in 2014 found that 23,688 people walked on the path every week, and that on average they walked 4.38 miles per week. The economic value of all this physical activity, they suggested, equated to £18.3m.

Wales Coast Path near Harlech

(photo Andrew Green)

In 2022 the Welsh Government set up a tenth anniversary review of the Wales Coast Path. Celebrating its success, the review pointed out the Path's still unrealised potential for improving physical and mental health, and warned about the impact rapid climate change might have in future on the Path and its walkers.[13]

Among the achievements of Welsh governments in the twenty-first century the Wales Coast Path ranks as an outstanding expression of self-confidence and national identity. The Path is now established as one of the most distinctive aspects of Wales today. It opens Wales up to its own inhabitants, enabling people to discover, or reconnect with, their own landscapes, language, culture and fellow-citizens. It helps breaks down the mental barriers that often separate 'north' and 'south' Wales. It attracts visitors from the rest of Britain, giving them insights into an under-known country. It receives international visitors and attention.

From the beginning the Path attracted not only casual and local visitors but also long-distance and even 'extreme' walkers and runners. In 2012 Arry Beresford-Webb became the first person to run the Path (and the Offa's Dyke Path), in 41 days. Other Path walkers have also published blogs or books of their travels. Their accounts show how far the experience tested their physical capacity, but also how it has allowed them to grow as individuals.[14]

A researcher, Amy Jones, used immersive fieldwork to investigate the experience of long-distance Wales Coast Path walkers, by walking alongside them and recording their conversations in diaries. She found that the walk had expanded their knowledge of Wales, and that it stirred in them many profound feelings about its landscape, culture and language. Some of them treated the experience as a secular pilgrimage, aimed at enlarging their view of the country.[15]

The Wales Coast Path has arguably done more to bring Wales together as a geographical entity than the government's mainly unsuccessful efforts to improve the inadequate road and rail connections between north, mid and south Wales. Its long, peripheral route, following the multiple indentations of the coastline, and the slowness with which a walker traverses it, offer a richer introduction to the diversity of the country than any faster, more direct road line. Beyond its physical reality the Path has grown in stature as a powerful symbol of an old Wales renewed.

Pilgrimage revived

The post-war long-distance paths had no particular direction or fixed destination, unlike the medieval pilgrim routes, which normally had as their end-point the shrine of a saint. But at the beginning of the twenty-first century the pilgrimage tradition was revived. The first stirrings of the new movement, though, came not from the churches but from writers. Robin Reeves, journalist, mountaineer and editor of *New Welsh Review*, had nurtured the idea of a new route from Tintern to St Davids, and after his death six friends combined to 'write the route' in the winter of 2001 and the spring of 2002, each covering a stage before handing the baton to another. In their book, *I know another way*, they track their way on foot through the physical landscape, together with the photographer Paul Davies, and give their very different responses to it.

Jim Perrin, who walks from Tintern to Cardiff, questions his motivation:

What, I wondered, does it mean to be a pilgrim, and why had I undertaken this journey, that so reeks of the self-proclamations of 'spiritual improvement', of the habits of those who crack their knees for no more serious purpose than to be thought better than the rest of us – the spiritual materialists, the self-styled gurus?[16]

before conceding the comfort and grace that pilgrims of the past have derived from their travelling. In Llansadwrn, Carmarthenshire, Jon Gower, another elegiac writer, notes the absence of fellow walkers:

A lone jogger lopes by, the only other person on foot I have seen during this stretch. When George Borrow walked around Wales he was forever bumping into people on the roads – tinkers, travellers, farmhands – but nowadays a man on foot is a notifiable incident.[17]

By contrast, the artist Osi Rhys Osmond strikes a more visionary note in his imaginary procession of past walkers, only a few of them pilgrims, making their way over Foel Drygarn in the Preseli Hills:

And what if all of history's walkers came along in just one day? Early tomb-makers, cosmic worshippers, lunar and solar luminaries, possibly even troops of post-crucifixion Romans, striding the ridges, put carelessly out of their strict formations by geology and greed, nervously ransacking burial sites in search of mythic treasures... Modern hikers, SAS yompers, lovers, star-crossed and otherwise, mountain bikers, crystal gazers, National Park rangers, pony trekkers, New Agers, archaeologists, naturalists, conservationists and geologists, shepherds, World War pilots, ley-liners, ornithologists and herders, dowsers, farmers, crashed hang gliders, grazers, poets, painters and unsuccessful bluestone movers.[18]

The Tintern to St Davids route animated the imagination of creative writers, by no means all of them believers, but it failed to develop into a regular pilgrim trail. Soon, though, more organised routes were set up by religious groups and individuals, supported by signposts and guidebooks, and often with material as well as spiritual aims in mind.

Chris Potter, dean of St Asaph, and his wife Jenny were inspired by walking the Camino pilgrim route to Santiago de Compostela to plan a similar, 130-mile North Wales Pilgrim Way, waymarked with the symbol of a Celtic cross, from Basingwerk Abbey in Flintshire to Ynys Enlli (Bardsey Island).[19] In August 2011 the first group of thirteen pilgrims arrived at Ynys Enlli after an eleven-day walk.

Other, less fully developed pilgrim routes sprang up. The Cistercian Way, a circular 650-mile walk linking the fifteen Cistercian abbeys of Wales, was first prospected by a group led by Madeleine Gray in 1998, on the 900th anniversary of the Cistercian order.[20]

The Gower Pilgrimage Way was established in 2022 to link seventeen historic Anglican churches of the Gower Peninsula, between Pen-clawdd and Bishopston. To mark the event a Pilgrimage Festival was held, complete with services, hymn singing, meditation, plays and talks. The St Thomas Way, devised in 2018 as a 'heritage route' between Swansea and Hereford, isn't a traditional linear pilgrimage but a series of short circular walks. It commemorates the curious story of William ap Rhys or William Cragh. He was an anti-Norman rebel who miraculously survived two attempts to hang him in Swansea in 1290, and later made a journey of thanksgiving to the shrine of St Thomas de Cantilupe in Hereford Cathedral. New pilgrimage ways also cross frontiers and seas, echoing their medieval predecessors. When the Wexford-Pembrokeshire Pilgrim Way was formed in 2022, linking Ferns Abbey and St Davids Cathedral via Wexford, Rosslare and Fishguard, its organisers placed much emphasis on its role in encouraging sustainable tourism. In the same year a large wood and metal sculpture of a pilgrim, striding forwards with a staff, was created by Glenn Morris and erected above the old Cistercian abbey of Strata Florida.[21]

Several pilgrims have published personal accounts of walking these new pilgrim routes, and others have been interviewed by academic researchers. It's clear that walkers have very varied motives for setting out: spiritual comfort or enlightenment, the company of fellow-pilgrims, a desire to connect with the natural world and explore new landscapes and cultures, as well as more material aims, such as raising money for charities. Pilgrims develop a similarly rich reservoir of experience as they travel, absorbing the landscape and history around them (going 'deep into a country'), interacting with other pilgrims (or alternatively enjoying solitude), as well experiencing internal emotional and spiritual change, and improved physical and mental well-being.[22]

Anne Hayward is a representative modern Christian pilgrim. At Easter 2015 she set out on a series of Welsh pilgrimages over three months, wanting 'a more peaceful, more reflective and happier place in my life'. She was interested in Welsh history and Welsh saints, and she was also eager to have 'significant conversations' with other travellers. Carrying as little as possible and willing to accept offers of help and gifts along the way, Anne started her daily walks after a morning prayer. Her aim was to visit pilgrimage sites at Holywell, Ynys Enlli, St Davids and Llandaf.[23]

The new pilgrim routes naturally attract committed religious believers. Their emergence at a time when religious belief in Wales and Britain has never been less widespread might look surprising. But it may be that pilgrimage routes and organised pilgrimages, often led by evangelists, provide a public demonstration of pride and endurance that churches feel they need to make in a largely indifferent world – just as religious processions did in the streets of late nineteenth century and early twentieth century Welsh towns. The same routes, however, are obviously followed by many non-believers, possibly attracted by their destination-oriented nature, by the consolations of 'slow travel', by the opportunity for self-healing, self-discovery and peace of mind. In the words of one pilgrim, 'in an age that finds it hard to deal with finding silence and tranquillity, there's more need for places that give us respite and peace.'[24]

Angry male visitors

In the decades after the Second World War, walkers, mainly male, continued to come to Wales to tackle routes of their own devising, away from the new long-distance and pilgrim paths. Their accounts tend to echo the narrative conventions of much older visitors, and they often share the preconceptions of their predecessors.

Thomas Firbank, a Canadian of part-Welsh extraction, toured Wales, mostly on foot, in 1952. He followed roughly the route used by George Borrow, though his book of his tour lacks Borrow's verve and surprise. In 1966 John Hillaby strayed into the borders of Wales on his journey on foot from Land's End to John o'Groats, following part of the Wye valley and Offa's Dyke. Though he knows some of the historical and literary background of the land he travels through, he feels qualified to generalise about 'the Welsh', while being cavalier with Welsh language spelling and pronunciation.[25]

In 1982, as part of a journey round Britain, the jaundiced travel writer Paul Theroux used railways to venture to the west coast of Wales, where walks gave him a chance to exercise his bile at the expense of the population. The Welsh are poor, and given to alcoholism and burning down English-owned cottages. They can ruin even attractive places: 'Llandanwg was lovely, which is why it was full of ugly caravans.' Bilingual road signs are 'a sop to nationalists', while bilingualism is no more than 'a form of schizophrenia, allowing a person to hold two contradictory opinions in his head at once'. Unconsciously, Theroux reprises here the rancorous satire of William Richards in his *Wallography*, three centuries earlier.[26]

In the warm summer of 1991 Anthony Bailey, an English writer and art historian, felt the need for a 'really long walk', and chose Wales, for no other reason than because it was the 'closest-to-hand foreign country'. Bailey walks from Cardiff to Bangor, but he avoids an established trail like the Cambrian Way, preferring to sacrifice mountain tops for a greater variety of terrain. Like Hillaby, he comes well-stocked with a reading knowledge of Wales, and he's well aware of his own travelling predecessors, like Edward Thomas and George Borrow. He may lack Borrow's humour and Thomas's introspection, but like them he uses his curiosity and mode of travel to talk to many people along the way: landlords, Irish travellers, teachers, farmers, sheep shearers and English settlers. What he hears and sees allow him to comment on many aspects of Wales in the early 1990s, a time of political depression and social change.

On the other hand, as a 'tolerant but nor overly knowledgeable' Englishman, Bailey misses much. His lack of Welsh and deafness to Welsh-language culture mean that he often mangles Welsh names and quotations. For all his openness he echoes the more crabbed of the early English visitors to Wales, with his crusty outlook and his impatience, especially with young people. Above all, his overall view of contemporary Wales tends to be bleak. Like Matthew Arnold and other English literary predecessors, he sees a distinctive Wales as belonging to the past, and Welsh people as now finally assimilated into British culture:

Their identity as citizens of the United Kingdom involved interests and preoccupations that are basically the same as those of people living in England, like taxes and television, snooker or snwker [sic].[27]

Before long, though, women began to walk long distances in Wales, bringing with them a warmth and sympathy so often lacking in their male predecessors.

Ursula Martin

With some exceptions, women had been absent from the ranks of long-distance walkers. Or so it seems to us today. Since most writing of walks was done by men, women's walking is badly under-represented in the historical record. In the twenty-first century, however, women have taken their place among the company of 'long walkers' and writers about walking. Much of the most penetrating and affecting writing about walking has come from women.

In winter 2011, in a Bulgarian village at the end of a three-month kayak journey along the Danube, Ursula Martin felt a sharp pain in her side. Back in Britain, she was diagnosed with ovarian cancer. A surgeon in a Bristol hospital operated to remove the whole of one ovary and part of the other. The treatment was successful, and Ursula was asked to return to Bristol from her home in Machynlleth for regular check-ups. Six months later she made the trip to hospital in Bristol on foot, following the River Severn from its source on Pumlumon, and returning home along the Wye. She treated it as a 'healing journey', proof that although her body had been invaded by cancer it was still capable of supporting her, and that she was still herself: 'I could still shoulder a bag and leave safety, go out and cope in the unknown.'

In March 2014 she set out on a much longer trip. Again, it was built around a timetable of check-ups in Bristol, but this time Ursula planned to 'fill in' the gaps between appointments by walking around Wales, using established long-distance paths. She walked 3,700 miles, over a period of seventeen months, and by the end had covered, in their entirety, the Severn Way, Offa's Dyke Path, Glyndŵr's Way, the Wales Coast Path, the Cistercian Way, the Cambrian Way, the Coast-to-Coast Path, the Mary Jones Path, and eight river valley routes (Severn, Conwy, Dee, Tywi, Teifi, Taff, Usk and Wye). These routes she deliberately planned as a single 'flow', one path leading naturally into the next, with diversions, resumptions and occasional rests along the way.

Ursula Martin's published account of her travels does much more than describe her route. In fact, she leaves out almost all of the external information that would make her book usable as a conventional route guide. Instead, she conveys an unusually intense, often visceral impression of the physical and mental exertions of 'extreme' walking. Her writing is frank. She's honest about her feelings about others, and especially about herself, her own fears, aversions and frequent sense of despair and failure – all of them transcended by a determination, never seriously shaken, to complete what she set out to do.

Ursula Martin

(*photo Ursula Martin*)

One practical motive for Ursula's walk was to raise money for an ovarian cancer charity. The internal, personal reasons for the journey are less explicit. One vital concern, following the shock of her cancer, was the process of self-healing. In the final words of the book she says,

> Part of healing is acknowledging hurt, part of healing is working at getting better, and part of healing is putting that painful time behind you, seeing that you no longer have to fear it. You're done with it; let it go, this trauma is no longer a necessary part of you. The end of healing comes when you can acknowledge that the hurt is over now, that it has gone – and left you different.[28]

There were many other attractions. The act of walking itself was an obvious pleasure, preferably on her own, and in rural and remoter areas (Offa's Dyke Path she finds too busy, 'a walker's motorway'). So too were the landscapes of Wales, the meetings with friends and strangers as well as the self-sufficient solitude, and the 'moments of splendour' and even ecstasy.

'I had no job', Ursula recalls, 'no money, no husband and no children'. Her walking was equally unencumbered. Her budget amounted to an average of £5 a day. She carried everything she needed in a rucksack on her back, except for two bamboo walking poles, each adorned with a flag. She planned to sleep overnight under the stars, or in a barn or polytunnel or some other shelter (a tent was reserved for the coldest and wettest months only).

Walking brings Ursula simplicity, pleasure and pain, as well as boredom. She translates into words the complex mix of experiences that result from spending day after day, usually all day long, putting one foot in front of the other:

> That's what I did, every day, I just walked, sometimes at a moderate speed, sometimes slowly. I walked and looked around me. Each day was stunning, surreal and memorable ... A lot of walking is tiredness. It's stopping frequently, whenever the

impetus slips a gear and the hovering pause pounces, compelling you to stop, turn around, watch the view and catch your breath. A lot of walking is an utterly empty-brained exhausted nothingness ... A lot of walking is automatic; it's letting your body function while your mind wanders in its own realm ... A lot of walking is time passing, small events amusing you for a second and then passing into insignificance ... I walked and walked and walked.[29]

Inevitably the unremitting routine soon takes its toll on Ursula's body. Her feet are the first to suffer, and they continue to trouble her till the end: at first, tendon aches, blisters and pressure pains from pounding hard surfaces; later, a serious pain around the arch and heel that she identifies as plantar fasciitis. There are other kinds of problem. Walking without enough water, especially in hot weather, leads to dehydration. Getting lost is a danger. Occasionally she walks into danger, as in the pathless bogs of the Cambrian Mountains. Rights of way are sometimes blocked or overgrown and impassable. Above all, bad weather can make walking a misery.

In moments of adversity, pain and exhaustion Ursula comes close to despair and abandoning her journey. She feels inadequate and amateurish, lugging an over-heavy rucksack, failing to meet her mileage targets, facing an apparently impossible distance to be covered. Low self-esteem, 'my historic traitor within', lack of respect for her own body, and a sense of underachievement conspire, it seems, to condemn her to another failure. Yet each time 'the chattering uncertainty of my fearful brain' urges her to give up, she rallies and pushes herself onwards, finding new inner strength and confidence in her ability to complete what she's begun. The determination comes from within, but Ursula also draws strength from the people she meets in the course of her trip who give her support, encouragement and comfort.

Ursula Martin is an extremist, as well as a completist: all gaps in the routes have to be filled later. Few others would contemplate, let alone carry out, her extraordinary plan for criss-crossing Wales in seventeen months. By the end, she admits, her walk had become a mania and she herself 'part wild ... a piece of the natural world ... uncaring of appropriate behaviour, of anything but walking'. The length, speed and intensity of her journey meant that she had to forego some of the pleasures enjoyed by a more conventional walker. She'd no time to let curiosity tempt her into following side-paths and by-ways, or to explore at leisure the history and culture of the localities she walked through. But her experience shows how one kind of walking has the capacity to test physical and mental limits, and to spur personal growth. Her walk gave her the chance to rediscover her complex identity as a Welsh woman:

> To be Welsh is to be local. To be intensely connected to one place, to know its history in great detail. I've walked the land of Wales because I love it and in loving it I've come to know it well but it's a different sense of nationality. Wales is my adopted country as well as my place of birth; I'm from here but not of here.[30]

Even before completing her Welsh adventure, she was already planning an even more ambitious trek, across the continent of Europe. The walking would continue (she'd go on to walk from Kyiv to Finisterre in 2018-21).

Hannah Engelkamp

The year before Ursula began her walk, her friend Hannah Engelkamp set out on another walk around Wales. If Ursula's journey was a true epic, Hannah's was a Quixotic or mock epic. Starting from Aberystwyth, she set out to walk, sometimes with family members or friends, along the entire Wales Coast Path and the Offa's Dyke Path. As an experienced long-distance walker, she was keen to use the Coast Path, opened only the year before, to explore Wales, and as a sociable person she was in need of someone to walk with. More unusual was her choice of walking companion: a five-year old donkey.

The donkey's name was Chico. He was still in the equivalent of his early teens, and arrived with the reputation of being watchful and nervous. Hannah had no previous experience of looking after donkeys, and Chico had no history of being managed. She took charge of him only weeks before she started out. On the positive side, she knew that donkeys were known for being 'companionable, stoical, strong, dependable – all of the traits you need in a good travel buddy'. In short, a donkey would be 'a porter, a companion, a crowd-pleaser and a good story'.

The negatives, on the other hand, were obvious. On the Coast Path there are over 400 stiles, and over 500 on the Offa's Dyke Path. As Hannah admitted, 'donkeys don't do stiles.' They have similar problems passing through kissing gates (almost 800 on the Coast Path) and over cattle grids. And by law they're barred from footpaths that are rights of way. Often, therefore, Hannah needed ingenuity and advanced map-reading skills to find donkey-friendly bridleways, cycle tracks, beaches and back roads lying parallel to the official paths. This necessity, though, was itself a blessing:

> I liked it that our route round Wales was self-assembled, determined by our energy levels, the weather, and offers of accommodation. We were spinning our own path behind us, not tied to a circuit ... we could walk for ever.[31]

A more serious difficulty, one that eclipsed all other anxieties on the trip, was donkey behaviour. The first half of the journey was dominated by the ever-changing relationship between Hannah and Chico, and the struggle between them to find a settled rapport.

Would they be able to walk at the same speed? Hannah had to learn to slow her pace to suit Chico, and put up with his frequent stops to eat wayside snacks. Would Chico survive the distance? A vet had checked him beforehand, but Hannah worried about the state of his hooves, and the chances of eating dangerous plants, like ragwort, privet and ivy. If he was nervous, how would he react to cars, cows, dogs, horses, narrow bridges and wading through water? Would he run away, or react badly to being tethered or corralled? Above all, how

Hannah Engelkamp and Chico

(*photo Hannah Engelkamp*)

could he be made to do what Hannah needed him to do? Sometimes he'd simply refuse to move, or would stand and bray loudly, or tread on Hannah's toes, or even trip her up.

Eventually, though, the two walkers learned to understand each other, and to rub along together amicably and with fewer problems. Like all couples they needed time apart, and while Chico took a break in a paddock near Bangor, Hannah walked, solo and carefree, round the Anglesey coast, 'a donkey walker without a donkey'. In the Marches she realised that she no longer needed to lead him with a rope; he could be trusted to follow her. But Chico was still a difficult character to decipher:

It took me a long time to read the signs of affection. People began to report that he was keeping an eye out for me if I went into a shop or out of sight, or that his ears twitched if he heard my voice, but it still looked to me like he didn't want to let on that he liked me. Perhaps this is just a donkey thing, but I suspect it might be a Chico thing – he is a bit of a diva. And if there's one thing people really love, me included, it's when the object of their affections is a little aloof. Anything hard-won is more precious.[32]

By the end a mutual affection had grown up between them – one that fell short of outright love, since Chico was rarely expressive of his intimate feelings. People who met him in his travels found him curious and endearing; he in turn appreciated their carrots and apples.

Hannah's original idea had been to average fifteen miles a day. She soon realised that, with Chico as fellow-walker, precise planning and high speeds were impossible, and eventually she found how to live for the moment, in slower, donkey time, and, like Chico, how to live simply and sustainably. She modified her original aim of sleeping wild under the stars, and nights were spent on campsites, in gardens and fields, and in caravans and houses. This was possible in part because, like Ursula Martin, she grew a network of supporters through social media and her blog, strangers who did her constant acts of kindness.

The complex, ever-changing relationship of Hannah and Chico describes, in comical, inter-species form, what happens when two human friends find themselves in each other's company on a long-distance walk. If Chico could, at different times, be stubborn and self-willed, uncooperative and sulky, gentle and modest, brave and determined, then he was only mirroring the spectrum of behaviours a human companion might display. Hannah's final verdict on Chico's company favoured her donkey above any possible human fellow-walker: 'you were more compliant than a human companion would ever have been under the same circumstances.'

After six months of mixed weather, donkey misbehaviour and countless human encounters, Hannah and Chico arrived back in Aberystwyth, along with a second donkey, Flo, in November 2013. Hannah had set out with no specific purpose in mind. She wasn't collecting money for charity, though people did offer her donations. She'd nothing to prove, though she suspected that she may hold the record as the slowest long-distance walker. And she hadn't aimed to embrace pain or hardship, though she loved living plainly. Quite simply, as she summed up her experience, 'I liked walking. I like Wales. I loved meeting people ... This was a big adventure, for its own magic.'

Environmental walkers

At around the same time as Hannah Engelkamp and Ursula Martin were tracing the perimeter of Wales, a third woman, Julie Brominicks, was walking the same route, via the Wales Coast Path and Offa's Dyke. An experienced hiker, she had two ambitions, to become a writer and to achieve a deeper appreciation of Wales. Her journey was completed in stages over twelve months, sometimes alone, sometimes accompanied by her partner, and her book about the experience, *The edge of Cymru*, was published over ten years later. Her narrative is interlaced with a long-considered meditation on two themes, the calamitous state of the natural environment, and her own complex sense of engagement with Wales.

Julie travels with a light backpack and a tight budget, often wild-camping and unafraid to trespass where she needs to. Like Martin and Engelkamp she's troubled by rain, heat and cold, and by pains, blisters and bleeding, but she finds constant delight in the natural world around her. Uncomfortable in the presence of external economic, political and military power, as at Castlemartin and Powis Castle, she'd rather talk to farmers, steel workers, fishermen and the many people who offer her generous help.

What causes Julie more pain than bodily discomfort is observing the multiple wounds inflicted by humans on the natural world. Along her walk, or from the front of her tent, she catches sight of hundreds of beauties – she can name dozens of the plants, birds and animals she meets – but by the end of the trip she's assembled an even longer catalogue of environmental abuse. Slurry and pollutants from poultry farms pour into rivers, numerous species of birds, mammals and fish are extinct or rare, factories pollute air and water, plastic litters beaches, hay-meadows are lost, public transport declines and cars

Julie Brominicks

(*photo M. Bromilow Photography*)

proliferate, nuclear power is revived at Wylfa, and land is lost to flooding. The horror that many earlier travellers reserved for industrialised south Wales, and even discouraged them from visiting, extends now to almost the whole country, and beyond.

Julie was brought up in England, but living in Wales has made her identify ever more closely with Wales and its people and the Welsh language. She's unusually sensitive to her incomer status ('being English bothered me'), and to her incomplete grasp of the Welsh language. Suspicious and sometimes hostile to those who disrespect the country and its culture, she often feels self-conscious when talking to Welsh-speakers, and reluctant to expose herself as a less than competent speaker. But as time goes on her anxiety and guilt subside, and a more nuanced view of her national identity emerges. Everyone living in Wales is some kind of 'immigrant', she understands, and kindness motivates people more than nationality.

Finally, she concludes that she's 'earned my right to walk with a carefree heart'. As with Ursula Martin, the experience of the long walk has been to rewild her: 'I felt wild', she writes, 'as the choughs exploding into the air, wild as the huge cliffs, spiralling foam, rocks like wrecks, and red kites patrolling the slopes.'[33]

Julie Brominicks belongs to a group of Welsh 'eco-pedestrians', who share an agonised concern for the future of the land they pass through. Between summer 2020 and summer 2021 the novelist Tom Bullough walked the course of 'Sarn Helen', the Roman road linking Neath and Caerhun, near Conwy. All through the walk he's conscious not only of the beauty of the countryside, but also how seriously it's threatened by human degradation of the environment – and by the failure to recognise the threat. He interrupts his story of the journey with records of online conversations he's arranged with climate scientists. They find it hard to disguise their despair at the planet's prospects. Just short of Caerhun he breaks his trip to attend a London magistrates' court, to defend himself, in vain, against a charge of demonstrating in London as a member of Extinction Rebellion. But all along Sarn Helen he takes comfort from the past of Wales, and especially the age of the Celtic saints. Illtud, Samson, Melangell and others seem to him to strike a more respectful balance and harmony between humans and their habitats.[34]

Around the same time Matthew Yeomans, a writer and journalist, set off from his home in Cardiff to walk to north Wales. He had a different route and a different aim. The Welsh Government had just announced plans for a National Forest for Wales, to create new areas of woodland and to restore existing woods. Yeomans plotted his own path that would link together existing woodlands, as one possible long-distance route for future forest-walkers. As a committed environmentalist he finds parts of the journey dismaying. Disrespect for the natural world is common. People strew sacks of household rubbish and builders' debris in Wentwood. New homes are built on the flood plain of the Usk. Above Maesteg bikers churn a green ridgeway into rutted mud. Large companies plant new woodlands, though only to use 'carbon offset' to cover up their carbon emissions. But, unlike Bullough, Yeomans takes heart from the many initiatives he meets with on his journey, like local treeing schemes. He recognises, as someone prone to anxiety and panic attacks, how immersion in woodland or forest can ease mental fears and produce happiness. And he looks forward to a time when 'natural capital' and 'rights of nature' might replace traditional economic and legal values, and when Wales, like Costa Rica, might place its natural environment at the centre of its national identity.[35]

Not every long-form walker strives for extended length. Others focus on concentration, exploring a specific area intensively. Rhian Parry combed the countryside of Ardudwy for her microscopic study of its place-names, *Cerdded y caeau*. 'It is only by walking the fields', she wrote, 'that we can notice the features of the land and realise that the names chosen are entirely appropriate.' And the post-war period saw a revival of the naturalist walker, figures such as William Condry and Jim Perrin. Others were generalists. Just before the Second World War Hope Hewett set out on a series of criss-cross walks through Merioneth. Travelling alone, with her terrier dog Jack, a light rucksack and no fixed destination, she disdained 'hikers', who tended to march in groups, over-rapidly and with excessive baggage.[36]

Later, as motor cars became the default mode of rural travel, walking as a way of exploring local areas intensively declined. In 1952 Llyfrau'r Dryw began to publish the 'Crwydro' series of twenty-one travel books by well-known Welsh-language authors, each title concentrating in detail on a particular county or region. The first, *Crwydro Ceredigion* by T.I. Ellis, came out in 1952, and all parts of Wales had been covered by 1976, when Aneirin Talfan Davies completed *Crwydro Bro Morgannwg*. Not one of the (all-male) authors chooses to walk as his main means of going from place to place. Each of them assumes that he, and his readers, will be using a car. Yet when a knowledgeable author uses feet rather than wheels, a closely-examined place can yield a rich tapestry of histories, stories and characters, as when Hefin Wyn roamed the coastal communities of his native Pembrokeshire for his book *Pentigily*, warmly written in his native dialect.[37]

Chapter 9:
Everyday walking and reflexive walking

The decline of walking

The post-war growth of long walking and recreational walking in Wales is striking. But its success masks a slow and catastrophic decline of walking in other aspects of life. Walking to work, walking to school, walking to the shops, walking to visit relatives or friends – all of these everyday forms of transport, so common in the 1940s and 1950s, have become rarities. Distance became measured in time, not in miles travelled. The motor car has become not just the dominant means of getting around, but a rampant monster that has gradually devoured walking, cycling, public transport – and people themselves. Even worse, the environmental costs arising from its manufacture, emissions and wider effects have made it a threat to the stability of our climate.

In 1951 there were 2.6m vehicles on British roads. Only 14% of households then owned a car. Seventy years later, in 2021, there were almost 40m vehicles on the roads, two million of them in Wales. A third of households owned two or more.[1]

People without access to cars were left isolated as public transport deteriorated. In Wales Dr Beeching's evisceration of the railway network in the 1960s removed hundreds of miles of track and cut north-south links uniting the country. The decline in bus services, accelerated by deregulation in the 1980s, was more gradual but even more damaging for those who had no car or chose not to use one. In the meantime, decisions on transport links, and the location of retail parks and other facilities, came to depend on an assumption that all households had the use of a car. Those who didn't were ignored and, in effect, disenfranchised.

More cars called for more roads. Concrete and tarmac have covered over more and more land in Wales, over 1,500 miles of them for the exclusive or near-exclusive use of motor vehicles. Those unlucky enough to live close to the busiest roads suffer not only from restrictions in their movement and threats to their safety when on foot, but also from noise and the usually unacknowledged health effects of air pollution from vehicle emissions.

Walking in general in urban areas became ever more dangerous and unpleasant, as vehicle volumes and emissions increased, and facilities for pedestrians failed to match the privileged public provision for motor transport. Fear, as much as perceived convenience, led many to abandon walking and cycling, even for short distances. Almost half of the people asked in a survey in 2021-2 reported that they walked or cycled less than once a week for non-recreational purposes. A mere 18% said that they walked for more than ten minutes every day.[2]

The lack of alternatives, along with the geography of Wales, means that almost 80% of people going to work here now do so by car – a higher figure than for any other part of the United Kingdom. In the early 1990s two-thirds of children walked or cycled to their local primary school, but by 2019 less than 44% did so. School gates become besieged twice a day by battalions of SUVs, as colossal as armoured personnel carriers, shooting diesel fumes into the faces of children. Beyond school, in their spare time, children are rarely allowed to wander without adult accompaniment, as was common in the 1950s. Welsh children, according to a research study, are among the least physically active in the world.[3]

The most serious personal cost of these trends is to health. Routinely inactive transport, added to sedentary forms of work and leisure, cause problems for the heart, lungs and other organs. Almost two-thirds of Welsh adults, and 12% of 4-5-year-old children, are overweight or obese, while 8% of Welsh adults have type 2 diabetes, the highest incidence in the UK. Almost 2,000 people in Wales die every year from air pollution, nitrogen dioxide and particulates, caused by road traffic; vulnerable social groups suffer more than others. The threat that motor vehicles pose for the health of the climate is even more serious. Transport, mainly cars, accounts for almost a quarter of Wales's annual greenhouse gas emissions, mainly carbon dioxide.

These problems were well known from early in the twenty-first century. Solving them was another matter. The Welsh Government aimed to develop policies to try to reduce car volumes. Its refusal in 2019 to build an extension to the M4 motorway and its 2021 moratorium on the building of new major roads recognised the truth that building new roads only succeeds in attracting more vehicles. In September 2023 it introduced a default 20mph to replace the previous 30mph limit in residential urban areas. It published a new transport policy, *Llwybr newydd*, in 2021. One of the policy's priorities was to 'encourage people to make the change to more sustainable transport', by moving them away from private cars to public transport, and supporting active travel. The plan set an ambitious target of 45% of journeys to be made by public transport, walking and cycling by 2040 (the figure was 32% in 2020). However, in the meantime, bus services have continued to deteriorate.

Promoting active travel had already been the subject of a Walking and Cycling Strategy in 2003, and the Active Travel (Wales) Act 2013. The Act required local authorities to improve facilities for everyday walking and cycling, supported by an Active Travel Fund. Despite these measures, and the introduction of local initiatives like 'low traffic neighbourhoods', 'school streets' and trial 20mph speed limits, evidence suggests there was no improvement over subsequent years in the numbers of adults or children choosing to walk. A Senedd committee in 2018 blamed this poor result in part on a failure to convince those who influenced and made decisions on transport.[4]

More locally, many specialist and community groups have done their best to give walking a higher profile, and walkers a better chance of thriving. The charity Living Streets, for example, has campaigned for years in Wales to enable more children to walk to and from school. Individual schools have put a lot of effort into practical measures to achieve the same aim. Ysgol Hamadryad is a primary school in Butetown, Cardiff that has worked with great energy to encourage walking to and from the school, including a 'walking bus', an

Walking bus, Ysgol Hamadryad, Cardiff
(Ysgol Gynradd Gymraeg Hamadryad)

accompanied walk from a car park to the school gates. Over 90% of children walk (or scoot or cycle) to school.[5]

Many other initiatives aim to promote walking locally. Some are planning walking and cycling routes to connect urban centres, including one to link Cardiff with Newport, only eleven miles apart. Using suggestions from volunteers, the Slow Ways initiative aims to create a network of walking routes connecting towns and cities across Britain. Local authorities have experimented with car-less residential streets to encourage cyclists and pedestrians. Annual 'car-free days' have been organised in the centre of Cardiff. The '15-minute city' concept holds that in urban areas most daily services should be within a quarter mile walk of one's home, to help increase walkability and reduce car dependency.[6]

When asked why they do not walk more than they do, people usually point to the car. Cars have many advantages: they're convenient, flexible, swift, and long-range; they needn't be shared with strangers; they provide shelter from Welsh rain and they hold less risk of serious injury than cycling or walking. Some of them are not just vehicles, but markers of pride and prestige – which explains why many cars are more grandiose and environmentally destructive than they need be. Many people are deterred from walking by their perceptions of the car's dangers, and by the usual distortions of the planned environment in favour of the car. All this means that attempts to encourage walkers must be linked, nationally and locally, with measures to curb the dominance of the car. The determination and resources to unlock these are dependent on a large cultural shift in public attitudes to the car and its alternatives, as well as brave decisions by governments and other authorities who understand the urgency of change.[7]

Workers still walk

Not only are workers increasingly unlikely to walk to their place of employment, few spend much of their time on their feet when they arrive. The numbers of people employed in manual work has decreased, especially after the headlong deindustrialisation of the Thatcher period and the advance of industrial robots. Most jobs now mean long hours sitting in front of a computer screen. Studies show that employees spend around 80% of their time sitting down.

In a few traditional occupations, walking has survived, apparently irreducible and untouched by robots. And a few new kinds of job have arisen, to give walking a new life, even if the walking in them may be oppressively regulated.

Walking is still a daily reality for postal workers. The monopoly for delivering post was scrapped in 2006, most parcels and other deliveries now arrive at houses by van, and most communication has become electronic. But postal workers still walk from door to door to deliver letters and parcels. In the past, rural postal workers walked long distances, sometimes along routes seldom used by others: there are several 'posties' paths' recorded throughout western Britain. Postal access to the South Stack lighthouse on Ynys Lawd, off the coast of Holy Island, was possible at first only by a cable and basket system, but in the 1930s a flight of stone steps and a suspension bridge were introduced. The postman, R.G. Rees, estimated that in six years of deliveries he'd walked up and down over 1.5m steps. In 1938 a Pathé newsreel captured him on film, adding doggerel verses as commentary:

There are many steps to clamber,
Four-O-three to be exact,
But the postman's got to climb 'em
And so far he's never slacked.

Up and up and up he trudges,
Each step nearer to the top,
Trust OHMS the postman,
Mr R.G. Rees can't stop.[8]

Around the same time Idris Mathias was a Cardigan postman who walked up and down the lower Teifi valley on his rounds. From 1945 he began to draw and colour, on a single roll of cartridge paper, a map, 58 feet long and a yard wide, of the course of the Teifi from Newcastle Emlyn to Cardigan Bay. He finished it nearly seventeen years later. On it he noted, in astonishing detail, the natural features and place-names he was familiar with from his walking routes, complete with exquisite illustrations of trees, animals, birds and insects.[9]

R.G. Rees, postman, South Stack, Anglesey, 1934, photograph
(*Royal Mail Group, courtesy of The Postal Museum*)

Manuscript map of the lower Teifi valley by Idris Mathias, 1945-62 (detail)
(Cymdeithas Enwau Lleoedd Cymru)

Today walking postal workers operate mainly in urban areas. Chris Baker has been delivering mail in Swansea for over twenty years (his father is also a working postie). When asked whether he enjoyed his role, he replied,

> I love the job ... Talking to the customers, playing my part in the community. Little things, but massive things, if that makes any sense. Seeing people. Working outdoors in the fresh air. And fitness is a massive part. If it wasn't for this job I'd be huge.[10]

Chris's day starts at 6.40am. At the central sorting office he prepares the mail for his own route. At around 8.30 he takes his van to the start of the route, and the walking begins. Each day he walks around seven miles or 15,000 steps, and covers 20-25 streets. He appreciates having control over how he makes his deliveries. He can walk at his own pace, which gives him enough time to talk to his customers, one of the elements of the job he values most.

Employee-walkers of a very different kind can be found in the huge sheds full of retail goods that exist to feed the appetites of online buyers. Customers seldom consider, when they open the door to receive a parcel they ordered only hours before, that its rapid journey began when a poorly-paid and highly-controlled 'picker' scurried along the length of a warehouse to locate the object of their desire.

The largest of these buildings in Wales, measuring 800,000 square feet, is the 'Amazon Fulfilment Centre' at Jersey Marine, to the east of Swansea. Swansea is one of over twenty similar centres, situated mainly in economically depressed areas of the UK. Amazon's success relies on two strategies: obtaining perfect satisfaction for customers, achieved through strict efficiency in operations, and offering the lowest possible prices, achieved by reducing costs, including taxes and labour costs, to the absolute minimum.

At peak times around 3,000 people work in the Swansea Centre. Amazon's owner, Jeff Bezos, may be one of the richest men in the world, but most of his Swansea workers earn little more than the official minimum wage. It's the working conditions, however, that have drawn most attention, especially from undercover journalists investigating the building. What they discovered was a picture of oppressive control and exploitation, and a place that may delight consumers but provides a less than fulfilling experience for workers.[11]

New recruits were told they could be required to walk up to fifteen miles a shift (each shift was ten and a half hours long). Their feet quickly developed blisters and sores as they were hurried from shelf to shelf and floor to floor, pushing a heavy trolley and closely monitored by computer handsets. The computers tracked their movements, logged the speed and accuracy of their selection, and reported their data to a central performance station. Workers were specified a target of 'picks' to be made in an hour, and the handset allowed a set number of seconds to find each pick on the shelf. In other words, data and algorithms dictated their working lives.

Most workers were not generally employed directly by Amazon but by agencies operating on its behalf, on zero-hours contracts and with the minimum of employee rights and benefits. Breaks were short, sickness wasn't tolerated, and nor were mistakes made by workers. Absence, illness, arriving late, failure to hit often unrealistic picking targets, talking in the aisles, over-long lunch breaks: all of these attracted 'points'. One or two points led to interviews and disciplinary action. Three points meant that staff were 'released' by Amazon.

Employees paid a heavy physical and mental price for being forced to work in such a harsh, algorithm-directed environment. They became exhausted in body and mind, were subject to constant and close discipline, and had almost no ability to control their own work. The experience of walking in an Amazon warehouse seems much closer to a prison treadmill than the steady tread of the postie.

Squeezed out of everyday activities like going to work or school, and almost eliminated from the way work people carry out their work, walking has increasingly taken on the form of a reserved or specialised activity.

An extreme example of this trend is the strange phenomenon of walking (and running and rowing) in the modern gym. As Rebecca Solnit has observed, a gym is configured in much the same way as a nineteenth century factory. Rows of machines stand in lines, occupied by Lycra'd men and women on treadmills, working their limbs and pumping their hearts in time to individualised music and videos. Behind them, more complex machines await those with more specialist muscles to be developed. In the factory, human muscles worked the machine; in the gym, the machine works the muscles. All contact with the world outside the gym walls, the natural home for walking, has been lost, or needs to be reinvented. One local gym announces that 'we even provide a running track, so that if you want to train your cardio off the machines and in the fresh air, you can have free use of our running track to do just that!'[12]

Rambling and mountaineering

'Reserved' walking activity that has become more and more popular is the use of open country for rambling, hillwalking and mountaineering. Ramblers' organisations have flourished, and today there are over forty Ramblers groups active in Wales. Other societies cater for particular needs, some national, some local. Since 1978, for example, Cymdeithas Edward Llwyd has arranged walks for Welsh speakers to discuss the natural world, while the Gower Society, established in 1949, runs several guided walks each month around its area. Since the 1970s gay and lesbian walking organisations have been set up. The needs of disabled walkers are beginning to be realised, for example by the replacement of stiles by gates on footpaths.

Historically members of BAME communities have been badly under-represented as country walkers, and new groups have been set up to encourage them to shed doubts they had about taking part in what they sometimes perceived as an activity that excluded them. In 2001 only 1.4% of visitors to the Bannau Brycheiniog National Park were from ethnic minorities. The National Park Authority worked with 'community champions' under the Mosaic Wales project to help improve participation, and in 2023 it appointed its first black board member, with the same aim.

Some of the barriers that face would-be BAME walkers became clear to Guy Kennaway, a white, upper middle-class Englishman who walked over forty miles along the Offa's Dyke Path in the company of a relation by marriage, Hussain Sharif. Hussain was an east African Muslim and came from a wholly urban background. Cows, walking boots, long distances, the looks of strangers – all these and more felt alien and uncomfortable to him at first.[13]

Less noticed and debated as an aspect of under-representation on the hills is social class. National parks in particular are less accessible to households without cars, or to those without the money for public transport to reach them from distant urban centres. Car-owners, by contrast, enjoy all too easy access to upland walking. In recent years vehicle congestion in the approach roads to Yr Wyddfa and other 'honey-pots' has become a headache for the Eryri National Park. Large increases in the number of walkers in Eryri – over 600,000 people now climb to the summit of Yr Wyddfa each year – have also taken a toll on the environment, including the walking routes. Too many footfalls lead to rapid erosion and scarring, and a constant need to repair and rebuild footpaths. There are strong arguments for encouraging walkers to bypass the obvious peaks like Yr Wyddfa and Pen-y-fan and explore less used parts of the National

Parks, or other upland areas like the Cambrian Mountains.

Mountaineers as well as mountain walkers continued to come to Eryri and other sites. For some in the immediate post-war period, Eryri offered a convenient training ground, as it had done for earlier Alpinists, for greater challenges abroad. Members of the 1953 Chomolungma (Everest) expedition, led by John Hunt, stayed at Pen-y-Gwryd while they tested themselves with oxygen equipment on the slopes in the winter months. In the 1950s many working-class climbers like Joe Brown and Don Whillans came from the cities and towns of Lancashire to Yr Wyddfa, to test themselves with routes on cliffs like Clogwyn Du'r Arddu. And in the years since, many more climbers have made names for themselves, often away from the classic sites. The sheer faces left by the old quarrymen at Dinorwig, for example, attracted small but fanatical bands of slate climbers.[14]

Visitors from outside Wales could become familiar with their favoured climbs and rockfaces in Eryri, but not many could command the wide but intensive knowledge of the mountains that local people nurtured in their daily lives. For climbers like Ioan Bowen Rees, Dafydd Andrews, Jim Perrin and Iolo ap Gwyn the peaks and slopes are a constant presence in their lives. The same is true of the farmers of Eryri. The poet, musician and stonemason Dewi Prysor was brought up on a hill farm in Cwm Prysor, west of the Arenig range, and has written vividly of how the mountains became a constant and natural part of his life:

> The hill farm extends to over two thousand feet, to the top of the eastern ridge of Gallt y Daren. On this land, between a thousand and two thousand feet, I spent a good chunk of my first eighteen years in the world. As well as shepherding, draining, ditching, fencing, building walls and saving sheep from snowdrifts, I would spend long summer days on my own on the mountain, cutting thistles with scythe and sickle on the slopes of Foel yr Wden and Yr Allt ... In these childhood years I got my mountain sense and came to know the moods and quirks of the mountains by second nature.[15]

Walking to Greenham Common

Another type of walking activity that survived into the late twentieth century was protest. Campaigns used marches as one means of expressing and amplifying public feeling against what they saw as unjust actions – the drowning of villages to build reservoirs, the divisive politics of Margaret Thatcher's government, threats to the Welsh language, and many others.

Walking was a crucial part of the campaign in 1981 against the installation of nuclear cruise missiles. In 1980 the UK government had announced the stationing of 96 cruise missiles in a US air base, RAF Greenham Common, near Newbury in Berkshire. Two women living in Carmarthenshire, Ann Pettitt and Karmen Cutler (later Thomas), set up, with two others, Women for Life on Earth, a Welsh group dedicated to opposing the weapons. The group, fearful and horrified by the increasing danger of nuclear conflict, decided to organise a ten-day, 120-mile protest walk from Cardiff to Greenham. The walk was led and populated almost entirely by women:

> But it wasn't an organisation, we were just Women for Life on Earth. Simple. And that could be one or 5,000. It could be just two – didn't matter. We couldn't have had a more varied group of women in their ages, their professions, where they came from, if we'd have hand-picked them all.[16]

Ann and Karmen feared that no one would join them in Cardiff, but in the event thirty-six women, and a few men and some small children, started out from City Hall on 26 August. The women were of varied ages, backgrounds, beliefs and experience. Some were experienced political activists; for others this was their first public protest. Few had trained for the physical challenges of the walk. Writing twenty-five years later, Ann Pettitt summarised the reasons why she marched:

> I love going on long walks. No, that's an understatement, I adore

going on long walks. I am just like an eager-beaver dog, wagging its tail at the door, in this respect. This is one of the reasons I liked the idea of walking to Greenham Common in 1981. We could have just driven down the motorway. It would have been quicker and a lot easier, but had we done so, none of the things that did happen, would have happened.[17]

'The things that did happen' included a busy send-off from Cardiff; banners and scarves in purple, green and white, made by the women themselves; hospitality, entertainment and accommodation from Quakers, CND, the local Labour Party, churches and chapels at each evening destination; and marching bands and songs. The weather was hot and the roads hard. One of the walkers volunteered to check feet every day for blisters. Local people tended to react to the walkers with bewilderment and mild curiosity, rather than enthusiastic support. The marchers were escorted by police, who sometimes tried in vain to modify their route or offer them lifts.

Greenham Common march banner, 1981
(Thalia Campbell / Amgueddfa Cymru – National Museum Wales)

An advance group of the women arrived at the front gate of RAF Greenham early in the morning of 5 September, and chained themselves to the fence. The sole policeman on guard mistook them for cleaners. Karmen delivered a statement, including the words, 'We have undertaken this action because we believe that the nuclear arms race constitutes the greatest threat ever faced by the human race and our living planet.' Officials continued to pay them little attention. Paradoxically, this indifference stung the women into a longer occupation of the site than they'd planned.

The walk itself had attracted little media interest, but once the women made it clear that they meant to stay and began to take action against the base, their presence started to be noticed. Outside the base they set up a peace camp to continue their protest (several camps grew up, at the different gates to the base), and occasionally they cut through the perimeter wires and broke into the base.

More women joined the protest. On 12 December 1982 thousands of women and men from all over the country took part in 'Embrace the Base', holding hands around the entire nine-mile perimeter of the site. This event helped make Greenham and its women household names by the time the cruise missiles were finally deployed in November 1983.

The Greenham march inspired a second protest walk, this time around 120 miles from Cardiff to RAF Brawdy on the Pembrokeshire coast, between 27 May and 5 June 1982. Brawdy included a US site that monitored the movements of Soviet submarines, and was seen as a key Soviet target for attack. The protesters, including a Greenham contingent, again called for nuclear disarmament, and set up a camp at the base for a time.

The peace camps became a national focus for opposition to nuclear weapons in the years to come. By 1991, following an arms treaty between the USA and the Soviet Union, all cruise missiles had been removed from Greenham, the Americans forces left soon afterwards, and today almost no trace of the military occupation remains. The women remained at Greenham until 2000. Their nineteen-year protest had helped harden public opinion against nuclear weapons, and radicalised two generations of women. Ann Pettitt attributed their achievement to their innocent faith in marching feet:

> We did this ... not because we were good at campaigning, but because we were bad at it; not because we went about things in a professional way, but because we were amateurs; not because we were clever, but because we were naïve. We wanted to stop the nuclear arms race, which was then the greatest threat to the human race and indeed to all life, and we thought marching down a road a long way would be enough to start people talking and thinking.[18]

The end of coal

A few years after the Greenham march the National Union of Mineworkers held a nationwide strike against the Conservative government's plans to close coal mines and destroy the power of trade unions. The government brought to bear all the instruments available to the state, including the police and the courts, to defeat the miners. The strike, which lasted from March 1984 to March 1985, ended in comprehensive failure, a failure that marked the end of large-scale industrial trade unionism in Britain.

The last strikers in Wales to return to work after the strike, on 5 March 1985, were the miners of Maerdy Colliery, long known for their militancy. They chose to do so by organising a march, as a symbol of solidarity, unity and determination, even in the hour of defeat. Not a single Maerdy miner had passed through the picket line throughout the strike.

On 4 March the Maerdy Lodge committee met to receive the news of the strike's end, and to plan the return to work. One of the officers announced the Union's aims for the following day:

> It will be an orderly return to work through the gates, united. The one thing we've got to do in the general meeting later on is to lift

the men up. We don't want a dejected workforce returning tomorrow ... We are still opposing pit closures. We are not a beaten workforce.[19]

Miners and their families and supporters gathered at 5.30 the following morning at the Maerdy Workingmen's Hall and Institute, the darkness pierced by television arc-lights and flashing cameras. At the signal the procession got under way, led by the Maerdy, Ferndale and Tylorstown colliery brass band. Next came the Maerdy Lodge banner, held high, and the 300 colliery workers and 700 relatives and supporters, including the mayor of Rhondda wearing her chain of office. Among them were more banners, including the banner of the support group of women who had been so crucial in sustaining the Maerdy miners throughout the year of the strike. They all walked uphill for a mile and halted at the colliery gates. Arfon Evans, the Lodge chairman, addressed the crowd from the pit bath roof. He assured the men that they were unbowed by defeat, and he warned

Miners returning to work, Maerdy, March 1985, by an unknown photographer
(Rhondda Cynon Taf Libraries)

the National Coal Board, 'you will not walk all over us, we will stand and fight for the pits and communities.' At 7.00am the sun came up, and the miners returned to work.

One of the miners, recalling the day, was aware of its historical continuities:

> I'm proud to say that my grandfather, who marched in the General Strike and the Miners' Strike in 1926, also marched with me in 1985 when we marched back to work. And I'll never forget that day. That was outside Maerdy Hall, and Maerdy Church was next door, and the bells were pealing, there was cameras from all over the world, there was a lot of people there, in preparation to walk back up the road to the colliery, united in arms ... the miners, everybody else working in the Maerdy Colliery, lots of the wives, lots of the children, everybody was united.[20]

The march was far from funereal. It was a defiant reassertion of the miners' resistance to the oppression of those in power, which dated back beyond the 1926 strike into the nineteenth century. Their feet were echoing those of generations of miners who had used the march to defend their livelihoods and communities. In December 1990 Maerdy Colliery, the last pit left in the Rhondda valleys, finally closed. Another procession took place, this time in the reverse direction, from the colliery to the Hall.

Still protesting

Popular protests were not confined to Welsh or British causes. Just as in the 1930s workers in Wales had united to oppose the rise of fascism in Spain, giving refuge to Basque refugees and providing fighters for the Republic in the civil war, so from the 1970s many came together to oppose the racist apartheid regime in South Africa. From 1981 Wales possessed a highly active group, the Wales Anti-Apartheid Movement (WAAM), organised by the South African émigré Hanef Bhamjee. In 1986 the Movement began an annual series of 'Soweto

Walks', named after the 1976 uprising by black schoolchildren in the township of Soweto.

The ten-mile Walk aimed to pull together supporters, from political parties, churches and other organisations, and to raise money for the anti-apartheid cause. It was also designed for enjoyment. Each year walkers gathered in the King George V Playing Field at St Donats on the south Glamorgan coast and strolled westwards along the coast path above the cliffs, past the lighthouse at Nash Point. Then they'd turn up the wooded valley of Cwm Nash and walk along the narrow lane leading to Monknash, stopping for food and a pint or two in a seventeenth century inn, the Plough and Harrow, before returning in the afternoon to St Donats.[21]

By this time the sponsored walk had been a very common activity, in all parts of Wales, and in aid of many different causes. Its initial growth in the 1970s mirrored in reverse the rapid decline in everyday walking: to potential sponsors, walking could be presented as effortful, even heroic, and therefore worth supporting.

Walking as art

Such is the power of motorised transport today that, beyond these kinds of 'paid' walking, protest marching and other survivals, most forms of non-recreational walking have come to be seen as exceptional and worthy of notice. They're conspicuous or even deviant. Those who practise them feel, or are made to feel, self-conscious. Even such a mundane act as walking to the shops looks and feels eccentric when most people take their cars.

There are some advantages in this for those who insist on walking. Since the 1960s, for some visual artists, beginning with Richard Long in his 'sculpture in time', *A line made by walking*, walking the land has become an established art form, and a noticeable and noteworthy act. Often it's a practice at odds with social conformity. The Belgian artist Francis Alÿs wrote that 'walking, in particular drifting, or strolling, is already – with the speed culture of our time – a kind of resistance.'

Since the 1990s the movement artist Simon Whitehead, from his home in Aber-cuch, north Pembrokeshire, has explored the possibilities of walking. Walking as movement lends itself naturally to performance art, but Whitehead uses walking to extend in many other directions: drawing, photography, film, writing and sound. In 1997, in 'Folcland', he walked a route on the Llŷn peninsula, stopping every hundred steps to pick one of the yellow tormentils that flourish on the slopes. After mounting twenty-two of the flowers in a single line on a wall, he was recorded in the process of writing on two rolls of paper, while sound and light played in the background; the paper became a 'landscape at sunset'. In 2002, in a work entitled '2mph', he loaded a stuffed goose on to a hand-cart and spent twenty-three days pushing the cart, with a fellow-artist and a dog, from west Wales to Smithfield Market in London, following the route of the old drovers.[22]

Since 2006 Whitehead has pursued a project centred on the Dulais, a small river that flows into Afon Cuch near his home. He wades along the length of the river's bed, carrying microphones, an amplifier and an electric guitar strapped to his back. Sounds are coaxed from the passing wind, from birdsong, and from flows and eddies in the water itself, after dipping the guitar's neck into the river. In the studio his sounds are processed and manipulated by a collaborator, Barnaby Oliver. The resulting tapes aim to capture complexities of the river's movements and frequencies. On 2 June 2022 he wrote about a meander in Afon Cuch:

> I wade downstream, coming across a fallen alder, its branches snagged up with grasses, sticks and plastic bags, making an accumulated tangle midstream ... The recording is short and intense – I hold the guitar's body and plunge its neck into the river bed beneath, I press into it with my weight and force. It begins to play in the river's flow, creating its own vectors in the water and sound.[23]

Younger walker-artists tend to have a powerful strain of eco-activism in their work. In 2016 Jess Allen, an Aberystwyth-based biologist, dancer, artist and aerialist, completed a five-day walk entitled 'Water treatment works'. Her route followed the course of mains water pipelines between a water treatment plant at Bontgoch and a visitor centre at Ynys-las. She carried with her a two-metre length of water pipe, a bottle of freshly treated water and two glasses, and she asked each person she met, 'if you had to make a promise to 'treat' water differently in future, what would it be?' Their responses were written on the pipe, and at the walk's end toasts were drunk with, and to, water. Allen started out as an environment activist, but became disillusioned with the anthropocentric aim of 'sustainability'. She realised that walking art in a rural setting, or what she calls 'tracktivism', is her best way of involving people in ecological debate, with its pathways of connection, its unexpected encounters with strangers, and its 'drawing' attention to ecological concerns. Her work was no longer about activism, but activating: encouraging others to care for the natural world through their engagement with matter.

Allen finds writing and walking to be uncomfortable companions:

Walking stimulates thought but ultimately brings me to a quiet stillness. It's a linear, directional, space-eatingly satisfying, multi-sensorial engagement with the world. It gives me energy at the same time as it exhausts me. Writing is an attempt to tether and order that thought, but it agitates me in the process. It's a non-linear chaos of words in my head emerging through the dam of my fingers, the sluice gate of the pen or keyboard, as a tamed stream of communication. It makes me restless at the same time as it saps my energy. They tire me in different ways but equally, so I can only do one or the other. I don't have the energy for both.[24]

Other pedestrian artists have more in common with the long-distance walkers of Chapter 8. Angela Maddock is a Swansea artist and teacher, working mainly with textiles. In October 2018 she set out to walk on her own from Carmarthen, via her childhood home in the English Midlands, to Middlesborough. The destination was chosen for her by her mobile phone, which suggested it whenever she keyed in the word 'middle'. It took twenty-six days to walk the 307 miles.

Angela was searching for a bodily parallel to processes familiar from her artistic practice: 'winding', 'spooling out' and 'unravelling'. Her slow, light-weight walking mirrored the slow and intermittent process of sewing with threads. On the way she paused to pick up fragmentary objects from her track, including fleece for spinning, and she created 'dorodangos', a Japanese tradition of moulding and polishing spherical balls of earth. As she walked, she kept an audio diary on her phone. Later, she worked up her notes into a handwritten journal of the trip, handwriting being another slow, individualised and bodily process.[25]

The journal tells of the journey's highs and lows, which included storms, dogs, giant blisters and dangerous roads. At one point Angela imagined a local newspaper headline 'Middle-aged woman found dead in a ditch was walking to Middlesborough!' Though she didn't travel as a pilgrim, arrival at the mouth of the Tees had some pilgrimage-like features. Entering the town she found a seemingly magical 'gold coin' on the ground – actually a chocolate coin in gold foil – and marked the walk's end by stroking one of the towers of Middlesborough's famous transporter bridge.

Other artists, rather than using walking as their expression, respond to the experience of walking in more traditional media. For many years, for example, Brendan Stuart Burns has walked and re-walked the beaches of St Bride's Bay, and its tides, land forms and light have worked their way into many of his paintings. In 2022 ten artists and poets were invited contribute to the celebration of the tenth anniversary of the Wales Coast Path. The artists worked in many materials, including paint, metal, embroidery and graffiti. Their works were shown in different venues around the Path, and guided walks were offered, starting from the venues.[26]

Another Swansea art teacher, Robert Newell, known for his large and meticulously drawn landscapes of Welsh mountains, embraces walking for its preparatory value and its ability to afford creative solitude:

Walking is integral to the working process. On mountains it often takes a good two hours to reach the location where I work on a drawing, repeatedly, some twenty to thirty times for each of the main drawings. Walking affords a heightened understanding of topography and scale that informs drawing itself. Being free to walk is at one with being free for the indeterminate attentiveness that constitutes aesthetic engagement.[27]

Rivers, rather than the sea or mountains, preoccupy the artist and letterer Valerie Coffin Price. For a book published in 2015, *A fold in the river*, she walked the length of the Taff, sketching passages of the water and the banks in response to poems about the river by Philip Gross – themselves the product of a walking journal. The resulting printed images are derived from photographs, watercolours and ink drawings. They track the river and its banks in colour and monochrome, incorporating typewritten fragments of text from the poems they surround.

A newer form of performance is the radio walk, pioneered by Horatio Clare in his 'Sound walk to Hay on Wye', first broadcast on BBC Radio 3 in 2017. In this four-hour walk Clare started from near Capel-y-ffin, climbed the steep hill to Hatterrall Ridge, and followed the ridge-top walk along the Offa's Dyke Path north to Hay Bluff and down to Hay-on-Wye. As he walked, a microphone recorded his impressions of the scenery, wildlife and history of the area, as well as ambient sounds and the sound of his own breathing and footsteps, creating for the listener the impression of walking alongside him as a companion.

Action walking of this kind has come to overshadow older kinds of performance by pedestrians. In summer 1947 a fifty-nine-year-old puppeteer called Walter Wilkinson set out on a journey from Newport to Cadair Idris, pushing in front of him a wooden barrow or hand-cart, laden with his puppet theatre, a tent and other camping equipment. It proved to be the last of a sequence of similar journeys, begun by Wilkinson in 1926 in the West Country of England. He wanders the roads slowly, avoiding steep hills if he can, and keeping out of the way of motor vehicles. Even before the consumer revolution multiplied the number of cars, he's painfully aware that the pedestrian is in danger on the open road in the post-war world:

> The startled blast of a near motor horn behind me made me scurry the barrow into the gutter, and a huge bus rolled by with only an inch to spare between its fat tyres and my toes. A lot of expressionless faces at the windows stared down at me, standing in the gutter with the barrow, and I stopped for a moment – well, I just stopped and stood still because my little pedestrian world had vanished in the momentary confusion.[28]

When he senses that he may have an audience, Walter sets up his stall, unpacks his puppets and puts on a 'peep show' for children and their parents. In Ebbw Vale he finds a twelve-year-old boy with experience of manipulating Punch. New Quay, by contrast, has never seen a puppet theatre before. At Tal-y-bont, north of Aberystwyth, he performs on the green. The Second World War casts a long shadow – ration books are still in use, shops are often bare of goods – and the harsh winter of 1946-7 is fresh in the memory. But almost everyone he meets is welcoming and friendly. Farmers are happy for him to pitch his tent in their fields, and, as payment, he's happy to lend a hand with haymaking. Walking through the green countryside, he feels exhilaration.

He knows, however, that it will not be long before such experiences will become hard to recapture:

> Walking is so odd, and so psychologically difficult nowadays, that a pedestrian is suddenly attacked by the feeling that he is missing something, that he is being left behind by all this rushing about on wheels, and not seeing enough of the world, as if the wheels always took one somewhere and never away from anywhere.[29]

As he describes himself, Walter is a mercurial character: lyrical but droll, sympathetic to the Welsh, but hostile towards rain, materialism, bullying landowners and careless motorists. He ends his tour by abandoning his barrow and climbing the summit of Cadair Idris, from where he surveys the land and sea in every direction, and 'all the waves of the sea of hilltops flowing eastwards'. Then he walks his cart all the way back to Machynlleth, only to see the train home pull out of the station without him.

Walter Wilkinson pulling his puppet handcart, undated, by an unknown photographer
(National Puppetry Archive)

Sixty-five summers later, another performer set out on a similarly quixotic trip. Delyth Jenkins, an experienced folk harpist, set off from St Dogmaels in August 2012 to walk the length of the Pembrokeshire Coast Path with a harp strapped to her back and a small rucksack to her front. She called her venture *Llais ar y Llwybr* (Voice on the Path): in Welsh a harpist 'sings' her harp, rather than 'playing' it. She planned to stop at points along the way and give impromptu concerts to other Path walkers, and also to 'sing for her supper' in the places where she stayed overnight.

Delyth knows that through her journey she's echoing an ancient Welsh tradition. For centuries poets and musicians – harpists, fiddlers, crwth players and others – would move from court to court, and from gentry house to gentry house, in search of new audiences, patrons and rewards. When she plays to people on the route of the Path the usual reaction is gratitude, and often tears.

As a musician Delyth is alert to the sonic landscapes of the Path. At Pwllygranat she's mesmerised by the splash of water cascading over a waterfall towards the sea. She records the stream, recollecting as she does so 'my mother who so loved the sound of running water'.

Her journey, in fact, is a double one: a physical, linear walk along the Path in the present, and a more episodic tour through her memories – of her childhood in Shropshire and her grandparents in Montgomeryshire, her relationship with the poet Nigel Jenkins, the end of the marriage and Nigel's death, her two small daughters, her previous jobs and holidays in Pembrokeshire, her recollection of snatches of songs, and poems by Waldo Williams and Dewi Emrys.

At the end of the walk she considers what her answers would be to the questions 'Why are you doing it?' and 'Are you depressed?'

> There is a link between depression and walking, and also perhaps with writing. Some notable depressives, who were also writers, are George Borrow and Edward Thomas. The poet John Clare, another depressive, said of footpaths, 'They give me joy as I proceed.' But there is a huge difference between depression and feeling downhearted. Walking the Pembrokeshire Coast Path brought me happiness and calm. Hardly ever during those seventeen days did I feel down, and with all the thrill of walking so close to the edge, there was never the slightest hint of wanting to go over.[30]

One of the other pleasures of her walk is meeting old friends, including the poet Emily Hinshelwood. Emily too has walked the Pembrokeshire Coast Path, marking places she passes through with short poems, as Delyth paused to play her harp. The poems begin at Amroth and continue via Angle, Skomer and Solva to St Dogmaels. They touch on many essential human experiences – vulnerability and love, cruelty and death, the exploitation of nature – but each takes its cue from a local coastal feature or event. The first poem, about the empty beach at Amroth at the end of a summer's day, recalls, without mentioning them, the imprinted feet of Mesolithic walkers found not far away on the shore of the Severn sea:

> Each footprint a journey
> turns the beach into dreamtime.

They collide, converge
in silent riot of unmet strangers ...[31]

Another author who has transformed the experience of long-distance walking into creative writing is Lloyd Jones. His novel *Mr Vogel*, at once picaresque, learned and fantastical, reflects an epic journey he made in 2002-3 around the circumference of Wales, his way of recuperating from a breakdown caused by alcoholism and extreme stress. In the book, narrative continuity and linear space are collapsed. So is the order of time, and along the way the reader meets many of the leading figures of Welsh walking, including Twrch Trwyth, Coleridge, Dic Aberdaron, Faraday, Borrow, Kilvert and William Gale. As a young child Jones spent a year strapped to a metal frame, to correct a hip condition, and walking, for him and his narrator, is a celebration of physical mobility and mental freedom.[32]

Psychogeographers

It's no coincidence that creative writing, as well as visual art, music and performance, has lighted on the act of walking as a powerful subject for exploration at a time when everyday walking has lost its ubiquity. Writing about walking took on a new energy in the late twentieth century age of the car. In large part this renaissance of literary walking was an urban phenomenon, with its roots in the wanderings of the Parisian '*flâneur*' and the London psychogeographer.

The *flâneur* is a figure created by the poet Charles Baudelaire in an essay published in 1863, and revived in the 1920s by the critic Walter Benjamin. He – the *flâneur* is generally male – saunters on foot without definite direction through the streets of Paris. He's part of the crowd but also a detached observer of the myriad details of modern urban life and people: a tramp, fop, scout, private eye and collector, 'botanising on the asphalt', in Benjamin's phrase, and open to every urban vibration. In the 1950s Guy Debord and fellow 'Situationists' invented a related Parisian figure, the psychogeographer, a street-walker with the more deliberate aim of mapping the areas of a city alongside the geographical, temporal and psychological connections to be found in them. Much of Debord's work was highly theoretical. A real life psychogeographer proved to be as rare a bird to spot as the *flâneur*.

In the 1970s psychogeography migrated to London, and became more practical. Its chief practitioner was Iain Sinclair, at first in long prose-poems including *Lud heat* (1975) and then in longer books starting with *Lights out for the territory* (1997). Sinclair scrutinises overlooked parts of the capital and lets his imagination play around their multiple connections, often historical or cultural, and sometimes occult. His writing is highly personal and often political, sharp in its denunciation of the effects of power on the city and its people. Walking is essential to this kind of exploration:

> Walking is the best way to explore and exploit the city; the changes, the shifts, breaks in the cloud helmet, movement of light on water. Drifting purposefully is the recommended mode, tramping asphalted earth in alert reverie, allowing the fiction of an underlying pattern to reveal itself'.[33]

In 2015 Sinclair, who grew up in Maesteg and holidayed in Wales in his childhood, published a book about a recent trip to Wales, entitled *Black apples of Gower*. Despite his memories from childhood and later visits, he's out of his usual element in walking along the south Gower coast. Although he can call up the ghosts of well-known local cultural figures like Dylan Thomas, Vernon Watkins and Ceri Richards, his narrative of rural travelling lacks the richness of reference built up over a lifetime spent in his adopted Hackney. In a critique of the traditional outsider's account of Wales, and a warning to himself, Sinclair accepts that imposing your own descriptions and meanings on another's landscape is futile:

> Identifying, like fully-paid up Romantics, some authentic wilderness, a rapture of gaze, is not our task. You don't bring

experience home like a souvenir. You listen and learn. You *confirm*. The walk does not require the walker.[34]

Lacking extensive, dense urban centres, Wales has little history of self-conscious urban walking, and no sightings of *flâneurs*. There's one Welsh writer, though, who has worked for years in the Sinclair tradition of close pedestrian readings of city streets. In 2020, during the Covid epidemic, the poet Peter Finch was encouraged by *London orbital*, Sinclair's account of following the route of the M25 motorway, to make his own circular tour, around the administrative boundary of the city and county of Cardiff. In the book of the walk, *Edging Cardiff*, Finch reproduces his clockwise journey in words, maps and pictures.

The edges of Cardiff embrace very different landscapes: sludgy rivers, quiet woods and fields, spreading housing estates, industry, both defunct and extant, and the vast tidelands of the Severn sea. History and archaeology continually poke through the texture of his narrative. He hunts down neglected prehistoric, Roman and medieval remains, like the Roman villa at Ely and Castell Morgraig, that have somehow survived the city's obsession with relentless growth and reinvention.

Today transformation continues at a rapid pace. Although the northern hills of the county remain rural, Finch senses everywhere the implacable appetite of the city for expansion. The eastern fringes bulge with new housing estates, occupied by 'shopless families who live here with their cars', and larger, gated villas, where pavements are scarce and where 'you stand back against the hedges to let the big Mercs and the white Teslas slide by'.

Beyond St Mellons Finch finds a welcome contrast to urban sprawl in the Wentloog Levels, low wetlands drained since Roman times by a complex network of reens and sluices. Always under threat from development, the Levels hold their own, and offer relief to the pedestrian eye:

The flatlands roll out before me, the evenly turfed fields dazzling with an almost luminescent green … The sky has suddenly enlarged. Its high and cloudless blue helps, but the main driver is the sudden lack of buildings, elevated roadways, bridge structures, hoardings, cranes, towers and all of the other enclosing appurtenances of the city.[35]

For the psychogeographer Cardiff offers less fertile ground than London. Its short history as a city hasn't yet laid down the accretion of myth and legend from which the imaginative walker can take flight. Peter Finch departs from Iain Sinclair in avoiding the hermetic and occult, and he adopts a less astringent political voice. But he's just as determined an excavator of history and chronicler of the present as Sinclair, and his camera-like eye makes no distinction between old and new, official and demotic, handsome and ugly.

Wales's second city also attracts a few archivists of urban walking. Rhys Trimble, another poet, avoids Peter Finch's conventional, annalistic narration in favour of a fragmentary, elliptical style, in his novel or prose-poem *Swansea automatic*. It's an account of a bus journey from Bangor to Swansea and his wanderings on foot round the city. With him is a dog called Annwn, tapes of friends talking, a Dictaphone to record his own passing thoughts, and a manual for writing published by the obscure 1970s school of US 'language' poets.

Rhys walks along Swansea's long seafront. He finds moving on foot at once a trance and a stimulant: 'walking brings a kind of parallel unconscious – like sleep but ambulatory – but not sleepwalking either – ideas come by the rhythm'. His eyes look upwards, to the prison, the SA1 tower, the Patti Pavilion and the names of ships written on the sea wall, but more often down, to pebbles, feathers and sand fleas on the beach, or Annwn's shit. The text that results, in English and Welsh, skitters down the page, jump-cutting from place to place, voice to voice, and present to past. Rhys and Annwn pause beside the Tower of the Ecliptic, once an observatory:

A woman is looking up at the building – I talk to her explain about the place a little bit from the research I've done – SWANSEA council's increasing the rent [ASTRONOMICALLY] and the astronomical society leaving with their telescope – the model of the solar system that's supposed to be inside the staircase ...

The woman has wandered off – it's a place I must have been in my childhood – walking past – wondering past – maybe laughing at it – its utopianism seeming naïve even then – now it has the benefit of dereliction.

[MUMBLES WALK] in the armpit of the curve Mumbles is here like a multicoloured bacteria. [Torrance's voice ghosting in on the tape] plaques of growth on a petri dish – up the arc – the peninsula – or maybe I've got a few biochemical terms –[36]

Unlike Peter Finch in Cardiff, Rhys Trimble brings only the resources of a passing visitor to the task of recording Swansea, beyond his childhood recollections. But his feet and his eye, and his ear for voices, live and recorded, combine to capture part of the essence of that city.

We shall end this journey in Swansea. The city has its own popular walking culture. When the track of the old Mumbles Railway, the earliest passenger railway in the world, was closed in 1960, it was eventually replaced by a broad promenade shared by walkers and cyclists. Residents and visitors gained a new way of tracking the long curve of Swansea Bay. Today cyclists sprint along the path, often faster than cars on the congested, fume-laden Mumbles Road. Walkers, meanwhile, long ago borrowed the art of the Italian *passegiatta*. They spend summer evenings sauntering along the path, ice-cream cones in hand, watching the sun setting and stopping to exchange news with groups of friends. Today, promenading, once the reserve of eighteenth-century aristocrats and gentlemen, is a common pastime for everyone – a democratic manifestation of the art of leisurely walking.

Afterword: The future of walking

If Wales has a long history of walking, what will the future bring?

The signs are mixed. On the positive side, walking in the countryside clearly appeals to more and more people. Wales now has a large network of long-distance paths and thousands of rights of way. The Ramblers have over forty active groups in Wales, and there are dozens of independent groups, many serving particular needs and constituencies. Walking holidays are popular. Large numbers of people walk without an affiliation to any group. All varieties of walking flourish, from strolling and dog-walking to long-distance hiking and mountaineering.

In some cases, walking has become too popular. Mountain peaks like Yr Wyddfa and Pen-y-fan attract so many visitors in summer that approach roads become clogged with traffic, footpaths suffer scarring and erosion, and the press and noise of bodies damage the serenity that most people come in search of.

The outlook for other kinds of everyday walking, especially in urban areas, is less certain. With some exceptions, street processions and marches in Wales have declined in number and size in recent years. Protests connected with employment are fewer because of increasing legal and other restraints on collective action by workers, and the destruction of earlier patterns of work with the coming of the 'gig economy'. Those seeking social and political change are more likely to campaign online through social media than take to their feet in the streets.

As for everyday walking, you only have to spend a few minutes on foot on an average town or city street to realise that it's occupied by more cars than ever in the past. Worse, over recent years, they've become inflated in size and pomposity. The largest, with their raised suspension, gigantic wheels and aggressive styling, look more like military vehicles than mere cars. They rule the road with a careless arrogance. Meanwhile, at the periphery of the driver's vision, the pedestrian stumbles hesitantly along the street, or struggles to cross it, assaulted by noise, aerial pollution and the threat of injury.

This looks an unequal contest – until we look at the situation, as we now must, from the point of view of the climate crisis. Transport accounts for more than a quarter of all greenhouse gas emissions in Britain, and emissions are still rising from year to year; the private car is the worst offender. The future, on this reading, is on the side of the pedestrian. In the new environmental calculus, it's the walker, treading lightly on the earth, who's moving towards a sustainable future, whereas the SUV driver clings stubbornly to the old, discredited world of fossil fuel engines and gas exhausts. (Electronic vehicles remove one source of pollution, but fail to banish others.)

In Wales the government has begun to rein in the car and encourage more sustainable transport. It ordered a halt to major new road building, it has introduced a default 20mph limit in residential urban areas, and it funds schemes to build better routes for walkers and cyclists. Interest is growing in other ideas that would shift transport modes towards active travel, like the 'fifteen minute' city, which locates the essentials of living within easy walking or cycling distance of any home, and re-allocating road space for people to stroll and children to play in.

Policies like these are limited but they're also ambitious, because they try to reverse almost a century of official presumption in favour of the car, a presumption accepted as if it were natural by almost everyone. They meet with fierce opposition from those who treat the unrestrained use of a car as tantamount to a human right. Large cultural changes will need to take place before people will be ready to abandon their cars or reduce the use of them and turn to less damaging forms of transport, like the bus, the bicycle and the human foot.

But a better balance between different modes of transport isn't impossible. In many cities and towns on the European continent walking and cycling are already the dominant forms, supported by reliable, clean and comfortable public transport. Cars are used only occasionally. It's true that Wales is hillier and more rural, but its current over-dependence on the private car isn't an inevitability.

There are many benefits of a shift to more sustainable transport.

Reduced car use would mean fewer accidents and deaths, less pollution from emissions and particulates, fewer destructive road building schemes, and a quieter and pleasanter environment for everyone. Out of their cars, people could rediscover the pleasures of pedestrianism, tasted momentarily during the period of Covid lockdown – stretching and testing the muscles, filling the lungs with clean air, finding new routes and making new acquaintances, lightening a sedentary but frenetic lifestyle with physical effort and a welcome slowness.

Another rediscovery could be the social and communal value of walking. Travel within the private pod of the car, sealed off from contact with the out-of-doors and with other people, mirrors the atomised social and economic world that has been made for us during forty years and more of individualism and neoliberalism. As Frédéric Gros wrote, 'the walker considers it a liberation to be disentangled from the web of exchanges, no longer reduced to a junction in the network redistributing information, images and goods.'[1] Learning to walk with others, as so many Welsh people have done in previous centuries, may open us to a better sense of how sharing can benefit everyone, and how it's worth joining with others to fight for a better world.

Walking alone, too, we should cherish, especially for those moments of transcendence that few other human activities can offer. On one hot, airless day in August 2020 I set out on foot along the northern part of the modern pilgrim path Pererindod Melangell.[2] Most medieval pilgrims probably took the easier route up the Tanat valley and through Llangynog, but I started from Llanwddyn, to the south, on the shore of Lake Efyrnwy. The journey took me across the open hills and through the forests of Hirnant and Llechwedd y Garth. I walked down through Cwm Llech and into Cwm Pennant. Up the valley was my destination, the church of St Melangell, the saint who protected in the folds of her clothes a terrified hare fleeing from the hunting dogs. At about the half-way point, at a bend in the track near Brwynen farm, an adult hare stopped suddenly ahead of me. For an instant we looked at each other, our eyes locked together. Then, just as suddenly, the hare bounded away out of sight. I stood there in silence, wondering at the sheltering power of the saint, before walking on up the track.

Hare painting: Carys Evans

Sgwarnog

In the midday heat,
Where the track bends –
Sgwarnog!
The instant before you spring away
Our animal eyes meet.
Will you wait? say mine.
Yours turn to flee,
Knowing fear,
Knowing I'm
No angel.

Appendix: Some walks in Wales

The number of possible walks in Wales is limitless, but here are brief details of some walks with connections to subjects and places mentioned in this book, for those who would like to experience them as well as read about them. The list includes lesser-known as well as well-established routes; distances vary from 1.5 miles to 870 miles.

Ann Griffiths Walk

An easy seven-mile walk in Powys along the River Efyrnwy, named after the eighteenth-century hymn writer Ann Griffiths (p.201–202). It begins at Pont Llogel, passes through Dolanog, site of the memorial chapel to Ann, and ends at Pontrobert, with a possible diversion to Ann's home, Dolwar Fechan. Along the way bronze 'open books' give information to the walker. Links to Glyndŵr's Way and Pererindod Melangell.

Route and description:
Ann Griffiths Walk, Llandrindod Wells, 2003.
https://ldwa.org.uk/ldp/members/show_path.php?path_name=Ann+Griffiths+Walk

Ardudwy Way

A waymarked route on paths, tracks and quiet roads between Llandecwyn and Barmouth (Gwynedd), crossing moorland on the western flanks of the Rhinog mountains. The Way is divided into three sections, Northern: Llandecwyn to Harlech (12 miles), Central: Harlech to Tal-y-bont (13 miles) and Southern: Tal-y-bont to Barmouth (8 miles).

Drovers used parts of the Way to herd animals east to the English markets (p.49–61). Walkers can in addition follow the fine drovers' track from Cors-y-gedol via Pont Scethin to Y Bontddu on the Mawddach estuary (p.55). Robert Graves explored the Harlech Dome in his youth and revisited it during the First World War (p.204–208).

Rhian Parry walked intensively across Ardudwy in researching her detailed survey of its place-names (p.271).

Route and description:
http://www.taithardudwyway.com/

Cadair Idris (Minffordd path)

A strenuous circular walk of around six miles, starting from Minfordd (Gwynedd), ascending to Llyn Cau, then climbing again to Craig Cau and Pen-y-gadair, returning via Mynydd Moel. Links with the Mary Jones Walk.

Cadair Idris instilled fear in John Byng (p.77) and reminded Joseph Hucks of Milton's Chaos (p.91). The writers Richard Warner (p.96), Thomas Love Peacock (p.100), Francis Kilvert (p.132–3), Jenkin Jones (p.142) and Alfred Tennyson (p.167) all reached the summit. Cadair also attracted artists like J.M.W. Turner (p.110), Cornelius Varley (p.110) and Richard Wilson (p.110), who painted Craig Cau from high on a path on Mynydd Moel, as well as the puppeteer Walter Wilkinson (p.295), the scientist Michael Faraday (p.146) and the rock climber O.G. Jones (p. 157).

Route and description:
https://snowdonia.gov.wales/walk/minffordd-path/

Glyndŵr's Way

A 135-mile National Trail through hilly and sparsely populated country from Knighton to Welshpool via Machynlleth (Powys) (p.251). Links to the Wales Coast Path, Offa's Dyke Path and shares a route with the Ann Griffiths Walk. The northern section passes through Ambrose Bebb's paradise, Cwm Nant yr Eira (Powys) (p.240–41).

Route and description:
Paddy Dillon, *Glyndŵr's Way*, 3rd ed., Kendal, 2024.
https://www.nationaltrail.co.uk/en_GB/trails/glyndwrs-way/

Henrhyd Falls and Nant Llech

From the National Trust car park near Coelbren (Powys) a path descends to Henrhyd Falls, visited by Michael Faraday in 1819 (p.145–6), and then follows the wooded valley of Nant Llech to its junction with Afon Tawe, a distance of 3.5 miles.

Route and description:
https://www.nationaltrust.org.uk/visit/wales/bannau-brycheiniog-brecon-beacons/henrhyd-falls-and-nant-llech-walk

Iolo Morganwg Heritage Walk

An easy six-and-a-half-mile circular walk starting in Cowbridge (Vale of Glamorgan), that visits sites familiar to Edward Williams, Iolo Morganwg (p.78–82), including Stalling Down, where Iolo assembled the first 'gorsedd of bards'.

Route and description:
https://www.visitthevale.com/walks/vale-trail-9

Y Lôn Goed

Y Lôn Goed (Gwynedd), a quiet tree-lined path, was originally laid out in the early nineteenth century as a track for transporting lime to upland farms in Eifionydd. It begins at Afon-wen and ends at Hendre Cennen near Bryncir, five miles to the north-east. It was celebrated in R. Williams Parry's poem 'Eifionydd' (p.236–8)

Route and description:
https://www.mudandroutes.com/routes/y-lon-goed/

Maen Madoc

A 1.5 mile linear walk in the Fforest Fawr (Powys) follows the Roman road from Blaen Llia to Afon Nedd Fechan (p.25) and passes the early Christian monument Maen Madoc (p.27).

Route and description:
https://gwallter.com/archaeology/maen-madoc.html

Mary Jones Walk

A reconstruction of the barefoot walk taken by the fifteen-year-old Mary Jones in 1800 from her home in Llanfihangel-y-Pennant to Bala (Gwynedd) to acquire a bible from Thomas Charles (p.136–8). This is a linear route of 28 miles, from the foot of Cadair Idris to Llyn Tegid, and is normally walked in three days. Links with Cadair Idris (Minffordd path).

Route and description:
Mary Thomas, *The Mary Jones Walk: Llanfihangel-y-Pennant to Bala*, [n.p.], [2009].
Des Marshall, *The Mary Jones Way: a 29 mile scenic & historic walk*, Machynlleth, 2017.
https://www.biblesociety.org.uk/uploads/content/projects/mary_jones_walk_guide.pdf

Newport Chartist Walking Trail

Two short urban walks in the city of Newport, taking in sites associated with the Chartist uprising of 1839 (p.118–19). Three years later, festivities, including a grand procession, to mark the open of the new Newport Dock were designed in part to expunge memory of the Rising (p.180–82).

Route and description:
https://www.newport.gov.uk/documents/Leisure-and-Tourism/

Newports-Chartist-Walk.pdf
https://www.newportrising.co.uk/digitaltrail

North Wales Pilgrim Way

Chris and Jenny Potter devised this reconstruction of the route medieval pilgrims took to reach Ynys Enlli (Bardsey Island). The Way begins at Basingwerk Abbey (Flintshire), visits many of the sites that catered for pilgrims, like St Winefride's Well, Holywell (p.38–9, 46, 89, 169–70) and Clynnog Fawr Church, and ends after 130 miles at Aberdaron (Gwynedd) (p.42, 62), the port for the sea passage to Ynys Enlli (p.33, 42–3, 256). The Way passes through Tremeirchion, where Gerard Manley Hopkins attended St Beuno's College (p.168–72). Links with the Wales Coast Path and Offa's Dyke Path.

Route and description:
Chris Potter, *North Wales Pilgrim's Way: the official guide to the Welsh Camino*, [n.p.], 2019.
https://pilgrims-way-north-wales.org/

Offa's Dyke Path

A National Trail between Sedbury, near Chepstow (Monmouthshire) on the Severn estuary, and Prestatyn (Flintshire) on the north Wales coast, following the course of Offa's Dyke. The Path was the second long-distance path to be opened, in 1971 (p.248–9). Links with the Wales Coast Path and Glyndŵr's Way.

Route and description:
Ernie and Kathy Kay and Mark Richards, *Offa's Dyke Path*, London, 2021.
https://www.nationaltrail.co.uk/en_GB/trails/offas-dyke-path/

Penrhys Pilgrimage Way

One of the pilgrim routes to the hill-top sanctuary of the Virgin Mary at Pen-rhys (Rhondda Cynon Taf), the Penrhys Pilgrimage Way, opened in 2018, begins at Llandaf Cathedral in Cardiff and moves north-west through Creigiau, Llantrisant and Tonyrefail, to reach Pen-rhys after 21 miles (p.40–42, 45–6).

Route and description:
http://www.penrhyspilgrimageway.wales/

Pererindod Melangell

A modern 15-mile pilgrimage walk to Pennant Melangell and Llangynog (Powys), starting at Pont Llogel and passing through Llanwddyn on Llyn Efyrnwy. The shrine of St Melangell was a destination for pilgrims from the Middle Ages (p.43–4). At Pont Llogel the walk links to Glyndŵr's Way and the Ann Griffiths Walk.

Route and description:
Pererindod Melangell: kites, cairns and churches: a walk to a saint's retreat below the Berwyn mountains, Llandrindod Wells, 2000.
https://ldwa.org.uk/ldp/members/show_path.php?path_name=Pererind od+Melangell

Snowdonia Slate Walk

The 83-mile Snowdonia Slate Walk was opened in 2017. The route begins with a short stage from Porth Penrhyn, Bangor to Bethesda (Gwynedd), and then loops in a circle around Eryri, visiting Llanberis, visited by Tennyson (p.167, 168), Waunfawr, Nantlle, Beddgelert, Croesor, Llan Ffestiniog, Betws-y-coed, Penmachno and Capel Curig before returning to Bethesda. The Walk offers many views of Yr Wyddfa and passes many of the quarries, like Penrhyn, that gave employment to slate workers (p.126–8). It also passes the old schoolhouse, the childhood home of T.H. Parry-Williams, in Rhyd-ddu (p.238–40).

Route and description:
Aled Owen, *Snowdonia Slate Walk*, rev. ed., Edinburgh, 2022.
https://snowdoniaslatetrail.org/

Teifi Valley Trail

This new 75-mile trail is currently in the course of development. When complete it will begin at the river's source in the Cambrian Mountains (Ceredigion) and end at its mouth beyond Cardigan, where it will link with the Wales Coast Path.

The Trail will pass through Strata Florida, visited by Gerald of Wales (p.33) and John Leland (p.67), from where the Monk's Trod leads over the mountains to Abbey Cwm-hir (p.35–6), the drovers' centre Tregaron (p.53) and the lower stretches of the river familiar to the map-maker Idris Mathias (p.277); Simon Whitehead 'walked his art' in a tributary, Afon Dulais (p.290).

More information:
https://walkersarewelcome.org.uk/2023/03/teifi-valley-trail/

Wales Coast Path

The Wales Coast Path (WCP) follows the whole coast of Wales for 870 miles from Chepstow (Monmouthshire) to Chester, including Anglesey. Opened in 2012, it incorporates earlier paths, including those in Pembrokeshire, Anglesey, Llŷn and Ceredigion, and links with Offa's Dyke Path and Glyndŵr's Way.

The WCP passes through Goldcliff (Newport), where Mesolithic footprints were found on the shore (p.19). The Soweto Walk passed along the south Glamorgan coast (p.288–9). In the estuary of Afon Nedd Gerald of Wales almost came in grief (p.32), and Rhys Trimble scoured the Swansea seafront (p.300–301) The WCP's earliest forerunner was the Pembrokeshire Coast Path, a National Trail planned by R.M. Lockley and opened in 1970 (p.245–8). Along its course Delyth Jenkins played her harp and Emily Hinshelwood wrote her poems (p.295–7). In 2008 Dic Jones marked in verse the opening of the Ceredigion Coast Path (p.251). At Harlech Coleridge and Robert Graves scaled the castle walls (p.90, 207). The WCP passes along both sides of the Menai Strait (p.53, 90, 127). George Borrow began his walking tour of Wales from Chester (p.161).

Route and description:
Paddy Dillon, *Wales Coast Path: Llwybr Arfordir Cymru*, 2nd ed., Kendal, 2022. (There are many other, more detailed guides available for separate sections of the Path.)
https://www.walescoastpath.gov.uk/?lang=en

Yr Wyddfa (Snowdon Ranger path)

The eight-mile Snowdon Ranger route is one of the earliest of the visitors' paths. Today, except towards its end, it's one of the quieter ones. Ascending yr Wyddfa from the west, it starts from Llyn Cwellyn, by the old Snowdon Ranger inn named after the guide John Morton (p.107, 128, 142), and climbs above Clogwyn Du'r Arddu to join the Llanberis Path to the summit.

Walkers taking the Snowdon Ranger path included Thomas Johnson (p.67–8), Samuel Taylor Coleridge (p.90), Ellen Weeton (p.104) and Jenkin Jones (p.142–3). Among others who reached the summit were Edward Llwyd (p.68), John Ray (p.68), Samuel Brewer (p.71), William Wordsworth (p.84), Elizabeth Smith (p.103–104), William Bingley (p.106), Frances Ridley Havergal (p.158) and George Borrow (p.162). Early Ordnance Survey engineers spent days together on the summit (p.174).

Route and description:
R. Russell Roberts, *A pocket guide to Snowdon / Yr Wyddfa*, 3rd ed., Frodsham, 2007.
https://snowdonia.gov.wales/walk/snowdon-ranger/

Notes

Introduction

[1] Rebecca Solnit, *Wanderlust: a history of walking*, London, 2001, p.3.
[2] Solnit, *Wanderlust*, p.5.

Chapter 1: Hunters, invaders and pilgrims

[1] https://www.bbc.co.uk/news/uk-wales-mid-wales-17353470
[2] Martin Bell, *Making one's way in the world: the footprints and trackways of prehistoric people*, Oxford, 2020, p.90-97; Kirsten Barr, 'Prehistoric avian, mammalian and H.sapiens footprint-tracks from intertidal sediments as evidence of human palaeoecology', PhD thesis, Department of Archaeology, University of Reading, 2018.
[3] Robert Macfarlane, *The old tracks: a journey on foot*, London, 2012, p.362-3.
[4] R. Alan Evans and Cécile Le Carlier de Veslud, 'Boom and bust in Bronze Age Britain: major copper production from the Great Orme mine and European trade, c.1600–1400 BC', *Antiquity*, vol.93, 2019, p.1178-96.
[5] Mike Parker-Pearson, Josh Pollard, Colin Richards and Kate Welham, 'Megalithic quarries for Stonehenge's bluestones', *Antiquity*, vol.93, 2019, p.45-62.
[6] Jim Leary, *Footmarks: a journey into our restless past*, London, 2023, p.209-19.
[7] C.A. Gresham and H.C. Irvine, 'Prehistoric routes across north Wales', *Antiquity*, vol.37, 1963, p.54-8.
[8] Martin Bell, Astrid Caseldine and Heike Neumann, *Prehistoric intertidal archaeology in the Welsh Severn estuary*, York, 2000, p.136-158: https://archaeologydataservice.ac.uk/archiveDS/archiveDownload?t=arch-281-1/dissemination/pdf/RR120.pdf; Andy Sherman, 'Recently discovered trackways in Swansea Bay', *Studia Celtica*, vol.45, 2011, p.1-25.
[9] https://www.archaeology.co.uk/articles/new-finds-from-the-pembrokeshire-chariot-burial.htm
[10] N.A. Page, 'Whitland Bypass Roman road', *Archaeology in Wales*, 36, 1996, p.72-3.
[11] Sir Cyril Fox, 'The re-erection of Maen Madoc, Ystradfellte, Breconshire', *Archaeologia Cambrensis*, vol. 95, 1940, p.210-16.
[12] One of the Margam stones is a milestone with the name of the Roman emperor Maximinus Daza (309-313), turned upside down and reused, some two centuries later, as a gravestone; it is inscribed in Latin with the name of Cantusus, son of Paulinus.
[13] 'The dream of the emperor Maxen', *The Mabinogion*, tr. Sioned Davies, Oxford, 2007, p.108.
[14] Thomas Taylor, *The Life of St. Samson of Dol*, London, 1925.
[15] W.H. Stevenson, *ed., Early scholastic colloquies*, Oxford, 1929, p.7-8.
[16] Stevenson, *Early scholastic colloquies*, p.5.
[17] Gerald of Wales, *The journey through Wales and The description of Wales*, translated with an introduction by Lewis Thorpe, Harmondsworth, 1978.
[18] Gerald of Wales, *The journey through Wales*, p. 130-31.

[19] Gerald of Wales, *The journey through Wales*, p. 182.

[20] Gerald of Wales, *The journey through Wales*, p. 184.

[21] Gerald of Wales, *The journey through Wales*, p. 236.

[22] W. Linnard, *Welsh woods and forests: a history*, Llandysul, 2000, p.29-31; Gruffudd ab yr Ynad Coch: *Gwaith Bleddyn Fardd a beirdd eraill o ail hanner y drydedd ganrif ar ddeg*, gol. Rhian Andrews, Aberystwyth, 1996, p.421.

[23] Andrew Fleming, 'The making of a medieval road: the Monks' Trod routeway', *Landscapes*, vol. 10, 2009, p.77-100.

[24] Fred Cowley, *The monastic order in south Wales, 1066–1349*, Cardiff 1977, p.120.

[25] Iolo Goch, *Poems*, ed. Dafydd Johnston, Llandysul, 1993, p.56-63.

[26] Kathryn Hurlock, *Medieval Welsh pilgrimage, c.1100–1500*, New York, 2018.

[27] Barry J. Lewis (ed.), *Medieval Welsh poems to saints and shrines*, Dublin, 2015, p.85. My translation.

[28] Tudur Aled, *Gwaith Tudur Aled*, gol. T.Gwynn Jones, Caerdydd, 1926, vol.2, p.523-8.

[29] Glanmor Williams, 'St Winifred's Well: Ffynnon Wenfrew', *Journal of the Flintshire Historical Society*, vol.36, 2003, p.32-51.

[30] William of Malmesbury, *Gesta regum Anglorum: the history of the English kings*, ed. R.A.B. Mynors, R.M. Thomson and M. Winterbottom, vol.1, Oxford, 1998, p.779-81.

[31] Madeleine Gray, 'Sacred space and the natural world: the holy well and shrine of the Virgin Mary at Penrhys', *European Review of History*, vol.18, 2011, p.243-60.

[32] Jane Cartwright, *Feminine sanctity and spirituality in medieval Wales*, Cardiff, 2008, p.56.

[33] Anne Elizabeth Jones, 'Gwilym Tew: astudiaeth destunol a chymharol o'i lawysgrif, Peniarth 51, ynghyd ag ymdriniaeth o'i farddoniaeth', University of Wales Ph.D. thesis, 1980, p.447-8.

[34] R. Gerallt Jones a Christopher J. Arnold (gol.), *Enlli*, Caerdydd, 1996; Jonathan M. Wooding (ed.), *Solitaries, pastors and 20,000 saints: studies in the religious history of Bardsey Island (Ynys Enlli)*, *Trivium*, vol. 39, 2010.

[35] Brynley F. Roberts, 'Enlli'r oesoedd canol', in R. Gerallt Jones a Christopher J. Arnold, gol., *Enlli*, Caerdydd, 1996, p.21-48; Gregory Fitzgerald, 'Pererindod i Ynys Enlli', *Trivium*, 4, 1969, p.17-20.

[36] *Montgomeryshire Collections*, vol. 82, 1994.

[37] M.Ll. Chapman, 'Transcript of the will of Morgan Herbert, Kt., dated 19 July 1526', *Montgomeryshire Collections*, vol. 82, 1994, p.126.

[38] Dafydd ap Gwilym, 'Pererindod merch', *Dafydd ap Gwilym.net*: https://dafyddapgwilym.net/eng/3win.php

[39] Hugh Latimer, *Sermons and remains of Hugh Latimer, sometime Bishop of Worcester, martyr 1555*, edited for the Parker Society by the Rev. George Elwes Corrie, Cambridge, 1844-45, vol.2, p.395.

[40] Letter from Nicholas Robinson, Bishop of Bangor, to Sir William Cecil, 7 October 1567, *Calendar of state papers domestic, Edward, Mary and Elizabeth, 1547–80*, ed. Robert Lemon, London, 1856, p.300-301.

[41] W.J. Hemp and C.A. Ralegh Radford, 'The Llanelltyd stone', *Archaeologia Cambrensis*, vol.102, 1953, p.164-8.

[42] Rice Merrick, *Morganiae archaiographia: a book of the antiquities of Glamorganshire*, ed. Brian Ll. James, Barry, 1983, p.100, 182-3.

Chapter 2: Drovers, loners and tourists

[1] William Coxe, *An historical tour in Monmouthshire*, London, 1801, vol.1, p.14.

[2] Caroline Skeel, 'The cattle trade between Wales and England from the fifteenth to the nineteenth centuries', *Transactions of the Royal Historical Society*, vol. 9, 1926, p. 135-58; Richard Moore-Colyer, *Welsh cattle-drovers*, 2nd ed., Ashbourne, 2006; Twm Elias, *On the trail of the Welsh drovers*, Llanrwst, 2018.

[3] Guto'r Glyn, 'Porthmona', *Guto'r Glyn.net*: http://www.gutorglyn.net/gutorglyn/poem/?poem-selection=044

[4] Tudur Penllyn, 'Ymateb Tudur Penllyn i Guto'r Glyn a'i gyngor i Syr Bened', *Guto'r Glyn.net*: http://www.gutorglyn.net/gutorglyn/poem/?poem-selection=044a&first-line=044

[5] 'Dafydd Jones, o Gaio', *Y Traethodydd*, vol.5, 1849, p.379, my translation. See also David Gosden, *Tears and laughter: following in the track of David Jones of Caio, hymn-writer, wit, drover*, Southsea, [n.d], p.9.

[6] Arthur Aikin, *Journal of a tour through north Wales and part of Shropshire, with observations in mineralogy, and other branches of natural history*, London, 1798, p.153

[7] In 1979 Wynford Vaughan Thomas was recorded on television riding this spectacular route on horseback:
https://www.youtube.com/watch?v=kqUA9wF5uco

[8] John Jones, *Cerddi Jac Glan-y-Gors*, gol. E.G. Milward, Abertawe, 2003, p.26-7.

[9] Edward Browne, of Aldbury Heath, Surrey, quoted in Caroline Skeel, 'The cattle trade', p.147.

[10] *Farmer's Magazine*, 1856, p.57.

[11] http://bulkeleydiaries.bangor.ac.uk/

[12] *Archaeologia Cambrensis*, ser.4, vol.1, 1870, p.192.

[13] *Carnarfon and Denbigh Herald*, 28 September 1850, p.4

[14] George Owen, *The description of Pembrokeshire*, ed. Dillwyn Miles, Llandysul, 1994.

[15] R.O. Roberts, 'Financial developments in early modern Wales and the emergence of the first banks', *Welsh History Review*, vol. 16, 1993, p. 291-307.

[16] *Carnarfon and Denbigh Herald*, 28 September 1850, p.4.

[17] Ellis Wynn, *Gweledigaethau y bardd cwsg*, gol. Patrick J. Donovan a Gwyn Thomas, Llandysul, 1991, p.111.

[18] Rhys Prichard, *Canwyll y Cymry*, London, 1681, p.149-50.

[19] Richard Phillips, 'The last of the drovers: Dafydd Isaac', *Transactions of the Honourable Society of Cymmrodorion*, 1968, p.110-21.

[20] Eiluned Rees, 'The Welsh book trade from 1718 to 1820', in Philip Henry Jones and Eiluned Rees, eds, *A nation and its books: a history of the book in Wales*, Aberystwyth, 1998, p.128-9.

[21] J. Breese Davies, 'Richard Jones y Llyfrau', *Cymru*, vol. 62, 1922, p.97.

[22] Evan David Jones, 'William Hope', *Dictionary of Welsh Biography*:
https://biography.wales/article/s-HOPE-WIL-1765?&query=itinerant&lang%5b%5d=en&sort=score&order=desc&rows=12&page=1;

[23] Arwyn Lloyd Hughes, 'Richard Jones, Aberangell (1848–1915)', *Journal of the Merioneth Historical and Record Society*, vol.8, 1980, p.447-9. Obituary: *Y Goleuad*, 26 Tachwedd, 1915, p.3.

[24] [William Roscoe], *Memoir of Richard Roberts Jones of Aberdaron*, London, 1822, p.13.

[25] *Y Gwladgarwr*, 26 Mai 1860, p.8.

[26] Richart Suggett, 'Vagabonds and minstrels in sixteenth-century Wales', in Peter Lake and Daniel Woolf, eds, *The spoken word: oral culture in Britain, 1500–1850*, Manchester, 2018, p.138-72.

[27] Thomas Williams, *Hanes bywyd Thomas Williams*, Llanrwst, 1854.

[28] *Newtown and Welshpool Express*, 30 May 1871, quoted in Rachael Jones, 'Crimes, courts and community in mid-Victorian Montgomeryshire', Ph.D. thesis, Aberystwyth University, 2015, p.101: http://pure.aber.ac.uk/ws/files/10907138/Jones_Rachel.pdf

[29] Dot Jones, 'Pauperism in the Aberystwyth Poor Law Union, 1870–1914', *Ceredigion*, vol. 9, 1983, p.86-7; Mary John, 'A sacking matter in Narberth: sentimental treatment of vagrants', *Journal of the Pembrokeshire Historical Society*, vol.13, 2004, p.43-56.

[30] Howell Harris, *Selected Trevecka letters (1747–1794)*, ed. Gomer Morgan Roberts, Caernarvon, 1962, p.21 (Howell Harris to Thomas Boddington, 20 October 1748).

[31] Adam Coward, 'Spiritual journeys: 'purposeful travel' and the writings of the Reverend Edmund Jones (1702–1793)', *Studies in Travel Writing*, vol.22, 2018, p.254-73.

[32] Thomas Johnson, *Mercurius botanicus ... pars altera*, London, 1649, p.7-8. My translation from the Latin.

[33] John Ray to Edward Lhwyd, 22 March 1692, *Further correspondence of John Ray*, ed. Robert W.T. Gunther, London, 1928, p.235.

[34] Brynley F. Roberts, Richard Sharpe and Helen Watt, eds., *The correspondence of Edward Lhwyd*: http://emlo-portal.bodleian.ox.ac.uk/collections/?catalogue= edward-lhwyd; see also Brynley F. Roberts, *Edward Lhwyd, c.1660–1709: naturalist, antiquary, philologist*, Cardiff, 2022.

[35] William Pryce, *Archaeologia Cornu-Britannica*, Sherborne, 1790, [p.246-7].

[36] Castell y Gwynt: William Camden, *Britannia*, ed. Edmund Gibson, London, 1695, col. 667; 'Next summer come twelve month': https://emlo-edit.bodleian.ox.ac.uk/ culturesofknowledge/transcripts/lhwyd/1696-09-14%20EL%20to%20Robinson% 20G%20154%20LBO.14%20P285.pdf

Caer Vorwyn: https://emlo-edit.bodleian.ox.ac.uk/culturesofknowledge/transcripts /lhwyd/1695-07-16%20EL%20to%20John%20Lloyd%20Pen%20427%20F43%20G% 20130.pdf

[37] Mark Lawley, 'Samuel Brewer': https://www.britishbryologicalsociety. org.uk/wp-content/uploads/2021/08/SAMUEL-BREWER.pdf

[38] John Skinner, *Ten days' tour through the isle of Anglesea, December 1802*, London, 1908, p.35.

[39] John Taylor, *A short relation of a long journey*, London: [n.p], 1653.

[40] William Richards, *Wallography, or, The Britton describ'd, being a pleasant relation of a journey into Wales*, London, 1682, p.89.

[41] Richards, *Wallography*, p.123.

[42] Michael Roberts, '"A witty book, but mostly feign'd": William Richards' *Wallography* and perceptions of Wales in later seventeenth-century England', in Philip Schwyzer and Simon Mealor, eds, *Archipelagic identities: literature and identity in the Atlantic archipelago, 1550–1800*, London, 2004, p.153-65.

[43] *A trip to North-Wales: being a description of that country and people*, London, 1701, p.2,3. The author claims to be 'E.B.', identified by some as Ned Ward or Edward Bysshe.

[44] Michael Freeman, *Early tourists in Wales: 18th and 19th century tourists' comments about Wales* is an extensive compilation of information about and writings by tourists: https://sublimewales.wordpress.com/

[45] Thomas Pennant, *The journey to Snowdon*, vol. 2, London, 1781, p.159-171.

[46] Malcolm Andrews, *The search for the picturesque: landscape aesthetics and tourism, 1760–1800*, Aldershot, 1989.

[47] George Lyttelton, *The works of George Lord Lyttelton*, London, 1776, p. 341-2.

[48] *Letters from Snowdon*, London, 1770, p.58-9. The author is often identified, wrongly, as Joseph Cradock.

[49] Charles Bucke, *On the beauties, harmonies, and sublimities of nature*, London, 1821, 2nd ed., vol 1, 1823, p.138.

[50] Charles P. Moritz, *Travels, chiefly on foot, through several parts of England, in 1782*, London, 1795, p.122; *Letters describing a tour through part of south Wales ... by a pedestrian traveller*, London, 1797, p.4.

[51] John Byng, *The Torrington diaries, containing the tours through England and Wales ... between the years 1781 and 1794*, ed. C. Bruyn Andrews, vol. 1, London, 1934, p.157.

[52] R.H. Newell, *Letters on the scenery of Wales ...*, London, 1821, p.2.

[53] Peter Howell Williams, 'Pedestrian peregrinations of Parson Plumptre through Wales in 1792, 1797 and 1799', *Denbighshire Historical Society Transactions*, vol.42, 1993, p.59-84.

[54] Elijah Waring, *Recollections and anecdotes of Edward Williams, the Bard of Glamorgan; or, Iolo Morganwg*, London, 1850, p.1-2. See also Geraint H. Jenkins, *Y digymar Iolo Morganwg*, Talybont, 2018; Geraint H. Jenkins (ed.), *A rattleskull genius: the many faces of Iolo Morganwg*, Cardiff, 2005.

[55] Edward Williams to Walter Davies (Gwallter Mechain), 13 May 1802, *The correspondence of Iolo Morganwg*, ed. Geraint H. Jenkins, Ffion Mair Jones and David Ceri Jones, vol.2, Cardiff, 2007, p.414 (Letter 605).

[56] I am indebted to Mary-Ann Constantine for showing me her transcription of Iolo's diary, and for her account of his walk in 'A journey out of London, 1802: Iolo Morganwg walks home', which forms chapter 3 of her book *Curious travellers: writing the Welsh tour, 1720–1820*, Oxford, 2024.

[57] Edward Williams, Journal, 1801, National Library of Wales, NLW 13174A, p.35r-v. Translation by Mary-Ann Constantine.

Chapter 3: Romantics, climbers and artists

[1] Herbert Wright, 'The tour of Coleridge and his friend Hucks in Wales in 1794', *Nineteenth Century*, vol.99, 1926, p.732-44.

[2] J. Hucks, *A pedestrian tour through north Wales in a series of letters*, ed. Alun R. Jones and William Tydeman, Cardiff, 1979.

[3] Samuel Taylor Coleridge, *Collected letters*, ed. Earl Leslie Griggs, vol.1, Oxford, 1956, p.82-95

[4] Coleridge to Robert Southey, 6 July 1794, *Collected letters*, vol.1, p.83-5.

[5] Joseph Hucks, *A pedestrian tour through north Wales in a series of letters*, London, 1795, p.4.

[6] Coleridge, *Poetical works*, ed. J.C.C. Mays, London, 2001, vol.1: Poems (reading text), part 1, p.69 (poem 69).

[7] Hucks, *A pedestrian tour*, p. 1.

[8] Coleridge to Robert Southey, 13 July 1794, *Collected letters*, vol.1, p.88.

[9] Coleridge to Southey, 13 July 1794, *Collected letters*, vol.1, p.89.

[10] Coleridge, *The notebooks of Samuel Taylor Coleridge*, ed. Kathleen Coburn, London, 1957, vol.1, entry 1207. To walk without a guide preserved for Coleridge his sense of the independent and self-sufficient artist: see Simon Bainbridge, *Mountaineering and British romanticism: the literary cultures of climbing 1770–1836*, Oxford, 2020, p.179.

[11] Coleridge, *Table talk*, ed. Carl Woodring, London, 1990, vol.1, p.149: 30 May 1830.

[12] Coleridge, 'The rime of the ancient mariner', part 3, stanza 6 (1834 edition).

[13] John Thelwall, *The peripatetic*, ed. Judith Thompson, Detroit, 2001, p.78.

[14] Coleridge returned to (south) Wales in 1802, though not on foot: 'S. Wales would needs appear flat & lame, as ditch-water', he wrote to his wife on 16 November. On Coleridge as a walker see Robin Jarvis, 'Landscape and locomotion: Coleridge the walker', *The Coleridge Bulletin*, n.s., vol.13, Spring 1999, p.35-51: http://www.friendsofcoleridge.com/MembersOnly/JarvisLandscape.html

[15] Coleridge, *Poetical works*, vol.1: Poems (reading text), part 1, p.124 (poem 73); see Arthur Johnston, 'The source of Coleridge's 'Imitated from the Welsh'', *Yearbook of English Studies*, vol.6, 1976, p.141-3.

[16] Robert Southey, *The life and correspondence of the late Robert Southey*, ed. G.C. Southey, London, 1850, vol. 2, p.218.

[17] Charles Shephard, 'A tour through Wales and the central parts of England', *Gentleman's Magazine*, vol.68, 1798, p.390.

[18] For many years pedestrians could expect a poor welcome at the better inns. In 1811 one English walker reported that at the Mackworth Arms in Swansea 'those under the rank of post-chaise travellers are unwelcome guests': Daniel Carless Webb, *Observations and remarks during four excursions made to various parts of Great Britain in 1810 and 1811*, London, 1812, p.354. Thomas Evans reported in 1819 that the wet and weary walker 'has sometimes to suffer the mortification of being received with coldness, treated with subordinate accommodations, if not refused admittance; obliged, perhaps, to accept the necessaries of a mere public house; or to proceed further.' (Thomas Evans, *Walks through Wales*, London, 1819, p.208.

[19] Richard Warner, *A walk through Wales in August 1797*, Bath, 1798, p.3-4.

[20] Paul Readman, 'Walking, and knowing the past: antiquaries, pedestrianism and historical practice in modern Britain', *History*, vol.107, 2022, p.51-73.

[21] Richard Warner, *Literary recollections*, vol.1, London, 1830, p.136.

[22] Hywel M. Davies, 'Wales in English travel writing, 1791–8: the Welsh critique of Theophilus Jones', *Welsh History Review*, 23, no.3, 2007, p.65-93.

[23] 'Cymro' [Theophilus Jones], 'Cursory remarks on Welsh tours or travels', *Cambrian Register for the year 1796*, vol.2, 1799, p.422.

[24] Theophilus Jones, *The history of Brecknock*, (1805), vol.1, Brecknock, 1805, p.26.

[25] Thomas de Quincey, *Confessions of an English opium eater*, 2nd ed., Edinburgh, 1856.

[26] Thomas de Quincey, 'Confessions of an English opium eater', *London Magazine*, September 1821.

[27] Damian Walford Davies, '"Sweet sylvan routes" and grave Methodists: Wales in de Quincey's *Confessions of an English opium-eater*', in *Wales and the Romantic imagination*, ed. Damian Walford Davies and Lynda Pratt, Cardiff, 2007, p.199-227. De Quincey took another walking tour in Wales in 1815.

[28] Cian Duffy, '"One draught from Snowdon's ever-sacred spring": Shelley's Welsh sublime', in *Wales and the Romantic imagination*, ed. Damian Walford Davies and Lynda Pratt, Cardiff, 2007, p.180-98.

[29] Thomas Love Peacock, *The letters of Thomas Love Peacock*, ed. Nicholas A. Joukovsky, Oxford, 2001, vol. 1, p.65. See also Lionel Madden, '"Terrestrial paradise": the Welsh dimension in Peacock's life and work', *Keats-Shelley Memorial Bulletin*, 36, 1985, p.41–56.

[30] Benjamin Heath Malkin, The *scenery, antiquities, and biography of south Wales*, 2nd ed., vol.1, London, 1807, p.113.

[31] Daniel Carless Webb, *Observations and remarks*, London, 1812, p.xiii.

[32] William Sandys and Sampson Sandys, 'Walk through South Wales in October, 1819', National Library of Wales, Cwrt Mawr MS393 C, pp. v-vi; William Chapman, 'Notes of a tour in north Wales', National Library of Wales MS 20138 A, p. 79; John Skinner, *Ten days' tour through the isle of Anglesea, December 1802*, London, 1808, p.66; J.T. Barber, *A tour throughout south Wales and Monmouthshire*, London, 1803, p.4.

[33] Robert Ker Porter, 'Journal of a tour in north Wales', National Library of Wales, NLW MS 12651, B, 15 July 1799: https://editions.curioustravellers.ac.uk/ doc/0012

[34] Catherine Hutton, 'Tour of Wales, 1796': National Library of Wales NLW MS 19079C: https://editions.curioustravellers.ac.uk/doc/0011. See Mary-Ann Constantine, '"The bounds of female reach": Catherine Hutton's fiction and her tours in Wales', *Romantic Textualities: Literature and Print Culture, 1780–1840*, vol. 22, 2017, p.89-103.

[35] Catherine Hutton, 'Tour of Wales, 1796', p.11.

[36] Catherine Hutton, letter to her brother, Shrewsbury, 21 September 1800, National Library of Wales MS 19079C, p. 138.

[37] Elizabeth Smith, Letter to Miss Hunt, Conwy, 26 May 1798, in Elizabeth Smith, *Fragments in prose and verse by a young lady, with some account of her life and character*, ed. Henrietta Maria Bowdler, 1808, p.106: https://sublimewales.wordpress.com/tourists-by-name/smith-elizabeth-1776-1806/

[38] Ellen Weeton, *Miss Weeton's journal of a governess*, vol.2: 1811–1825, ed. Edward Hall, Newton Abbot, 1969, p.388.

[39] Weeton, *Miss Weeton's journal*, vol.2, p.390-91.

[40] Weeton, *Miss Weeton's journal*, vol.1: 1807–1811, p.168-9.

[41] William Bingley, *A tour round north Wales, performed during the summer of 1798*, London, 1800, vol.1, p.iv.

[42] Bingley, *A tour round north Wales*, 2 vols, London, 1800; William Bingley, *North Wales*, 2v., London: 1804. The 1804 edition has been abridged and edited, with an introduction, by Monica Kendall (Bristol, 2023). See also Jim Perrin, *Snowdon: the story of a Welsh mountain*, Llandysul, 2012, p.132-40.

[43] Dewi Jones, *The botanists and guides of Snowdonia*, new ed., Pwllheli, 2007.

44 Helen Pierce, 'Francis Place, 1647–1728, and his early sketches of Wales': https://curioustravellers.ac.uk/en/francis-place-1647-1728-and-his-early-sketches-of-wales/

45 J.M.W. Turner, *Academic sketchbook* (1798–9), *Hereford Court sketchbook* (1798) and *Studies for pictures* (1798–1802) (all Tate Gallery).

46 Cornelius Varley, 'Narrative written by himself', Victoria and Albert Museum, National Art Library, MSL/1984, 74: https://editions.curioustravellers.ac.uk/doc/0016. See also Andrew Green, 'Cornelius Varley in Wales': https://gwallter.com/art/cornelius-varley-in-wales. htm.

47 Edward Pugh, *Cambria depicta: a tour through north Wales, illustrated with picturesque views by a native artist*, London, 1816, p.v-vi. See also John Barrell, *Edward Pugh of Ruthin, 1763–1813: 'a native artist'*, Cardiff, 2013.

Chapter 4: Rebels, workers and believers

1 British Library, Add. MSS, 15027, ff.79-80.

2 Thomas Evans, *Walks through Wales*, London, 1819, p.63.

3 Mary Morgan, *A tour to Milford Haven in the year 1791*, London, 1795, pp. 120-121.

4 Hugh Evans, *Cwm Eithin*, Lerpwl, 1931, p.3.

5 William Matthews, *The miscellaneous companions: being a short tour of observation and sentiment, through a part of south Wales*, Bath, 1786, vol.1, p.131; Elizabeth Rand, 'Tour of north Wales, 1827', National Museum Wales MS 207044.

6 *The Welshman*, 23 June 1843, p.2.

7 Eric Hobsbawm, 'The machine breakers', in *Labouring men: studies in the history of labour*, London, 1964, p.7-26.

8 Andrew Green, 'The Cyfarthfa Philosophical Society': https://gwallter.com/history/the-cyfarthfa-philosophical-society.html

9 Francis Kilvert, *Kilvert's diary: selections from the diary of the Rev. Francis Kilvert*, ed. William Plomer, new ed., London, 1960, vol. 2, p.78.

10 In Bala at the end of the nineteenth century, knitting by men and women was a common sight in the open air: 'You see none idle, going out, or returning home; riding or walking, they are occupied in this portable employment' (John Evans, *Letters written during a tour through north Wales in the year 1798*, 3rd ed., London, 1804, p.68.)

11 Sir Richard Phillips, *A morning's walk from London to Kew*, London, 1817, p.228.

12 D.C. Rees, *Tregaron, historical and antiquarian*, Llandysul, 1935, p.124.

13 John Williams-Davies, 'Merched y gerddi: a seasonal migration of female labour from rural Wales', *Folk Life*, vol.15, 1977, p.12-23; John Williams-Davies, 'Merched y gerddi: mudwyr tymhorol o Geredigion', *Ceredigion*, vol.8, 1978, p.291-303; William Linnard, 'Merched y gerddi yn Llundain ac yng Nghymru', *Ceredigion*, vol.9, 1982, p.260-63.

14 *Cambrian*, 25 April 1890, p.8; see Delyth Lloyd, 'The Penclawdd cockle industry', *Gower*, vol.35, 1984, p.12-25.

15 Thomas Jenkins, *The diary of Thomas Jenkins of Llandeilo, 1826–1870*, ed. D.C. Jenkins, Bala, 1976.

16 A quarryman might take a 'llwybr llwynog', or secret 'fox's path' if he was late

for work and wished to avoid a penalty: R. Emrys Jones, 'Casgiad o dermau chwarel', *Bulletin of the Board of Celtic Studies*, vol.20, 1964, p.245.

[17] R. Merfyn Jones, *The north Wales quarrymen, 1874–1922*, Cardiff, 1982.

[18] *Report of the Departmental Committee upon Merionethshire slate mines*, London, 1895, p.45.

[19] Rhiain Bower, 'Baricsio: the slate quarrymen's barracks of north-west Wales', *Journal of Architecture*, vol.23, 2018, p.137-161; Emyr Jones, *Canrif y chwarelwr*, Dinbych, 1964, p.44-48.

[20] Morgan Richards, *Slate quarrying and how to make it profitable*, Bangor, 1876, p.104.

[21] Ivor E. Davies, 'The manufacture of honestones in Gwynedd', *Transactions of the Caernarvonshire Historical Society*, vol. 37, 1976, p.80-86.

[22] Jim Perrin, *Snowdon: the story of a mountain*, Llandysul, 2012, p.171-272.

[23] George Borrow, *Wild Wales: its people, language and scenery*, London, 1862, chapter 81.

[24] Philip Dunham, '"An angel satyr walks these hills": landscape and identity in Kilvert's diary', in P.S. Barnwell and Marilyn Palmer, eds, *Post-medieval landscapes*, Macclesfield, 2007, p.169-84.

[25] *Looking back: a Kilvert miscellanea*, Hereford, 1969, p.15.

[26] Francis Kilvert, *Kilvert's diary: selections from the diary of the Rev. Francis Kilvert*, ed. William Plomer, new ed., London, 1960, vol. 1, p.34.

[27] *Kilvert's diary*, vol.1, p.41-2.

[28] *Kilvert's diary*, vol.1, p.83.

[29] *Kilvert's diary*, vol.1, p.307.

[30] *Kilvert's diary*, vol.1, p.79.

[31] *Kilvert's diary*, vol.1, p.357.

[32] *Kilvert's diary*, vol.1, p.360.

[33] *Kilvert's diary*, vol. 2, p.86.

[34] *Kilvert's diary*, vol. 2, p.349.

[35] *Kilvert's diary*, vol. 2, p.145, 159-60.

[36] David Lockwood, *Francis Kilvert*, Bridgend, 1990, p.135.

[37] *Reports of the commissioners of inquiry into the state of education in Wales*, London, 1847, p.38.

[38] Richard Thomas, *Cofiant a thraethodau duwinyddol y Parch. R. Thomas (Ap Vychan), Bala*, gol. M. D. Jones a D. V. Thomas, Dolgellau, *c.*1882.

[39] Robert Oliver Rees, *Mary Jones, y Gymraes fechan heb yr un Beibl a sefydliad y Feibl-Gymdeithas*, Dolgellau, [1879].

[40] [Mary E. Ropes], *The story of Mary Jones and her bible*, London, 1882.

[41] Edward Morgan, *John Elias: life, letters and essays*, Edinburgh, 1973, p. 16.

[42] E. Wyn James, 'Thomas Charles, Ann Griffiths a Mary Jones' in D. Densil Morgan, gol., *Thomas Charles o'r Bala*, Caerdydd, 2014, p.135-56.

[43] D.J.V. Jones, '"A dead loss to the community": the criminal vagrant in mid-nineteenth-century Wales', *Welsh History Review*, vol.8, 1976, p.312.

[44] *Second annual report of the Poor Law Board 1849*, London, 1850, p.100.

[45] David Edmondes-Owen, 'The tramps' chaplain: the simple annals of a Welsh hermit', *Journal of the Kilvert Society*, no.32, March 2011, p.78-82.

⁴⁶ Hugh Evans, *Cwm Eithin*, Lerpwl, 1931, p.53.

⁴⁷ 'Merlin', 'Leaves from a criminal notebook', *Red Dragon*, vol.5, 1884, p.248.

⁴⁸ Huw Walters, 'Hen broffesor', *Y Casglwr*, rhif 8, Awst 1979, p.10-11:
http://www.casglwr.org/yrarchif/8hen.php

⁴⁹ Jenkin Jones, 'An account of tours in England and Wales made in 1819 and 1836
by Captain Jenkin Jones, R.N.', National Library of Wales, NLW MSS 785A.
Reprinted in part in *Transactions of the Historical Society of West Wales*, vol.1, 1912,
p.97-144: https://archive.org/details/westwaleshistorioɪhist/page/96/mode/2up

⁵⁰ Jones, NLW MSS 785A, p.102-3. Jones refers to the song 'King Henry and the
miller's song', in which the miller of Mansfield complains about sharing a bed
with the King's farts.

Chapter 5: Scientists, mountaineers and writers

¹ Michael Faraday, *Michael Faraday in Wales, including Faraday's journal of his tour
through Wales in 1819*, ed. Dafydd Tomos, Denbigh, [1972], p.24.

² Faraday, *Michael Faraday in Wales*, p.32.

³ Faraday, *Michael Faraday in Wales*, p.32.

⁴ Faraday, *Michael Faraday in Wales*, p.40.

⁵ Faraday, *Michael Faraday in Wales*, p.74.

⁶ Faraday, *Michael Faraday in Wales*, p.97.

⁷ Anne Lister, *I know my own heart: the diaries of Anne Lister, 1791–1840*, ed. Helena
Whitbread, London 1988, p.145 (29 August 1821).

⁸ 'Anne Lister's diary: tour of North Wales 11-27 July 1822', transcribed with an
introduction by Kirsty McHugh and edited by Elizabeth Edwards, Tuesday 23 July:
https://editions.curioustravellers.ac.uk/pages/show.html?document=0023.xml&fb
clid=IwAR0v8dArKsHVjizRvR7I5W_r7MzeXDn666N1A48sUvjkchM2iGRmP08oK
8c

⁹ Anne Lister, *I know my own heart*, p.210.

¹⁰ Charles Darwin, *The autobiography of Charles Darwin, 1809-82*, ed. Nora Barlow,
London, 1958, p.53-4.

¹¹ Charles Darwin, letter to W.D. Fox, 29 July 1828:
https://www.darwinproject.ac.uk/letter/?docId=letters/DCP-LETT-45.xml;query=
fox%2029%20july%201828

¹² A. Patchett Martin, *Life and letters of the Right Honourable Robert Lowe, Viscount
Sherbrooke*, vol. 1, London, 1893, p.19-20.

¹³ Charles Darwin, letter to J.S. Henslow, 18 May 1832:
https://www.darwinproject.ac.uk/letter/?docId=letters/DCP-LETT-171.xml;query=
j%20s%20henslow

¹⁴ Thomas Roberts, *The Welsh interpreter*, London, 1831, p.vi.

¹⁵ *Black's picturesque guide to North Wales*, new ed., Edinburgh, 1870, p.4.

¹⁶ Edwin Lees, *The botanical looker-out among the wild flowers of England and Wales
...*, London, 1851, p.462.

¹⁷ *Wrexham and Denbighshire Advertiser*, 26 August 1882, p.8.

¹⁸ R. Merfyn Jones, 'The mountaineering of Wales', *Welsh History Review*, vol. 19,
1998, p.48.

[19] Charles Kingsley, *Two years ago*, London, 1890, ch.21.

[20] Maria Vernon Graham Havergal, *Memorials of Frances Ridley Havergal*, London, 1887, p.94.

[21] Jim Perrin, *Snowdon: the story of a Welsh mountain*, Llandysul, 2012, ch.7: 'Colonizing the vertical'; Alan McNee, 'The haptic sublime and the 'cold stony reality' of mountaineering', *19: Interdisciplinary Studies in the Long Nineteenth Century*, vol. 19, 2014: https://doi.org/10.16995/ntn.697

[22] Borrow's walking speed was swift, a characteristic he shared with many writers, including William Wordsworth, Charles Dickens and Lewis Carroll.

[23] George Borrow, *Wild Wales, its people, language and scenery*, London, 1955, p.279 (ch.54).

[24] *Cornhill Magazine*, vol.7, January-June 1863, p.137.

[25] Edward Thomas, *George Borrow: the man and his books*, London, 1912, p.6.

[26] Alfred Tennyson, *Poems*, London, 1846: 'The golden year'. For Tennyson in Llanberis see https://gwallter.com/literature/tennyson-in-llanberis.html

[27] Alfred Tennyson, *The letters of Alfred Lord Tennyson*, vol.2: 1851–1870, ed. Cecil Y. Lang and Edgar F. Shannon, Oxford, 1987, p.158: Emily Sellwood Tennyson's journal, 8 September 1856.

[28] Gerard Manley Hopkins, *The journals and papers of Gerard Manley Hopkins*, ed. Humphry House and Graham Storey, London, 1959, p.258.

[29] Hopkins, *Journals and papers*, p.260.

[30] Damian Walford Davies, *Cartographies of culture: new geographies of Welsh writing in English*, Cardiff, 2012, p.43-77.

[31] Gerard Manley Hopkins, *The poetical works of Gerard Manley Hopkins*, ed. H. Mackenzie, Oxford, 1990, p.125.

[32] Hopkins, *Poetical works*, p.148-9.

[33] Hopkins, *Poetical works*, p.139.

[34] *The letters of Gerard Manley Hopkins to Robert Bridges*, ed. Claude Colleer Abbott, London, 1935, p.226-9; *Further letters of Gerard Manley Hopkins*, ed. Claude Colleer Abbott, 2nd ed., Oxford, 1956, p.177.

Chapter 6: Map-makers, protesters and poets

[1] *Carnarvon and Denbigh Herald*, 23 September 1848, p.2.

[2] J.G. Kohl, *England, Wales and Scotland*, London, 1844, p.68.

[3] Institute of Civil Engineers, [obituaries, 1862]:
https://www.gracesguide.co.uk/Robert_Kearsley_Dawson

[4] *Western Mail*, 9 May 1894, p.4.

[5] Hugh Evans, *Cwm Eithin*, Lerpwl, 1931, p.162.

[6] John Townsend: *The Cambrian*, 20 August 1825, p.3; Francis Kilvert, *Kilvert's diary: selections from the diary of the Rev. Francis Kilvert*, ed. William Plomer, new ed., London, 1960, vol. 1, p.355.

[7] *Western Mail*, 26 July 1877, p.3.

[8] *Western Mail*, 2 February 1885, p.3.

[9] *South Wales Daily News*, 4 November 1885, p.4.

[10] *South Wales Daily News*, 18 September 1896, p.3.

[11] *Western Mail*, 9 June 1903, p.3.

[12] Personal correspondence from T. Alexander Wade.

[13] Paul O'Leary, *Claiming the streets: processions and urban culture in south Wales, c.1830–1880*, Cardiff, 2012.

[14] *Monmouthshire Merlin*, 2 January 1841, p.3. Troops were stationed in Newport for some years after 1839, in case of a resumption of trouble: see David Osmond, 'After the rising: Chartism in Newport, 1840-48', *Gwent Local History*, vol.9, 2005, p.8-52.

[15] Gwyn Jones, *Times like these*, London, 1936, p.58-9.

[16] *Cardiff Times*, 7 September 1866, p.5.

[17] B.L. Coombes, *These poor hands: the autobiography of a miner working in south Wales*, London, 1939, p.31-2.

[18] Coombes, *These poor hands*, p.32-3.

[19] Watcyn Wyn, *Adgofion*, Merthyr Tydfil, 1907, p.34-5. My translation.

[20] Ben Davies, *Ffrwythau dethol*, Llandysul, 1938, p.35. My translation.

[21] *Evening Express*, 8 June 1898, p.3.

[22] *The Cardiff Times*, 18 June 1898, p.6.

[23] *South Wales Echo*, 8 August 1898, p.2.

[24] *Tarian y Gweithiwr*, 30 June 1898, p.5. My translation.

[25] Individuals tramped the industrial streets to preach the ILP message. Walter Hampson ('Casey'), an itinerant Irish entertainer and 'vehicle for socialist propaganda', walked through south Wales in 1911, wearing a black velvet coat and carrying only a fiddle and a walking stick. As well as performing on stage he wrote articles for the ILP newspaper, the *Labour Leader*. See Liam Harte, *The literature of the Irish in Britain: autobiography and memoir, 1725–2001*, Basingstoke, 2009, p.106-10.

[26] *Y Genedl Gymreig*, 16 December 1885, p.4.

[27] *Western Mail*, 20 June 1908, p.6.

[28] *Evening Express*, 27 June 1908, p.4.

[29] *Women's Franchise*, 9 September 1909, p.767.

[30] *The Vote*, 8 October 1910, p.285.

[31] Graham Martin, 'The culture of the women's suffrage movement: the evidence of the McKenzie letters', *Llafur*, vol.7, nos 3-4, 1998–9, p.110.

[32] *The Common Cause*, 11 July 1913, p.237.

[33] *Barry Dock News*, 18 July 1913, p.5.

[34] *Cambrian Daily Leader*, 8 December 1914, p.6.

[35] Rev. Stephen Baker, vicar of Usk, *Monmouthshire Beacon*, 23 November 1872, p.5.

[36] *The Cambrian*, 4 October 1878, p.5.

[37] Tom Ridd, 'Thomas y Lan', *Gower*, vol. 15, 1962, p.61-6; Andrew Green, 'Greening Swansea: a forgotten pioneer': https://gwallter.com/history/greening-swansea-a-forgotten-pioneer.html; Robert Skinner, 'Parc Llewelyn: John Dillwyn Llewelyn's people's park', *Gower*, vol. 57, 2006, p. 59-69; J. Alun Owen, *Swansea's earliest open spaces: a study of Swansea's parks and their promotors in the nineteenth century*, Swansea, 1995.

[38] Among the new town parks were Llandrindod Wells (Rock Park, 1867), Aberdare (Aberdare Park, 1869), Mold (Bailey Hill Park, 1870), Llandudno (Happy Valley,

1887), Cardiff (Roath Park, 1894), Newport (Belle Vue Park, 1894), Tredegar (Bedwellty Park, 1901) and Merthyr Tydfil (Cyfarthfa Castle, 1909).

[39] The Precipice Walk had its origins in a path through a large private estate, Nannau, like others, such as those at Hafod, Ceredigion and the Torrent Walk at Brithdir.

[40] Howard C. Jones, 'Aberystwyth cliff railway', *Ceredigion*, vol.8, 1979, p.408-12.

[41] *Carnarvon and Denbigh Herald*, 12 October 1888, p.5.

[42] Owen M. Edwards, *Cartrefi Cymru*, Gwrecsam, 1896, p.139. See also M. Wynn Thomas, 'O.M. Edwards: keeping track of the *gwerin*', in *The nations of Wales, 1890–1914*, Cardiff, 2016, p.75-109; Hazel Walford Davies, *O.M: cofiant Syr Owen Morgan Edwards*, Llandysul, 2019; Aidan Byrne, '"He will bid me cross the border": George Borrow's *Wild Wales*, O. M. Edwards's *Cartrefi Cymru* and the imagined nation', *Studies in Travel Writing*, vol.18, 2014, p.148-159; Gramich, Katie, '"Every hill has its history, every region its romance": travellers' constructions of Wales, 1844–1913', Benjamin Colbert, ed., *Travel writing and tourism in Britain and Ireland*, Basingstoke, 2012, p.147–63.

[43] Edwards, *Cartrefi Cymru*, p.13.

[44] Edwards, *Cartrefi Cymru*, p.47-8.

[45] Jean Moorcroft Wilson, *Robert Graves: from Great War poet to Good-bye to all that (1895–1929)*, London, 2018; Richard Perceval Graves, *Robert Graves: the heroic assault, 1895–1926*, London, 1986; Mary-Ann Constantine, 'Rocky acres: Robert Graves, Harlech and the Great War', *Planet*, no.215, 2014, p.56-67.

[46] Robert Graves, *Good-bye to all that*, London, 4th ed., London, 1966, p.29.

[47] Robert Graves, *Good-bye to all that*, p.30.

[48] Robert Graves, *Good-bye to all that*, p.30.

[49] Robert Graves, *Complete poems*, ed. Beryl Graves and Dunstan Ward, vol. 1, London, 1995, p.83-4.

[50] Graves, *Good-bye to all that*, p.246.

[51] Graves, *Complete poems*, vol. 1, p.268.

[52] Graves, *Good-bye to all that*, p.254.

[53] Edward Thomas, *Edward Thomas and Wales*, ed. Jeff Towns, Cardigan, 2018.

[54] In a letter to his wife, Helen, Thomas describes in detail a day's walk of over thirty miles in October 1914 from Ammanford to Swansea via Carreg Cennen, Gwynfe, Brynaman and Pontardawe: Edward Thomas, *Letters to Helen, and an appendix of seven letters to Harry and Janet Hooton*, ed. R. George Thomas, Manchester, 2000, p.74-80.

[55] Jean Moorcroft Wilson, *Edward Thomas, from Adlestrop to Arras: a biography*, London, 2015, p.136-7.

[56] Edward Thomas, *Beautiful Wales*, London: 1905, p. 99 ('January').

[57] Thomas, *Beautiful Wales*, p.143 ('June').

[58] Edward Thomas, *The Icknield Way*, London, 1916, p.1.

[59] Lucy Newlyn, '"The shape of the sentences": Edward Thomas's tracks in contemporary poetry', in Guy Cuthbertson and Lucy Newlyn, eds, *Branch-lines: Edward Thomas and contemporary poetry*, London, 2007, p.65-82.

[60] Edward Thomas, *Richard Jefferies: his life and work*, London, 1909, p.151.

[61] Edward Thomas, *Swansea village*, Swansea, 2019.

[62] Edward Thomas, *The collected poems of Edward Thomas*, ed. R. George Thomas, Oxford, 1978, p.267.
[63] Edward Thomas, *Collected poems*, p.313.
[64] Edward Thomas, *Collected poems*, p.367.
[65] Edward Thomas, *Collected poems*, p.481.
[66] David Jones, *In parenthesis*, London, 1937, Part 1: 'The many men so beautiful'.

Chapter 7: Miners, hikers and patriots

[1] Sean O'Connell, 'The social and economic impact of the car in interwar Britain', Ph.D. thesis, University of Warwick, 1995, p.205:
http://wrap.warwick.ac.uk/36384/1/WRAP_THESIS_O%27Connell_1995.pdf
[2] J.S.Dean, *Murder most foul ...: a study of the road deaths problem*, London, 1947, p.[12-13].
[3] Kate Roberts, *Traed mewn cyffion*, Aberystwyth, 1936, p.65. My translation.
[4] E. Llwyd Williams, *Crwydro Sir Benfro*, vol.1, Llandybïe, 1958, p.13. My translation.
[5] Kate K. Liepmann, *The journey to work: its significance for industrial and community life*, London, 1944, p.127-9.
[6] Bert Coombes, *These poor hands: the autobiography of a miner working in south Wales*, London, 1939, p.154.
[7] Gwyn Jones, *Times like these*, London, 1936, p.11.
[8] Rhys Davies, *Jubilee blues*, London, 1938, p.200.
[9] 'The jazz bands of 1926', Cynon Valley Historical Society, *Hanes*, 35, 2006, p. [5-6]:
https://cvhs.org.uk/hanesarchive/2006_Hanes_35.pdf
[10] British Pathé, film ID 706.16: Unemployed miners' march 1927:
https://www.britishpathe.com/video/unemployed-miners-march
[11] David Lloyd Davies, letter to James Hawes, 10 January 1928, Amgueddfa Cymru – National Museum Wales, Big Pit Museum:
https://museum.wales/articles/1651/The-Letter-in-the-Lamp-The-South-Wales-Coal-Miners-Hunger-March/
[12] Claude Stanfield, Account of the hunger march from Merthyr Tydfil to London, 1936, written on 23 postcards, Richard Burton Archives, Swansea University, SWCC/MNA/PP/108/14.
[13] Neil Evans, '"South Wales has been roused as never before": marching against the means test, 1934–36', in David Howell and Kenneth O. Morgan, eds, *Crime, protest and police in modern British society: essays in memory of David V.J. Jones*, Cardiff, 1999, p.184.
[14] Gwyn Thomas, *A Welsh eye*, London, 1964, p.21.
[15] *Aberdare Leader*, 9 February 1935, p.8.
[16] Gwyn Thomas, *A Welsh eye*, p.18-21, 24.
[17] Lewis Jones, *We live*, London, 1939, p.241, 243.
[18] *House of Commons debates*, 11 November 1936, vol.317, col.959.
[19] Sydna Ann Williams, '"Law, not war – hedd nid cledd": women and the peace movement in north Wales, 1926–1945', *Welsh History Review*, vol. 18, 1996, p. 63-91.
[20] *Report of the peacemakers' pilgrimage through England, Scotland and Wales to London*, May-June 1926, London, 1926.

[21] David Hollett, *The pioneer ramblers, 1850–1940*, [n.p.], 2002.

[22] Blatchford's clubs were mainly confined to England, but his journalism was influential in Wales; Aneurin Bevan, for example, was drawn to socialism as a young man in part by reading *The Clarion*.

[23] David Prynn, 'The Clarion Clubs, rambling and the holiday associations in Britain since the 1890s', *Journal of Contemporary History*, vol.11, 1976, p.65-77.

[24] Cecil C. Granville, '50 years walking with Newport Ramblers', *Gwent Local History*, no.55, 1983, p.41.

[25] W.P. James, 'Cader Arthur', *Welsh Outlook*, vol. 8, 1921, p.114.

[26] Coombes, *These poor hands*, p.177.

[27] James Hanley, *Grey children: a study in humbug and misery*, London, 1937, p.25.

[28] Pyrs Gruffudd, David T. Herbert and Angela Piccini, 'In search of Wales: travel writing and narratives of difference, 1918–50', *Journal of Historical Geography*, vol.26, 2000, p.589-604.

[29] H.A. Piehler, *Wales for everyman*, London, 1935, p.9-10.

[30] Patrick Monkhouse, *On foot in north Wales*, London, 1934, p.2.

[31] Monkhouse, *On foot in north Wales*, p.135-6

[32] John C. Moore, *Tramping through Wales: in search of the red dragon*, London, 1931, p.30.

[33] Moore, *Tramping through Wales*, p.28.

[34] Moore, *Tramping through Wales*, p.90.

[35] Jim Perrin, *Menlove: the life of John Menlove Edwards*, London, 1985.

[36] William T. Palmer, *The splendour of Wales*, London, 1932, p.136. See Pip Hopkinson, 'A brief history of the Climbers' Club: a personal view': https://www.climbers-club.co.uk/wp-content/uploads/2016/03/cc-history.pdf

[37] R. Williams Parry, *Cerddi'r gaeaf*, Dinbych, 1952, p. 2. My translation.

[38] Alan Llwyd, *Bob: cofiant R. Williams Parry, 1884–1956*, Llandysul, 2013, p.451. My translation. The photographs were taken by Geoff Charles and are now in the National Library of Wales.

[39] T.H. Parry-Williams, 'Y Lôn Ucha', in *O'r pedwar gwynt*, Dinbych, 1944, p.33.

[40] T.H. Parry-Williams, 'Dieithrwch', in *Ysgrifau*, Llundain, 1928, p.64-7. See also R. Gerallt Jones, *T.H. Parry-Williams*, Caerdydd, 1999, p.31-7. My translation.

[41] Ambrose Bebb, 'Y cerddwr a'r ffordd', *Heddiw*, vol.1, no.2, 1936, p.47. My translation.

[42] Bebb, 'Y cerddwr a'r ffordd', p.48.

[43] Evelyn Lewes, *Out with the Cambrians*, London, 1934, p.63-4.

[44] Lewes, *Out with the Cambrians*, p.49.

[45] Steve Dubé, 'George Eyre Evans, 1857–1939: the self-appointed leader', *Carmarthenshire Antiquary*, vol.91, 2005, p.51-60.

[46] E.G. Bowen, 'George Eyre Evans, 1857–1939', *Carmarthen Antiquary*, vol.1, part 1, 1941, p. 5-10.

[47] Mortimer Wheeler, *Still digging: interleaves from an antiquary's notebook*, London, 1955, p.80-82.

[48] Paul Readman, 'Walking, and knowing the past: antiquaries, pedestrianism and historical practice in modern Britain, *History*, vol.107, 2022, p.51-73.

Chapter 8: Long walking and slow walking

[1] Ministry of Town and Country Planning, *Report of the National Parks Committee (England and Wales)*, London, 1947, p.67; Tom Stephenson, 'Wanted: a long green lane', *Daily Herald*, 22 June 1935, p.10.

[2] *House of Commons Debates*, 31 March 1949, National Parks and Access to the Countryside Bill, col.1485.

[3] Damian Walford Davies, 'Ronald Lockley and the archipelagic imagination' in Nicholas Allen, Nick Groom and Jos Smith, eds. *Coastal works: cultures of the Atlantic edge*, Oxford, 2017, p.131-60.

[4] Ronald Lockley, 'Notes by Mr R.M. Lockley on his maps of the Pembrokeshire Coast Path', typescript held by the Pembrokeshire Coast National Park Authority.

[5] Robin S. Henshaw, 'The development and impact of formal long-distance footpaths in Great Britain', Ph.D. thesis, University of Edinburgh, 1984, vol.1, p.179-82.

[6] John H. Barrett, *The Pembrokeshire Coast Path*, London, 1974, p.1.

[7] 'Pembrokeshire Path pioneers at County Show', *Tenby Observer*, 12 September 2016:
https://www.tenby-today.co.uk/news/pembrokeshire-coast-path-pioneers-at-county-show-464684

[8] Barrett, *Pembrokeshire Coast Path*, p.2.

[9] Frank Noble, *The Shell book of Offa's Dyke Path*, rev. ed., London, 1972, p.11.

[10] [David McGlade], 'The Offa's Dyke Association at 50: the early years', Offa's Dyke Association, *Newsletter*, no.136, Winter 2018, p.3-6.

[11] A.J. Drake, *Cambrian Way: the mountain connoisseur's walk: a practical guide and handbook*, Cheltenham, 2008. A different north-south route was followed in 2010 in a remarkable walk by a group with McArdle Disease: see Stacey L. Reason, *One step at a time: walking with McArdle Disease*, 2nd ed., Droxford, 2016:
https://www.iamgsd.org/_files/ugd/c951b2_b3358d69a7484de88eo8dfo7088cf9o4.pdf

[12] Dic Jones, *Yr un hwyl a'r un wylo: cerddi Dic Jones*, gol. Elsie Reynolds, Llandysul, 2011, p.78. My translation.

[13] Wales Coast Path Review Group, *A review of the Wales Coast Path on its 10th anniversary: recommendations for future development*, Cardiff, 2022:
https://gov.wales/sites/default/files/publications/2022-05/wales-coast-path-tenth-anniversary-review.pdf

[14] Early Wales Coast Path completists: https://www.walescoastpath.gov.uk/latest-news/hall-of-fame/?lang=en. Blogs include: Alan Dix: https://alanwalks.wales/, Gareth Axenderrie https://garethswelshwalk.wordpress.com/, Andrew Green https://gwallter.com/the-wales-coast-path-complete, Charles Hawes https://charleshawes.veddw.com/wales-coast-path/. Books include: Tom Davies, *A Welsh wander: an epic trek right around Wales*, Talybont, 2017; Steve Plant, *A wander around the coast of Wales: a 870-mile walk following the coastal path of Wales from north to south*, Peterborough, 2014; Christian Lewis, *Finding Hildasay: how one man walked the UK's coastline and found hope and happiness*, London, 2023; Eirlys Thomas and Lucy O'Donnell, *Slow walking the Wales coast path*, Cardiff, 2021; Beryl Vaughan, *Milgi Maldwyn: atgofion am daith ar hyd arfordir Cymru*, Caernarfon, 2017.

A much earlier hiker, Rosie Swale, walked 1,375 miles round the circumference of Wales in the winter of 1967: Rosie Swale, *Winter Wales*, Carmarthen, 1989.

[15] Amy Jones, 'Walking Wales: exploring the experiences of people who walk the Wales Coast Path', Ph.D. thesis, Swansea University, 2020, p.214: https://cronfa.swan.ac.uk/Record/cronfa56844

[16] Jon Gower, ed., *I know another way: from Tintern to St Davids*, Llandysul, 2002, p.8.

[17] Gower, *I know another way*, p.99.

[18] Gower, *I know another way*, p.133-34.

[19] Chris Potter, *North Wales Pilgrim's Way: the official guide to the Welsh camino*, [n.p.], 2019; Peter Stanford, *Pilgrimage: journeys of meaning*, London, 2021, Ch.7: North Wales Pilgrim's Way: Celtic revival. For a discussion of pilgrims' motivations and experience in walking the route, see Richard Scriven, 'A 'new' walking pilgrimage: performance and meaning on the North Wales Pilgrim's Way', *Landscape Research*, vol.46, 2021, p.64-76.

[20] Madeleine Gray, 'The Cistercian Way': http://www.medio-evo.org/madeleine.htm; Penrhys Pilgrimage Way: http://www.penrhyspilgrimageway.wales/

[21] Gower Pilgrimage Way: https://gowerma.org/gower-pilgrimage-way/; St Thomas Way: https://thomasway.ac.uk/; Catherine A.M. Clarke, ed., *The St. Thomas Way and the medieval march of Wales: exploring place, heritage, pilgrimage*, Leeds, 2020; Wexford-Pembrokeshire Pilgrim Way: https://wexfordpembrokeshirepilgrimway.org/.

[22] Richard Scriven, 'A 'new' walking pilgrimage', p.64-76.

[23] Anne Hayward, *A pilgrimage around Wales: in search of a significant conversation*, Talybont, 2018.

[24] Aled Lewis Evans, *Llwybrau llonyddwch*, Llandysul, 2015, p.v. My translation.

[25] Thomas Firbank, *A country of memorable honour*, London, 1953; John Hillaby, *Journey through Britain*, London, 1968.

[26] Paul Theroux, *The kingdom by the sea: a journey round the coast of Great Britain*, London, 1983.

[27] Anthony Bailey, *A walk through Wales*, London, 1992, p.282.

[28] Ursula Martin, *One woman walks Wales*, Dinas Powys, 2018, p.380.

[29] Martin, *One woman walks Wales*, p.57-9.

[30] Martin, *One woman walks Wales*, p.356-7.

[31] Hannah Engelkamp, *Seaside donkey: a wayward walk round Wales*, [n.p.], 2015, p. 260.

[32] Hannah Engelkamp, 'Could this be love?', *Seaside donkey blog*, 21 October 2013: http://seasidedonkey.co.uk/could-this-be-love/

[33] Julie Brominicks, *The edge of Cymru: a journey*, Bridgend, 2022, p.234.

[34] Tom Bullough, *Sarn Helen: a journey through Wales, past, present and future*, London, 2023.

[35] Matthew Yeomans, *Return to my trees: notes from the Welsh woodlands*, Cardiff, 2022.

[36] Rhian Parry, *Cerdded y caeau*, Talybont, 2022; Hope Hewett, *Walking through Merioneth*, Newtown, [1939].

[37] Hefin Wyn, *Pentigily: crwydro Llwybr Arfordir Sir Benfro*, Talybont, 2008.

Chapter 9: Everyday walking and reflexive walking

[1] Welsh Government, *Road traffic 2021*, Cardiff, 2022: https://www.gov.wales/road-traffic-2021- html#:~:text=In%202021%2C%20the%20number%20of,by%201.5%25%20to%202.0%20million.

[2] Welsh Government, *Active travel (walking and cycling), April 2021 to March 2022*, Cardiff, 2022: https://www.gov.wales/active-travel-walking-and-cycling-april-2021-march-2022-html

[3] Amie B. Richards et al., 'Wales 2021 Active Healthy Kids (AHK) report card: the fourth pandemic of childhood', *International Journal of Environmental and Public Health*, July 2022: https://pubmed.ncbi.nlm.nih.gov/35805795/

[4] Welsh Assembly Government, *Walking and cycling strategy for Wales*, Cardiff, 2003: https://apps.caerphilly.gov.uk/LDP/Examination/PDF/W94-Walking-and-Cycling-Strategy-for-Wales.pdf; Active Travel (Wales) Act 2013: https://www.legislation.gov.uk/anaw/2013/7/contents/enacted; National Assembly for Wales Economy, Infrastructure and Skills Committee, *Post-legislative scrutiny of the Active Travel (Wales) Act 2013*: https://business.senedd.wales/documents/s75863/Report %20-%20Post%20 Legislative%20Scrutiny%20of%20the%20Active%20Travel% 20Wales%20Act%202013%20PDF%201.3MB.pdf

[5] Dafydd Trystan, *Developing an active travel school: the Ysgol Hamadryad story*, [n.p., n.d]: https://keepingcardiffmoving.co.uk/wp-content/uploads/2020/09/Ysgol-Hamadryads-Active-Travel-Journey-Eng.pdf

[6] Living Streets Wales: https://www.livingstreets.org.uk/about-us/wales; Slow Ways: https://beta.slowways.org/

[7] Prof. Ian Walker of Swansea University, an authority on the social psychology of driving, has researched the forces that result in cars being regarded as the normal, default mode of transport: see Ian Walker, Alan Tapp and Adrian Davis, 'Motonormativity: how social norms hide a major public health hazard', *International Journal of Environment and Health*, vol. 11, 2023, p.21-33.

[8] Pathé film of Mr Rees climbing the steps from South Stack lighthouse: https://www.britishpathe.com/video/lighthouse-and-postman-issue-title-ohms/query/Holyhead

[9] Idris Mathias, 'Manuscript map of the lower Teifi valley', digitised by the National Library of Wales: https://www.library.wales/discover-learn/digital-exhibitions/maps/idris-mathias-manuscript-map-of-the-lower-teifi-valley#?c=&m=&s=&cv=&xywh=25209%2C 1352%2C1030%2C793

[10] Conversation with Chris Baker, Swansea, 23 January 2023.

[11] Carole Cadwalladr, 'My week as an Amazon insider', *Observer*, 1 December 2013: https://www.theguardian.com/technology/2013/dec/01/week-amazon-insider-feature-treatment-employees-work; 'Amazon: the truth behind the click', BBC Panorama, 25 November 2013: https://www.youtube.com/watch?v=JwrUYS9UTeU

[12] Rebecca Solnit, *Wanderlust: a history of walking*, London, 2001, p.260-66.

[13] Guy Kennaway and Hussein Sharif, *Foot notes*, London, 2021.

[14] Peter Goulding, *Slatehead: the ascent of Britain's slate-climbing scene*, Aberystwyth, 2020.

[15] Dewi Prysor, 100 *Cymru: y mynyddoedd a fi*, Talybont, 2021, p.11. My translation.

[16] Interview of Ann Pettitt and Karmen Thomas recorded by Nicky Arikoglu in 2019: https://greenhamwomeneverywhere.co.uk/ann-pettit-and-karmen-thomas/

[17] Ann Pettitt, *Walking to Greenham*, Dinas Powys, 2006, p.1.

[18] Ann Pettitt, *Walking to Greenham*, Dinas Powys, 2006, p.310.

[19] ITV Cymru / Wales broadcast of Maerdy Lodge meeting, 4 March 1985, National Library of Wales: https://www.youtube.com/watch?v=VFrOhV_lR_8

[20] Anonymous Maerdy miner, Media and Memory in Wales project, Aberystwyth University (People's Collection): https://www.peoplescollection.wales/items/461524

[21] https://gwallter.com/politics/to-soweto-by-way-of-the-plough-harrow.html

[22] Simon Whitehead, 'A complex experiential map: 22 Tormentil', *New Welsh Review*, no.69, 2005, p.77-80.

[23] Afon Dulais project: https://materialthinking.net/commissions/simon whitehead/. See also Simon Whitehead, *Walking to work*, Abercych, 2006.

[24] Jess Allen: https://allinadayswalk.org.uk/2013/07/30/wild-sleeping/

[25] Angela Maddock, [Journal of a walk from Carmarthen to Middlesborough], 21 October 2018, Macclesfield to Levenshulme, author's manuscript, [2018]. The exhibition, 'Sometimes all you can do is walk', was held at Oriel Myrddin, Carmarthen between March and May 2019.

[26] *Celf coast 10*, Llanfyllin, 2022

[27] Robert Newell: https://robertnewellartist.co.uk/. Other notable 'walking artists' include Kyffin Williams (Eryri and Anglesey) and Roger Cecil (Ebbw Fach). An earlier twentieth century artist who tramped miles in the cause of his art was the Llanelli-born painter J.D. Innes. With Augustus John he became obsessed with Arenig Fawr near Bala, taking 'long rambles over the moors in search of the magical moment' and returning with sketches of the mountain (Augustus John, *Chiaroscuro: fragments of autobiography*, London, 1952, p.203).

[28] Walter Wilkinson, *Puppets in Wales*, London, 1948, p.7-8.

[29] Wilkinson, *Puppets in Wales*, p.134.

[30] Delyth Jenkins, *That would be telyn: walking the Pembrokeshire Coast Path with my harp*, Talybont, 2019, p.134-5. In 2003 the folk duo Filkin's Drift set off with their instruments on a 'sustainable' walking tour (CERDD//ED) of the entire Wales Coast Path: https://filkinsmusic.com/cerdded/

[31] Emily Hinshelwood, *On becoming a fish*, Bridgend, [2012], p.7: 'Sandscape after hours'. See also Emily Hinshelwood and Delyth Jenkins, *Salt on my boots: harp and poetry inspired by the Pembrokeshire Coast Path*, audio CD, Swansea, 2019. Another artist to take inspiration from the Path was the theatre director and performance pioneer Cliff McLucas, best known for his work for Brith Gof; before his premature death in 2002 he was working on *Prosiect Ogam, rhwng ei dau fôn*, a 'deep map' of the Pembrokeshire Coastal Path. Offa's Dyke Path is the setting for James Rice's novel *Walk* (London, 2022), which tells the story of two friends, unfit, ill-equipped, penniless and emotionally troubled, who stumble their way from Prestatyn to Llangollen. In 2023 the poet Ifor ap Glyn walked from Cardiff to Caernarfon, performing his poems in venues during the evenings en route, in a journey he called 'Sha thre / Am adra' ('Going home').

[32] Lloyd Jones, *Mr Vogel*, Bridgend, 2004. Walking is at the heart of two of his other novels, *Mr Cassini* (Bridgend, 2006) and *Y daith* (Talybont, 2011). See also *Literary atlas of Wales: Mr Vogel*: http://www.literaryatlas.wales/en/novels/mr-vogel/
[33] Iain Sinclair, *Lights out for the territory: 9 excursions in the secret history of London*, London, 1997, p.4. See also Merlin Coverley, *Psychogeography*, Harpenden, 2010.
[34] Iain Sinclair, *Black apples of Gower: stone-footing in memory fields*, Toller Fratrum, 2015, p.66.
[35] Peter Finch, *Edging the city: a journey round the border of Cardiff*, Bridgend, 2022, p.169. See also Peter Finch, *Edging the estuary*, Bridgend, 2013.
[36] Rhys Trimble, *Swansea automatic*, Llangattock, 2015, p.51.

Afterword: The future of walking

[1] Frédéric Gros, *A philosophy of walking*, London, 2014, p.4-5.
[2] https://ldwa.org.uk/ldp/members/show_path.php?path_name=Pererindod+Melangell

Index

Note: page numbers in italics indicate illustrations; references to information in notes are given thus: 319 n.28.